The Collaboration Equation

Mushtak Al-Atabi

PENGUIN BOOKS
An imprint of Penguin Random House

PENGUIN BOOKS

Penguin Books is an imprint of the Penguin Random House group of companies whose addresses can be found at global.penguinrandomhouse.com

Published by Penguin Random House SEA Pte Ltd
40 Penjuru Lane, #03-12, Block 2
Singapore 609216

Penguin Random House SEA

First published in Penguin Books by Penguin Random House SEA 2025

10 9 8 7 6 5 4 3 2 1

ISBN 9789815280937

Typeset in Garamond by MAP Systems, Bangalore, India

www.penguin.sg

PENGUIN BOOKS

THE COLLABORATION EQUATION

Dr Mushtak Al-Atabi serves as the Provost and CEO at Heriot-Watt University Malaysia. He is the author of *Think Like an Engineer*, *Leading with Stories*, and *Driven by Purpose*.

Regarded as the pioneer of the use of the CDIO (Conceive, Design, Implement, Operate) educational framework in Malaysia, he offered one of the first Massive Open Online Courses (MOOCs) in Asia in 2013.

His online classes have attracted thousands of students from across 150 countries. He speaks at international conferences and consults for multinational corporations, universities, banks, and private companies.

Mushtak is a Fellow of the Institution of Mechanical Engineers (UK), a member of the board of directors at the British Malaysia Chamber of Commerce, and the chairman of Vice-Chancellors' Council of Private Universities in Malaysia.

ADVANCE PRAISE FOR *The Collaboration Equation*

'After discovering the fundamental organizing principles of life, they often appear simple. But this should never deceive us, as the simple is frequently very challenging to achieve. In *The Collaboration Equation*, Mushtak Al-Atabi states the eternal principle: for us to collaborate, we need both shared purpose and mutual trust. He eloquently and convincingly shows how this principle applies to the whole spectrum of life, from bacteria to multinational corporations.

Books like this are essential reads for leaders, particularly at a time when collaboration is a vital necessity.'

—Dato' Sri Dr Idris Jala
CEO, PEMANDU Associates

'Discover why 1 + 1 = ∞ when minds, machines, and nature unite. Drawing from decades as a leader who sees trust as our greatest currency, the author makes a passionate case: "Collaborate to save the world". To heal our planet's fractured ecosystems and steer AI's meteoric rise, we must radically cooperate; the future is not just an equation to solve alone, it is a sum we write together.'

—Datuk Dr Yvonne
Chairman, Standard Chartered Bank Malaysia

To all my family members, teachers, students, friends, and partners: Thank you for the mutual trust we have and the purpose we share. You are a living testament to the Collaboration Equation.

Contents

Introduction

There is no doubt that humans are very special.

As a species, we managed to dominate the world and harness its resources. Applying our minds and using science, humans were able to comprehend how the universe works and use this knowledge to build technologies that improved many aspects of our lives.

From the beginning of time, people developed ways to work together and organize their efforts to deliver feats that went well beyond the capabilities of individuals.

All this progress, however, was not without adverse side effects. Today, we are faced with an array of existential challenges that include the ecological emergency, the rampant inequality, and the multitudes of political and geopolitical conflicts. Even our most brilliant technologies have the potential to turn against us if we do not get our house in order.

Our existence today is defined by a number of key paradoxes. Among them are the following:

1. While we have never been as rich as we are now in our history, we have unprecedented levels of debt and inequality.
2. Although we have never been as globally connected and integrated as we are today, we are facing alarming levels of polarization and geopolitical conflict among nations and within individual countries.

3. Despite, and sometimes because of, the significant progress we've made in technological advancements, environmental degradation is escalating to unsustainable levels.
4. Although our armies have weapons that can destroy the whole world a few times over, we are not feeling any safer or more secure.
5. Even though digital information technology and social media promise to connect us all and enable us to flourish, mental health issues and loneliness afflict an increasing number of people.

What is clear is that having more information, knowledge, and intelligence does not necessarily mean that we are wiser, more empathetic, or more compassionate. In the same vein, possessing material wealth and power does not necessarily make us stronger, more resilient, or more robust.

Despite all the knowledge we have amassed about our physical world, the real challenge remains to know and understand ourselves and how we can collaborate and work together, for this holds the potential for us to survive the power we have.

Observing what has been happening around the world over the past couple of centuries, it is not surprising to see many adopt the viewpoint that life fundamentally revolves around competition. This perspective spans various domains, from personal ambitions and societal norms to the realms of business dynamics and international geopolitics.

In these contexts, competition and overt conflict often appear not just prevalent but seemingly unavoidable. The language and ethos of rivalry permeate through the literature of success and progress even when describing the natural world, exemplified by terms like 'survival of the fittest' and the 'law of the jungle'.

These expressions seem to endorse the idea that competition, struggle, and confrontation are the foundational principles governing life, dictating the course of evolution and driving forward human aspirations and achievements.

Further examining this observation, one might consider how such competitive dynamics have historically been viewed as the catalysts for inventiveness and development. In the business world, for instance, competition is often the crucible within which groundbreaking innovations, products, and services are forged. The relentless pursuit of excellence and market dominance can lead to significant technological advancements and operational efficiencies.

Similarly, in the realm of geopolitics, nations vie for influence, control of vital resources, and strategic advantages to ensure that they can achieve stability, security, and prosperity for their citizens.

This competition-anchored frame of mind that prevails among our leaders, teachers, and role models has undeniably fuelled progress, yet it has also contributed to the setbacks we mentioned earlier, such as environmental degradation, inequality, as well as wars and conflicts. If we are serious in our quest for a world that is sustainable, equitable, and enjoyable, we must realize that it is time for us to re-examine our reality, our connections with our world, and our relationships with one another.

The central question that we might ask is: Could there exist another organizing principle as an alternative to an absolute competitive framework? We are looking for an organizing principle that is more profound and universally applicable through underscoring life in the wide span of its complexities and nuances.

Contrary to what appears on the surface, life is not a zero-sum game. Amid the competitive overlay of life, generosity, altruism, compassion, and kindness do exist. Their impact on shaping the history of the world may have been underestimated, but it is both deep and real. They facilitate the emergence of shared purpose and enable mutual trust to be established and, in the process, set the scene for the non-zero-sum mechanisms to result in unprecedented value creation.

While the goodness of these elements has generally been recognized in and of itself, as the majority of us prefer to live in communities that are trusting, kind, and generous, the link between their presence and the creation of original business value is not very well established.

This book argues that while using competitive principles to explain life contains elements of truth, this approach offers a rather limited interpretation of the complex fabric of existence and that beneath the surface of competition lies a rich undercurrent of harmony and symbiosis. Even in the natural world, mutualistic relationships are abundant, where we see different species coordinate and cooperate for mutual benefit, illustrating that cooperation is as much a part of the evolutionary process as competition. Plants and pollinators, such as flowers and bees, engage in mutual support, each aiding the survival and propagation of the other.

In human societies, the capacities for coordination, cooperation, and collaboration—forming communities and networks, building shared resources, and working towards common goals—have been instrumental in our survival and success. These capabilities allowed talents and resources to be pooled and synergized, facilitating the creation of new and enhanced values that no individual or one group of people could muster alone. The achievements of civilizations are built not just on the competitive spirit but on the foundational pillars of collaboration, shared knowledge, and collective effort.

Even in the mathematical world of game theory, algorithms that prioritize cooperation when interacting with other algorithms appear to yield better results in the long term than algorithms that are programmed to prioritize their own benefits and exploit their opponents.

The emergence of global challenges, such as climate change, pandemics, conflicts, technological disruptions, and resource scarcity, further underscore the limitations of a purely competitive worldview. These issues demand a collective approach that transcends individual, organizational, and even national interests. The path forward, it seems, requires a delicate balance between competition and collaboration. Recognizing the value of competitive endeavours in driving progress, while embracing collaborative strategies for the common good, might be the dual approach needed for sustainable development and global harmony.

This expanded perspective invites a re-evaluation of the principles that we consider to be fundamental in organizing life and progress. This book suggests that alongside competition, principles such as coordination, cooperation, and collaboration are equally vital forces shaping the world. There is a need to recognize the power of these collaborative principles and be more intentional in creating the space for them to play a larger role in our future. Embracing this broader view could unlock new pathways for addressing the grand challenges facing humanity, leading to a more sustainable, equitable, and enjoyable world for all of us.

This work is an attempt to make the case for collaboration as a foundational and universal organizing principle in relationships at multiple levels, offering a framework for comprehending, forecasting, and driving global dynamics. It aims to facilitate and support a shift towards more effective leadership paradigms through collaboration. In doing so, the book will delineate the essential elements that facilitate collaborative efforts, empowering leaders and individuals to recognize and embrace collaboration as a viable and effective strategic choice.

To expose the biological, social, and psychological underpinnings of collaboration, we will present examples from both the natural world and various aspects of human experience. This approach not only highlights the innate propensity for collaboration in the natural world and human society, but also underscores its potential as a transformative force in leadership and organizational practices.

Whether in one-on-one relationships, within teams and groups, or even among nations, collaboration is a vital dynamic that ought to be cultivated across various contexts. It is the foundation for fostering understanding, enhancing creativity, and driving collective success.

The principles, frameworks, and models proposed in this book are designed to be versatile and adaptable, making them applicable in all these settings to maximize effectiveness and achieve higher levels of success.

Part One

The Anatomy of Collaboration

Collaboration is not only a necessary part of life; it is the very foundation of it. Humans were able to become the dominant species on Earth because of their superior ability to collaborate with each other. At a time when new and unparalleled levels of collaboration are required to deal with the multitude of existential challenges we face, we seem to suffer from a crisis of collaboration. The lack of shared purpose and mutual trust is sowing the seeds of more polarization and conflicts at systemic levels.

In the opening section of this book, we aim to analyse the fundamentals of humans' tendency to collaborate and establish the groundwork for identifying and comprehending the biological, psychological, social, and mathematical factors that explain what facilitates or hinders coaction and collaboration in their different manifestations, aiming to uncover the guiding principles that decipher the phenomena of coordination, cooperation, and collaboration.

We will further explore the subtleties of various levels of collaborative efforts, examining the nature and depth of these levels, as well as the inherent barriers that may obstruct the initiation or progression of collaborative endeavours.

We argue here that the unique ability of human groups to create and maintain intersubjective realities through developing, believing, and sustaining group narratives enables the emergence of mutual trust and shared purpose, which are the key ingredients of long-lasting collaboration.

While there is an intuitive recognition that collaboration, shared purpose, and mutual trust are important to address the key challenges of our age, there is also the prevailing feeling that trusting other parties may be the naïve thing to do as those who initiate trust may end up being ripped off.

This is a very complex space where psychology, values, enforcement, and pragmatism intertwine.

As these words are being typed, the global collaborative outlook seems bleak as we have two active wars in Ukraine and the Middle East while the trade war between China and the US is threatening to expand and heat up. Despite all of that, there is hope as we are approaching a reckoning that collaboration is our only way out. There are increasing indicators that we are on the cusp of an age of purpose, trust, and collaboration. However, this direction of travel is not inevitable, and hence, intentional leadership will need to play the role of the catalyst to bring this reality to bear sooner.

The chapters in Part One of the book will lay out the principles and the theoretical and foundational pillars essential for understanding the concepts discussed in the subsequent parts of the book. As readers progress, they will encounter an array of examples, practical techniques, and insights intended to deepen their comprehension and their ability to apply the materials presented in their own lives.

This structured approach ensures a thorough understanding, paving the way for the effective implementation of the principles and strategies outlined in the following chapters.

Chapter 1

The Collaboration Paradox

'The world is very different now. For man holds in his mortal hands the power to abolish all forms of human poverty and all forms of human life.'

—President John F. Kennedy
Inaugural Address,
Washington D.C. 20 January, 1961

Humans are not the strongest, fastest, or highest endurance species on Earth. Our senses of hearing, smelling, and vision are not extraordinary when compared to many other animals. We do not possess exceptional capabilities like the night vision that cats have, the ability to regenerate lost body parts that salamanders have, or the long life spans that tortoises have.

So, what is the secret behind the remarkable performance of this species that called itself Homo Sapiens?

This is what we will examine further in the coming sections.

Types of Reality

Before addressing the above question, it is important to briefly discuss the concept of reality, as it plays a significant role in the explanation. Reality can be defined as the state of things as they exist in the world, and it manifests at different levels. The most fundamental level is 'physical reality', often referred to as 'objective reality'. This encompasses the physical world that exists independently of human consciousness, perception, or belief, including everything that can be measured and observed—such as matter, energy, and the laws of physics.

For example, if there is a tree in the forest, it exists regardless of whether or not I believe in its existence. Similarly, if someone jumps from the twenty-fifth floor of a building, the law of gravity will inevitably pull them to the ground, irrespective of their beliefs about gravity. A molecule of water has two Hydrogen atoms and one Oxygen atom; this is real whether we know about the chemistry of water or not.

Another form of reality is called 'subjective reality' or 'perceptual reality' and refers to how individuals perceive and interpret the world around them based on their senses, experiences, beliefs, and emotions. Subjective reality exists in the mind of a conscious individual, allowing different people to have different perceptions of the same situation, event, or object. This can relate to how we taste food; a delicacy to someone may be a source of disgust for another, and extend to matters related to political inclination, where the election of a certain politician to the office may be the best outcome for some, while others may see it as almost the end of the world.

Subjective reality covers our feelings and emotions as well, including pain and pleasure. While subjective reality may seem confined to the individual person and have a limited bearing on the real world, it is, in fact, rather consequential as it affects the foundation of our motivations and how we engage with the world.

Another very powerful level of reality is 'social reality', which is sometimes called 'constructed reality' or 'intersubjective reality'. This type refers to the shared beliefs, norms, practices, and even myths and misconceptions that shape a group's or society's understanding of what is real. It results when certain concepts are held simultaneously in the minds of a group of individuals, yielding the creation of a network of minds that can think, exchange information, and operate together.

In his book *The Construction of Social Reality*[1], John R. Searle describes intersubjective reality as 'the objective facts in the world that are only facts by human agreement. In a sense, there are things that exist only because we believe them to exist. I am thinking of things like money, property, governments, and marriages.'

Examples of categories of intersubjective reality include religious and cultural beliefs, social norms, and institutions that influence how we interact with one another. This unique human ability to construct complex intersubjective realities, with the potential of connecting large groups of individuals together, is foundational to human superiority over other species. It is rooted in the human capacity to communicate and exchange information, linking brains in super information networks. Our political, religious, and financial systems are rooted in these intersubjective realities, imbuing concepts and objects with unique values.

Take, for example, the concept of money that was mentioned by John Searle. A banknote with a denomination of $1, $10, $20, or $100 has no innate value in and of itself. However, the global acceptance of this banknote as an item of value and the trust that the Federal Reserve Bank and the US government will back this banknote give it its acceptability.

Another example is the status of certain places or cities as being holy for the followers of a certain religion. While others may only see the objective reality of the place represented by its stones, buildings, and roads, the believers feel the spiritual energy and sense the connection with a higher power in their holy places.

It is useful to mention here that the subject of reality is a complex one, and there are many books and theories dedicated to studying it. The above brief description is only aimed at providing a simplified account within the context of this book.

This ability of humans to create and sustain intersubjective realities represents a crucial factor in creating our success in dominating life on earth through enabling our proclivity to connect and organize ourselves into highly adaptive collaborative networks of multiple individuals. These networks can vary greatly in size, from small bands hunting on the African savanna and teams participating in sports games, to multinational corporations producing consumer products or even entire nations.

No matter how strong, intelligent, or dedicated an individual may be, there will always be significant limitations to what they can achieve alone. Many of the conveniences we take for granted today rely on the knowledge, skills, and expertise of countless individuals that we do not know and may never meet in person.

For instance, producing a cup of coffee requires specialized knowledge in planting, growing, harvesting, processing, and brewing coffee cherries and beans—a body of knowledge that has been accumulated and refined over generations. People who have specialized knowledge in these multiple domains somehow formed the complex networks that enabled them to coordinate their efforts to bring coffee from the farm to your cup. Members of these networks apply their knowledge and efforts, trusting that they will receive their dues and knowing that their work supports a global industry. These networks span multiple continents, time zones, and individuals who may never meet each other, but the intersubjective reality that they belong to keeps them together.

The story begins at a coffee plantation somewhere. Once the coffee cherries are harvested, additional expertise is necessary for processing them to extract the coffee beans, as well as for drying and milling the beans using specific tools and machinery. Only after these steps can the beans be roasted, ground, and brewed to create a delicious cup of coffee. This account of the journey of the coffee is not complete without recognizing the roles of all people along the supply chain who run the markets where commodities are traded, control the quality, as well as those who run the stores and drive the trucks that carry coffee at different stages of the process.

While on the surface, an observer may see coffee beans moving through the network and changing form as they are processed, with a deeper look at the network of people who played their roles in making the cup of coffee a reality, one can see that, ultimately, what is being exchanged is trust, knowledge, information, and value. These ultimately keep the network together.

At each node in the network, individuals need to contribute and apply their knowledge and expertise. Moving the coffee through the network also requires exchanging information about the price, type, and condition of the commodity. The quality of the exchanged information is dependent on the nature of the relationship between different nodes and the prevalence of trust between them.

What holds true for coffee applies to many other products and services that are made possible by our remarkable organizational capabilities, which enable us to collaborate effectively in large groups. These capabilities are anchored in our unique capacity to use language and storytelling to develop shared realities and common beliefs, effectively connecting the minds of many individuals with the objective of achieving common goals. It is worth mentioning here that people simultaneously belong to multitudes of networks that vary in their goals, coherence, and the strengths of their connections.

Emphasizing the foundational role of language, John R. Searle made the case[1] that to have intersubjective realities at all, 'a society must have at least a primitive form of language, that in this sense the institution of language is logically prior to other institutions. On this view, language is the basic social institution in the sense that all others presuppose language, but language does not presuppose the others: you can have language without money and marriage, but not the converse.'

While cooperative behaviour in large numbers is routinely exhibited by other species—such as ants and bees—the cooperation demonstrated by these species is rigid in scope and limited in context. Ants can only work together to collect food, build large colonies, and defend them. Bees, on the other hand, can build hives and make honey.

'If a beehive is facing a new threat or a new opportunity, the bees cannot reinvent their social system overnight in order to cope better. They cannot, for example, execute the queen and establish a republic,' wrote Yuval Noah Harari, the author of *Sapiens*.[2] Other species may hunt cooperatively, which requires working flexibly together, but this often happens in small, tightly-knit groups of blood-related animals like a pride of lions.

A very similar observation about the role of language and the uniqueness of humans was made by Adam Smith two and a half centuries ago, when he attempted in the *Wealth of Nations*[3] to make the case for the collaborative division of labour, writing:

'This division of labour, from which so many advantages are derived, is not originally the effect of any human wisdom, which foresees and intends that general opulence to which it gives occasion. It is the necessary, though very slow and gradual, consequence of a certain propensity in human nature, which has in view no such extensive utility: the propensity to truck, barter, and exchange one thing for another.'

He then went on to affirm the role of language: 'Whether this propensity be one of those original principles in human nature, of which no further account can be given, or whether, as seems more probable, it be the necessary consequence of the faculties of *reason* and *speech*, it belongs not to our present subject to inquire. It is common to all men, and to be found in no other race of animals, which seem to know neither this nor any other species of contracts.'

What enables large numbers of humans to collaborate in a versatile manner is our unique ability to connect with other humans, including those whom we do not know in person or are not genetically related to us, creating mutual trust bonds and shared purpose with a large number of individuals. This capacity to connect many minds, even if they are not in the same locale, resulted in the establishment of far-reaching networks of individuals with the potential to exchange information, adapt to changing environments, and summon strengths that far exceed what a single individual can muster.

As discussed earlier, this phenomenon is enabled by our unique knack for creating intersubjective realities, processing abstract thoughts, the rich language we use, and ultimately, our ability to create and believe the collective narratives and stories we tell about our teams, tribes, organizations, nations, and the world.

The Storytelling Species

We have always known that human brains are wired for stories. The moment children are able to speak and comprehend language, their number one request is, 'Tell me a story.'

Even when we try to memorize lists of random objects, it is easier to do so by converting them into stories. Stories are not merely a source of entertainment, but essential enablers for us to understand ourselves and the communities we belong to and connect with others around us. Later in the book, we will discuss how effective storytelling is becoming an essential human skill in an age that is defined by disruptive technologies.

As mentioned earlier, stories that are collectively told and believed by groups of people can be the basis for establishing the group's information and communication system, enabling the building and enhancing of a shared sense of purpose, as well as the establishment and deepening of mutual trust. This represents the foundation for collective action and collaboration. Stories represent the cultural containers for knowledge, skills, values, and local wisdom. Through these stories, a group can build an identity, teach its members how to fish and what kind of plants are safe to eat, and also communicate what is important to the group, such as taking care of their environment and respecting their elders.

Whether in one-on-one relationships, within teams and groups, or even among nations, effective and sustained collaboration will necessitate having some form of a joint narrative that will enable shared purpose and mutual trust to emerge.

From the dawn of history, when humans had to confront and endure all types of dangers, obstacles, and the unforgiving natural world to survive, there were always questions like, 'Who controls nature?', 'Who are we?', 'Where did we come from?', and 'What happens after we die?'

Interestingly, millennia after our ancestors asked these questions, while we now understand the natural order better, we are still asking the same questions about who we are, what our origin is, and what our destiny is. The only way to address such questions is through telling stories. We can almost imagine bands and tribes of prehistoric humans, gathering around a campfire with a wise person—a master storyteller— answering existential questions with stories about how superbeings created our tribe and where grandma went when she died.

These master storytellers were highly respected members of the community. As they told their tales, they invented words and language as they went, often inspiring pride in the uniqueness of one's tribe, hope for a better life in the hereafter, and fear of committing sins that will invite the wrath of the superpowers in charge of the world.

As they told these stories, which they heard from generations of storytellers before them, they weaved the minds of their listeners into a united fabric, establishing a deep sense of identity for the group and inner peace for the individuals, reassuring them that their life is not an undertaking in vain.

The stories can serve practical and mundane purposes, too, such as communicating the best places to hunt, rallying the group to fight its enemies, celebrating important skills to learn, and enshrining the values of the group. These collective stories told for generations after generations, build the channels for information exchange, establishing the foundation of a group's shared purpose and mutual trust that makes working together much easier.

It is useful to mention here that while stories support the information and communication systems that serve to connect the group members, they do not all have to be positive, accurate, or even factual.

For example, groups may hold the belief that the earth is flat, their group is superior to other groups, or that their religion is the only true religion. Sometimes, these stories are designed to prevent mixing with other competing human groups, and they can have nasty content about how bad members of the other groups are. These beliefs will manifest as the intersubjective reality of the group and find their roots in the stories told by its members. At the small group level, the harmful impacts of a negative story are often confined to the group and its local context. As the group size grows, the negative impacts of harmful stories mount up.

We know of many instances from history where these negative stories had devastating outcomes, including the administering of apartheid and committing genocide.

When a Lunar Eclipse Defeats an Army

Towards the end of the Peloponnesian Wars in 413 BCE between Athens and the Sicilian city-state of Syracuse, the Athenian army was battered and reached the realization that the campaign they were waging was a miscalculation and an egregious act of overreach.

At the end of August 413 BCE, after two years of fighting and many thousands of casualties, the Athenians decided to withdraw their forces and go home. To maximize their chances of a successful retreat, the Athenians packed their ships and equipment discreteely and were ready to slip away before their enemy noticed. On the night of 28 August, there was a lunar eclipse, turning the colour of the moon over Sicily to a dark blood-red.

Seeing this terrifying scene, Nicias, the Athenian leader, and his men believed that this was a bad omen and the gods were showing disapproval of the timing of their retreat. This was confirmed after consulting the priests, who advised to delay the retreat for another twenty-seven days. The hesitation and delay of the Athenian manoeuvre made the Syracusans realize that the Athenians were trying to retreat, making their ships sitting ducks in the harbour.

In a demonstration of how intersubjective reality can be disconnected from objective reality and totally dependent on the mindset of the group harbouring it, the Syracusan forces interpreted the lunar eclipse in a more favourable light, seeing it as a sign that the gods were on their side, giving them confidence for the fight.

Needless to say, this did not end well for the Athenians, who suffered a decisive defeat at the hands of the Syracusans.

It is truly fascinating how the exact same natural phenomenon, a lunar eclipse, can be perceived in such drastically different ways by two groups of people. This clearly shows how the narratives we have inside our heads can literally shape our worldview and form our mindsets. They help create a network by building the channels and connections between individuals, enabling them to act in unison. The nature of the stories we tell ourselves shapes the world we live in. Our stories can build our resilience or lead us to give up, and can sow the seeds of collaboration or animosity.

Networks and Stories

In the context of collaboration, the previous sections were dedicated to establishing the importance of the stories we tell in connecting us, forming the pathways and channels through which we exchange information, and shaping the way we perceive our world and the role of others in it.

Stories mould group identities and guide their interaction with other groups. When a group is relatively small, the information exchange is mainly done orally, allowing these foundational collective stories to be told, evolved, and passed on. In prehistoric eras, the oral tradition represented a sufficient information and communication system to keep small networks of people coherent and maintain a sense of shared purpose and mutual trust among their members.

For a group identity to emerge, when the networks' sizes grew, as people came together to form larger communities, the collective stories needed to grow in sophistication and scope and be preserved and transmitted in a written format in order for them to remain the foundation for group harmony and help regulate people's affairs.

No wonder, then, when the world's first civilizations started to coalesce as bands of people came together to grow crops, build cities, and trade, epic myths of creation were narrated and written down on clay tablets. The Enuma Elish, for example, is one of the oldest known written creation myths, which comes from ancient Babylonian and Sumerian texts, dating back to around 2000 BCE. It describes the creation of the world and humanity by the god Marduk from the remains of the defeated goddess Tiamat.

The advent of written language was a monumental revolution that transformed our ability to process information and communicate across distance and time. This new system of information and communication technology laid the groundwork for modern life as we know it today. It facilitated the recording of debts, making credit possible and allowing for the documentation of property rights, which established the concept of private ownership.

The first written documents were clay tablets with cuneiform symbols. They gave way to ink handwritten words on skin and paper, then to the printed word, and finally to the electronic signals in the cloud. While the concept of written documents remained the same throughout these developments, every new technology gave the documented content the ability to travel wider and faster, which had a large impact on the potential to connect and network.

Without a doubt, this growing network and narrative complexity spun off an industry for maintaining, narrating, and interpreting these texts and documents, giving birth to the profession of priests and the construction of temples.

Clearly, to maintain social order and productive coordination, cooperation, and collaboration among members of society, people needed to believe in the shared value of not stealing their neighbours' properties, not polluting the communal sources of water, and other desirable social behaviours.

For those who would steal anyway, they needed to recognize that a higher authority, say the king or the ruler, would punish them if they were to get caught. Understandably, this meant that a larger, more complex society needed a more comprehensive information and communication system for it to maintain its collective narratives and function effectively. This system would include the legal, cultural, and social norms expected by society.

It is worth reiterating here that a legal system, for example, may be carved in stone like the Code of Hammurabi or reside in the mind of a ruler or priest who can deliver the judgement, but either way, people need to believe that there will be consequences if the law is broken for it to have the deterrence effect. The feeling about the effectiveness of a legal system is an example of how a collective story is held by a group of people, resulting in the creation of an intersubjective reality. The same can be said about the financial system and how our joint belief in the value of money and faith in financial institutions create a situation where trust keeps credit flowing and the whole financial system afloat.

When we collectively believe in our economic, legal, and political systems, we can collaborate with those who have trust in these systems, even if we do not know them in person or are not related to them by blood. We can trade and exchange services because we believe that we will be paid for our goods and work, and that the money we will receive is accepted by others when we want to exchange it for what we want. We also believe that banks will give us back our money upon request, and when our rights are breached, we can go to the authorities and ask for help.

There are, of course, multiple examples when people stop believing and trusting the positive intersubjective reality of the systems of society. When people doubt the stability of the banks, the integrity of the legal system, and the honesty of their politicians, these are usually signs of decline, lack of economic development, and deterioration of human flourishing.

A Broken Promise

'It is impossible that old prejudices and hostilities should longer exist while such an instrument has been created for the exchange of thought between all nations of the earth,' Charles Briggs and Augustus Maverick wrote in their 1858 book titled *The Story of the Telegraph and a History of the Great Atlantic Cable.* They went on to proclaim: 'How potent a power, then, is the telegraphic destined to become in the civilization of the world. This binds together by a vital cord all the nations of the earth'.[4]

This optimistic view that the latest information and communication technology will enable the exchange of information and will lead to a deeper understanding between us will appear repeatedly in our history. Two world wars and a Cold War later, the emergence of social media was predicted to increase our connectivity, facilitating the prevalence of peace and prosperity.

Needless to say, it failed to live up to these lofty expectations. While the Internet and social media were thought to be systems that would enable truth to prevail and people, particularly across political, racial, religious, and ideological divides, to trust each other more, the digital space seems to be having more than a fair share of hate, conspiracy theories, and fake news.

It is important to realize that a key characteristic of all the information and communication systems that we use to organize ourselves and enable collaboration is that they can be hacked to do a lot of damage and even sow the seeds of disunity and fragmentation. This is true for the oral tradition, written documents, postal service, printing press, telegraph, radio, television, social media, and ultimately AI.

Imagine manipulative master storytellers in the prehistoric era, who could use their gifts to spread rumours that could destroy mutual trust and undermine the sense of shared purpose that group members have. This could have disastrous effects not only on the potential of collaboration, but also on the very survival of the group. This potential for being manipulated and causing real harm increases exponentially as the networks and the information and communication systems that support them grow in size and sophistication.

That is why, as our ability to organize ourselves increases, we need higher levels of wisdom, compassion, and mature leadership to make sure that we nurture the mutual trust and inspire shared purpose necessary to control our technologies and realise their positive potential.

The Collaboration Paradox

As outlined earlier, the larger the network of people, the richer and more sophisticated the stories and the information exchange systems that connect them need to be. A small band of people living in the savanna will relatively easily establish a shared purpose of survival through hunting together and relying on each other to protect themselves. They build mutual trust on the basis of being related to one another. The proverbs, wisdom, and stories told by such a community will be directly related to their survival together in their environment.

Zooming out to the national level reveals new degrees of complexity in the stories and narratives necessary to maintain a robust societal fabric. These narratives include an origin story that highlights the nation's uniqueness and illustrates how citizenship of that nation connects individuals to a broader community of compatriots.

This sense of connectedness forms the basis for citizens to pay taxes, knowing that their contributions will benefit fellow citizens who may not be genetically related to them, or willingly join the army to fight for their country. Numerous stories and narratives are essential for this intersubjective reality we call the nation-state to take root and endure. These include financial, political, and judicial narratives, among others. These national stories were spread and enabled at a large scale in the seventeenth and eighteenth centuries by advanced technologies such as the railroad, the telegraph, and the radio.

These national stories serve as the information systems that connect different members of society and shape the national identity. Just like group stories, they do not all have to be positive, accurate, or even factual to perform their connective functions. Examples of extreme national narratives that led to war and destruction include prejudice against others, fascism, and nazism. While they may enable collaboration within the national borders, these prejudicial mindsets undermine the development of transnational shared purpose and trust-building across borders and make collaboration between nations impossible and the potential for conflict rampant.

It is apparent that through the combinatorial effect of our collaborative efforts, empowered by our unique ability to build networks, we were able to achieve outstanding feats that started with controlling fire and inventing the wheel and culminated with the development of AI. The economic value that humanity created and the growth that it achieved are mind-boggling. All this progress, as outlined earlier, had some serious negative side effects.

At this historical moment, when our species has unsurpassed levels of military might, economic resources, and technological capabilities while facing global challenges and disruptions, we require collaboration at much higher levels, inspiring a shared sense of purpose and nurturing mutual trust across borders and political, ideological, and religious trenches. This will ensure that we are able to use our resources to benefit us and make us happier and healthier, rather than weaponize them and use them against each other.

This necessitates the weaving of fresh narratives and stories that adopt empathy and compassion as the best strategies for survival. In order to ensure that we can survive and thrive, we need to utilize our creativity and imagination to conjure new intersubjective realities, in which we see the other as an opportunity rather than a threat. This requires that we transcend our immediate and selfish needs and focus on the needs of our bigger tribe, humanity. A story in which every human being is a valued member of the human family, worthy of love, respect, and appreciation, is possible. When enough of us believe in this story, it can become a reality.

What got us here is our ability to collaborate, enabled by information and communication systems that kept the fabric of society together. We recognize that our collaborative project thus far has created a lot of negative externalities, but what we need now is not less collaboration but even more. We need to go back to basics and remember, regardless of our race, religion, gender, or nationality, when we look at the sky at night, we sometimes ask ourselves who we are, where we came from, and where we are going. This should serve as a reminder that we are in this world together, and it is worth our effort to prioritize saving our world and taking care of each other.

The arc of history is clear: As the size of human groups needed to connect and work together increases, more effective technology is needed to maintain the information flow and communication of stories necessary to preserve the shared purpose and mutual trust. The information and communication technology has always been a double-edged sword. Stories can inform, educate and connect, but they can also be used to misinform, mislead, and divide.

Paradoxically, the more powerful the information technology we use, the more people it can connect and also the bigger the potential damage it can create. The direction of travel for our ability to organize massive numbers of people to do both bad and good is increasing as our connecting information technology has improved from the clay tablets, printing press, telegraph, radio, and railroads to social media. Our latest and most disruptive technology, AI, has the potential of helping us address our grand challenges and realize our full potential and simultaneously could lead to achieving the very opposite. It can help us unlock phenomenal levels of productivity, creativity, and discovery that can help us address our existential challenges.

In the wrong hands, AI also has the potential to destroy collaboration by undermining mutual trust. With easy access to very high-quality deepfake content, we may reach a stage where we cannot trust what we see or hear on our devices. This is indeed a very dystopian vision that we need to recognize and actively work to avoid by focusing on our humanity and building the right culture, policies, and institutions that will ensure that humans remain at the centre of this exciting development.

The role of leadership in ensuring that we will continue to collaborate for the right reasons is central. This book is an attempt to help establish the intellectual and practical ecosystem for the right leadership paradigms to prevail.

This hope and faith in leadership are not the result of an idealistic or naïve view of the world. Collaboration is so critical and essential that we need now to double down on this ability and understand how we can cultivate it as a key element of our leadership toolbox. We need to understand what initiates collaboration, how to sustain it, and how to take it to the new levels necessary to survive and thrive in this century. While we may be experiencing a crisis of collaboration, we need to remember that it is in moments of crisis when true leaders usually enable collaboration to emerge.

In the coming parts of this book, we will discuss how we can build such a collaborative world. We are not predestined for mere destructive competition. Developing the deep wisdom of seeing our diversity as a source of strength can help us unleash our highest potential and direct our resources and disruptive technologies to solve our most existential challenges, such as the climate emergency, inequality, and potential pandemics.

Chapter 2

The Collaboration Equation

'Individually, we are one drop. Together, we are an ocean.'

—Ryunosuke Satoro

When teaching Business Negotiation to my MBA students, one exercise that consistently captivates their attention is the timeless scenario of the Prisoner's Dilemma, a construct rooted in Game Theory. The hypothetical situation features two individuals detained by the police on suspicion of committing a relatively serious crime.

Despite their inability to substantiate the detainees' involvement in the crime, the investigating officers proposed a strategy with a high likelihood of securing at least one conviction, if not two. Each prisoner was separately presented with the proposition: 'You have two options: confess to the crime or remain silent. If both of you confess, each will receive a two-year jail sentence. Should you confess while your partner does not, you will be released after providing testimony that incriminates your partner, who will then receive a three-year jail term. If you choose not to confess, but your partner does, you will endure the sentence while your partner goes free. However, if neither of you confesses, both will be convicted of a minor charge, resulting in a one-year jail term for each.'

Initially, it may seem instinctive for both prisoners to prioritize their own freedom in such a dilemma by choosing to confess and hoping that the other prisoner will remain silent. Yet, this introduces a paradox: If both prisoners act solely in their own interests, they will inevitably both confess and end up spending the maximum jail sentence. The optimal, or win-win, scenario for the prisoners—where both serve the minimal sentence—necessitates a collective silence, a strategy that, while individually less appealing, benefits both parties collectively. Achieving this outcome will first require the establishment of a shared purpose, prioritizing the collective benefit over individual gain.

Now, even if a shared purpose is established, this will not be the end of the story, as the ultimate common success will hinge on another delicate balance—mutual trust. Even with premeditated coordination, each prisoner must place trust in the other to uphold their end of the silent bargain. The exercise, steeped in the intricacies of human behaviour, lays bare the perennial struggle between individual gain, the need for shared purpose, and the indispensable mutual trust required for actions that serve the greater good.

Although the stakes and complexities may vary, the fundamental mechanisms underlying collaborative dynamics are akin to those at play in the classic prisoner's dilemma. They are universally applicable whether the collaboration involves two people writing a book, a construction team erecting a building, or multiple nations organizing the FIFA World Cup.

The Mathematics of Cooperation

When being involved and interacting with others, the eternal question remains: When should we cooperate, and when should we be selfish and prioritize our own interests?

To mathematically answer this question, Professor Robert Axelrod of the University of Michigan turned to Game Theory, where he ran a round-robin tournament to test fourteen different algorithms plus a random decision-making computer programme.[5]

The competition was a computer-based Prisoner's Dilemma where algorithms were pitted against each other in a series of rounds. In each round, opposing algorithms had two choices: to cooperate or defect (exploit the other algorithm). If both algorithms chose to cooperate, they shared the points of the game. If both chose to defect, they would both be punished and lose points, but if one of them chose to defect while the other cooperated, the defecting algorithm would be rewarded with extra points, while the cooperating side would be punished by a deduction in points. The winning algorithm would be the one with the highest number of points at the end of the tournament. The competing entries for the tournament came from all corners of the intellectual world and were designed by psychologists, sociologists, mathematicians, political scientists, and economists.

To the surprise of Professor Axelrod, the winning algorithm was one that carried the name 'Tit-For-Tat'. The strategy of this algorithm was straightforward: to start with cooperation and then simply copy the previous move of the opponent algorithm.

Further investigation of different strategies kept on resulting in similar outcomes, further indicating that being 'nice' is not only the moral thing to do, but it is also a very practical strategy for success. The study concluded that successful strategies have the following qualities:

1. **Being nice:** These winning strategies join the game with no intention of exploiting the other players. They start with a cooperative offer that seeks a win-win outcome.
2. **Being forgiving:** When an opponent changes their stand from defecting to cooperating, the successful strategy welcomes this change and starts playing nice again.

3. **Being retaliatory:** When the opposing player attempts to exploit, a successful strategy implies the need for immediate punishment.
4. **Being clear:** The behaviour of starting with cooperation, rewarding it, and punishing defection should be made crystal clear to the opponent by not behaving in any ambiguous manner.

Guided by the well-established findings above, in the negotiation course I teach as part of the MBA curriculum, we embrace a philosophy that emphasizes collaboration over confrontation whenever possible. Our approach encourages students to seek mutually beneficial, creative, and collaborative solutions rather than adopting a stance of aggressive negotiation. The negotiation zone is not viewed as a zero-sum space, but rather a non-zero-sum territory where value can be generated, expanded, and enhanced through creative collaboration with other party or parties.

To achieve that, we advocate for a negotiation style that not only aims to deliver the desired results but also places a strong emphasis on fostering positive relationships with those across the table. A key tenet of this approach is the focus on understanding the purpose of each party as they go into negotiation, not only their positions on issues such as price, interest rate, etc.

Often, negotiators miss that the positions we take on the negotiated issues do not exist in a vacuum, and rather, they are there to serve our deepest interests and sense of purpose. More on this will be shared later in the chapter on collaborative negotiation.

This philosophy acknowledges the reality that not all negotiators play fair, and some will resort to tactics of aggression or manipulation. That is why our students are equipped with the skills to identify such tactics and assert themselves when necessary.

Central to our teaching is the understanding that negotiation is fundamentally about finding common ground and building trust, demonstrating that collaboration between parties with seemingly opposing interests is not only feasible but also preferable for achieving lasting and fruitful results.

As we outlined in the previous chapter, humans largely perceive the world through the stories they tell themselves about themselves and about how the world works. These stories shape both their subjective and intersubjective realities. To set the scene for successful collaboration, leaders have the responsibility for formulating the language, narratives, and intersubjective realities that recognize the goodness in others and create the space for the possibility of having common goals with them and trusting that they will deliver their part of the bargain.

Beyond business negotiation, when exploring some of our most pressing challenges—the climate emergency—and our most promising opportunities—the development of AI—human collaboration stands as the only viable way ahead for successfully addressing the challenges and realizing the opportunities. Reversing environmental degradation entails that we all make painful changes to our lifestyles and economic activities, and this will require the confidence and trust that others will be doing the same for humanity to stand a real chance at success.

As AI, particularly when it gets to be fuelled by quantum computing, holds both the promise of solving our major challenges and the risk of being used as a weapon of mass destruction in geopolitical and commercial conflicts, individuals, organizations, and nations need to establish the institutions that cultivate mutual trust so that further development can be carried out without fear and worry.

The Prisoner's Dilemma reflects a broader truth about human nature, particularly when faced with opportunities and challenges of unprecedented magnitude. It is worth reemphasizing here that mutual trust, while necessary, is not sufficient for collaboration to emerge.

Other key enablers of collaboration are the alignment and drive created by a shared purpose. This shared purpose acts as a compass, guiding individuals and groups towards a common direction and imbuing them with the needed motivation to achieve their collective goals. The articulation, mutual understanding, and embracing of this purpose clarify the path forward and serve as a powerful catalyst, enabling parties to harness their collective strengths and work in unison. Such a unified approach accelerates the journey towards achieving shared objectives and enhances the synergy and cohesion among the participants, laying a solid foundation for sustained collaboration and collective success.

Mutual trust is essential for collaboration as it fosters a sense of belonging, encourages open communication, increases engagement, and enables risk-taking. It facilitates candid dialogue, which is essential for addressing issues, brainstorming ideas, and resolving conflicts. Team members who trust each other feel safe expressing dissenting opinions, which can lead to innovative solutions.

Taking all of the above into consideration, we can propose a formula for successful and sustained collaboration. A formula that encapsulates the key collaborative dynamics can be helpful to leaders and practitioners by providing them with an easy-to-access mental tool they can use to initiate collaboration and diagnose situations when collaboration is missing.

The proposed 'Collaboration Equation' is given below:

$$\text{Collaboration} = \text{Shared Purpose} \times \text{Mutual Trust}$$

It is worth mentioning here that the different terms of this equation are not entirely independent of each other and could dynamically influence one another. Trust and purpose can be interdependent, and growing one could lead to the growth of the other and vice versa.

However, there are situations when shared purpose and mutual trust are independent, and the presence of one does not necessarily imply the existence of the other. In these situations, the presence of either mutual trust or shared purpose can be used to create room for growing the missing factor and expanding the landscape to enable collaboration to happen.

For example, when warring nations reach the realization that they will be better off aiming at peace, a precarious collaboration to end the war begins. The start will usually be the formation of the mutual goal and shared purpose of stopping the fighting in the minds of the political leaders of the warring nations. On the battlefield and the political front, trust-building exercises would be afoot, often enabled by mediators that both warring parties trust. When sufficient trust is built, and as the shared purpose of peace-making is sustained, collaboration can be initiated, and a peace treaty may be signed.

More examples will be shared and discussed in the coming chapters.

It is important to recognize that as we endeavour to demonstrate the universality of collaboration as an organizing principle and produce a general framework for the analysis and understanding of value-adding interactions between individuals and groups, we may need to adopt a broad definition of both shared purpose and mutual trust. This is particularly true as we attempt to verify the Collaboration Equation for other non-human forms of life.

The concept of a shared purpose in the context of this book encompasses the collective goals or objectives pursued by groups and individuals motivated by a range of underlying reasons. In human settings, this pursuit is often intentional, rooted in conscious decisions and a clear sense of agency. In contrast, animals and insects are primarily driven by instinct, acting on innate behaviours that guide their contributions towards common objectives.

Meanwhile, bacteria exhibit a shared purpose through biochemical motivations, engaging in actions driven by chemical signals and responses. This diverse array of motivations underlines the complexity and universality of shared purpose across different forms of life.

Trust is defined as the belief in the reliability, truth, ability, or strength of someone or something, marked by the anticipation of positive outcomes amidst uncertainty.[6] When it comes to humans and human groups, trust encompasses multifaceted constructs influenced by factors such as personal agency, ethical values, legal frameworks, and societal norms. We will explore the dynamics of nurturing mutual trust in the human context in detail in Chapter 7.

In the non-human realm, however, trust among animals, insects, and single-cell organisms is primarily built upon mutual recognition. This recognition is facilitated through various means, including chemical signals like pheromones, and genetic relatedness, allowing these organisms to establish trust based on inherent or learned recognition mechanisms.

Generally, as we ascend in our investigation of the interaction between groups and individuals from simple single-cell organisms to complex humans, the meanings of purpose and trust acquire more depth and sophistication as concepts such as will, choice, and agency start to colour and enhance them.

As hinted earlier, besides the optimum collaborative state when both shared purpose and mutual trust are abundant, there exist many situations and examples when shared purpose, mutual trust, or both are in short supply. Such scenarios will be explored in subsequent chapters.

In circumstances where both shared purpose and mutual trust are scarce, the likelihood of conflicts erupting increases significantly. Conversely, when there is alignment on a shared purpose, yet trust is absent, cynicism often becomes a prominent response, undermining the potential for successful collaboration. Alternatively, when there is mutual trust without a unified vision or shared goals, confusion tends to set in, stalling any meaningful progress. This exploration highlights the delicate balance required between shared purpose and mutual trust for effective collaboration and success.

Therefore, a fundamental role of effective leadership is to inspire a sense of shared purpose by crafting a compelling vision and setting impactful objectives that people can rally around. Additionally, cultivating mutual trust is crucial. This can be achieved by creating a culture of safety and inclusion, thereby laying the groundwork for fruitful collaboration.

In such collaborative environments, characterized by a shared purpose and a culture of inclusivity and trust, teams can harness the competencies, talents, and resources of diverse individuals and groups. This enables them to transform their collective purpose into a positive global impact and achieve performance levels far surpassing what any single individual or group could accomplish alone.

While this chapter is focused on the nature of collaboration and the importance of shared purpose and mutual trust for it to emerge and be sustained, the following chapters will explore examples of coordination, cooperation, and collaboration that can happen between individuals of different species and make a case for the Collaboration Equation as describing one of the most fundamental and universal organizing principles both in the natural world and within human relations.

This will hopefully prepare the grounds for more of us to advocate for collaboration as a first option and to view it as a viable strategic alternative for achieving individual, organizational, and societal objectives and aspirations.

Chapter 3

The Collaborative Spectrum

> 'Coming together is a beginning; keeping together is progress; working together is success.'
>
> —Henry Ford

In busy city centres around the world, the operation of major intersections is usually entrusted to pre-programmed traffic lights as they regulate the flow of vehicles and pedestrians like a well-conducted orchestra. However, imagine one day, these lights malfunction, plunging an intersection into chaos. Without the guiding red, yellow, and green signals, drivers, in a bid to reach their destinations swiftly, attempt to navigate the crossing simultaneously.

Each driver, prioritizing their own urgency, inches forward, eyeing gaps that barely exist. Cars, buses, and motorcycles create a chaotic situation governed by impatience rather than rules. Horns blare in a cacophony of frustration and confusion, but no one advances significantly.

As vehicles jostle for space, an inevitable gridlock ensues. Cars are now stuck in a traffic jam, with no room to manoeuvre or retreat. The intersection, usually a fluid conduit for traffic, becomes a static maze of metal, exhaust, and frustration.

This scenario is a classic representation of a breakdown in communal coordination and cooperation. When the sense of shared purpose and mutual trust, maintained by well-designed, impartial, and mutually agreed-upon traffic light operation, evaporates, each driver begins to prioritize their immediate benefit over the collective order, and the system collapses, leading to a situation where everyone is worse off. This underscores the importance of coordination and the potential consequences that result from its absence. Just as with traffic, many aspects of life require a balance between individual desires and the greater good.

The busy intersection and the potential for gridlock are metaphors for the vast landscape of human interactions, of which the concepts of coordination, cooperation, and collaboration stand as exemplars of collective effort. Often used interchangeably, these terms, in reality, represent distinct states of interaction and joint action, each marking a point on an ascending scale of sophistication, integration, and potential. Among the reasons why we sometimes do not differentiate between coordination, cooperation, and collaboration is the fact that all three require some levels of shared purpose and trust to emerge and that their manifestations are similar: individuals working together.

In a world increasingly defined by complex and interconnected challenges, understanding these nuances is not just academic curiosity but a requirement for leadership precision that is necessary for the achievement of the challenging goals that we need to deliver. It is important here to acknowledge that interactions between individuals and groups are often dynamic, complex, and continuously changing, which makes it difficult to pinpoint precisely the thresholds of coordination, cooperation, and collaboration.

Furthermore, the overlap of these three states indicates that coordination is a precursor for cooperation, and both coordination and cooperation are harbingers for collaboration. Nonetheless, it is helpful to attempt to describe these three interactive states so that we can analyse them further.

Coordination

At the outset, coordination appears as the foundational layer in this triad. It is the art of aligning actions and decisions, ensuring that the cogs of an organizational machine, whether human or natural, turn in harmony towards a common goal, resulting in sufficient shared purpose and trust for coaction to emerge. This is the realm of schedules, plans, and directives, where the emphasis is on reducing redundancy and avoiding conflict.

Yet, while essential, coordination is a mere precursor to more profound forms of interaction. It is the script that guides the players, but not the play itself. Navigating a busy intersection under the guidance of traffic lights is an example of coordination in practice, which is characterized by a minimal level of integration between the different players, in this case, the drivers. All they need to do is obey the instructions of the centralized traffic light system, which operates based on a pre-programmed pattern for the system to work until it doesn't, that is.

Other living beings, from bacteria to migratory birds and hunting whales, have the ability to coordinate their actions to achieve their common objectives, too. Coordination often happens when the choice is made to do one's part in a collective effort to deliver a sought-after outcome. When humpback whales engage in a coordinated hunting technique known as 'bubble net feeding,' several whales swim in a spiral and blow bubbles to create a 'net' that traps a school of fish or krill.[7] Then, the whales swim upward with their mouths open to consume the concentrated prey. Interestingly, coordination can, at times, happen without conscious effort.

People walking in crowded areas often adjust their pace and direction unconsciously to avoid collisions, creating a fluid movement pattern through crowded spaces like busy sidewalks or train stations.

In extreme cases, coordination can be the result of coercion. Dictators and managers of forced labour camps can force people to work or march in unison. They may even get them to display impressive spectacles such as meticulous parades and accurate marching. Often, the shared purpose of the group is to avoid punishment as they have trust that any failure will be severely dealt with. These are, of course, bad examples and are mentioned here for illustration purposes. Coerced coordination is never sustainable, as proven by the multiple examples of the chaos that often succeeds the fall of a totalitarian regime.

Cooperation

Ascend a step further, and we enter the realm of cooperation. Here, individuals not only align their actions but also willingly and intentionally share and exchange resources and information, enabling a higher level of integration. It also features sufficient trust to allow for a decentralized decision-making practice, where decisions are made independently but with consideration for mutual benefit. Cooperation is characterized by a sense of the existence of a common long-term goal and mutual benefit: the understanding that working together yields better results than working in isolation.

It is the soil in which the seeds of deeper trust begin to germinate and sprout, nurturing a landscape where shared purpose takes root. However, it is still a transitional stage, often limited by individual or departmental immediate priorities.

A racing car pit stop is a breathtaking example of how precision, speed, and teamwork can deliver operational magic and where every second shaved off the clock can mean the difference between winning and losing. During a Formula 1 or NASCAR race, a pit stop is a high-pressure, meticulously synchronized operation that involves the flawless and simultaneous execution of multiple tasks in a matter of seconds.

As the race car stops in the pit lane, a highly trained pit crew springs into action. Each member of the team has a specific role honed through relentless practice. Tyre changers equipped with pneumatic guns race to each wheel, swiftly removing and replacing the tyres. This task alone involves a team of three for each tyre: one to operate the pneumatic gun, one to remove the tyre, and another to fit the new one.

Simultaneously, other specialists have crucial roles. A technician might adjust the front wing angle for better aerodynamics, while another checks and adjusts the suspension settings based on the driver's feedback and track conditions. If refuelling is allowed, a refueller plugs in a high-speed fuel rig to top up the tank within seconds.

The synchronization extends to timing and communication. The crew chief oversees the entire operation, ensuring that each task is performed seamlessly and in perfect sync. Communication headsets link the team, with spotters and engineers providing real-time data about the race and other competitors, ensuring the driver and the car are optimally prepared for re-entry to the race.

This pit stop performance is the pinnacle of cooperation, where the collective efforts of each team member are crucial. The choreographed precision ensures that the car spends a minimal amount of time stationary. Any mishap, no matter how minor, can cost valuable seconds and potentially the race itself.

Thus, a well-executed pit stop is not just a routine service but a critical strategic element in the race, demonstrating the power and effectiveness of teamwork under intense pressure.

Bees, ants, lion prides, and other species consistently engage in sophisticated cooperative behaviours to navigate challenges and achieve collective objectives such as producing honey, foraging for food, and hunting. These activities are not only essential for their survival, but also show remarkable adaptation to their changing environments. For instance, bees and ants show cooperation and organizational skills that are tightly focused on specific goals, such as optimizing resource collection and efficient nest building.

However, the adaptability of these species, while impressive, is inherently limited to their biological programming. The behavioural patterns of ants and bees, for example, are highly specialized and rigidly dictated by their genetic makeup. It is inconceivable to imagine that ants or bees might spontaneously decide to use their organizational skills for purposes outside their evolutionary imperatives, such as exploring new and innovative ways to use resources or altering their social structures. Their activities and goals are pre-defined by their genetic coding, without the flexibility seen in human pursuits, where creativity and abstract thinking allow for a vast range of aspirations and adaptive strategies.

This comparison highlights the unique human capacity to transcend biological programming and pursue an almost limitless array of goals and adaptations in response to environmental and social changes.

Collaboration

The peak of this coaction spectrum is collaboration: a state that transcends mere alignment of actions or sharing of resources.

Collaboration is the alchemy that has the potential to transform individual contributions into a collective masterpiece. It involves deep engagement, a fusion of perspectives, and a shared ownership of both goals and outcomes. In a collaborative environment, the boundaries between 'my work' and 'our work' blur, creating a fertile ground for innovation where the collective output is decidedly greater than the sum of its individual parts.

This is where the whole becomes unequivocally greater than the sum of its parts. While collaboration entails coordination and cooperation, it surpasses them through profound integration, shared decision-making, and continual open communication to maintain constant alignment. Collaborative groups can address novel and unprecedented challenges and can pivot their capabilities and even culture to adapt their strengths to changing conditions. Defined in this way, collaboration is reserved for humans and has not been observed in other species. That is why ants, bees, and other animals are still living in the same way as they were for millennia while humans practised medicine, wrote poetry, and split the atom.

To be fair, one needs to admit that humans also used their collaborative flare to fight destructive wars, bring about environmental degradation, and create unprecedented inequality. Yet, the inherent flexibility of collaboration means it can be harnessed to strive for any goal passionately pursued. This adaptive capacity positions collaboration as our greatest hope, empowering us to leverage our collective talent and creativity to address the monumental challenges of our era.

The table below outlines and summarizes the different aspects of the triad of coaction.

	Coordination	Cooperation	Collaboration
Definition	The process of organizing individuals or groups so that they work together properly and well by following agreed-upon rules and guidelines.	The process of working together towards shared goals, formally or informally, under flexible rules and with a mutual benefit being the driving force.	Deeply working together in a way that is central to all parties' interests, often enhancing shared meanings and values.
Objective	To ensure resources and efforts are used efficiently, avoiding overlap and conflict.	To achieve individual objectives alongside others, with shared resources or information.	To realise a shared purpose or produce a unique outcome that could not be accomplished independently.
Level of Integration	Low – Coordination often involves aligning schedules, resources, and activities to avoid conflict.	Medium – Cooperation involves sharing resources and information but can operate independently.	High – Collaboration involves a deep, collective determination to reach an identical objective, often requiring shared workspaces.

	Coordination	Cooperation	Collaboration
Communication	Directive – involves assigning tasks and ensuring adherence to plans.	Open and informal – sharing information and resources freely but with separate contributions.	Intensive and ongoing – requires constant communication and negotiation to create and maintain shared understanding and progress.
Decision Making	Centralized – with decisions often made by leaders or based on pre-established policies.	Decentralized – decisions are made independently but with consideration for others' roles and mutual benefit.	Shared – decisions are made collectively with all parties involved in the negotiation and consensus-building process.
Outcomes	Efficiency in executing predefined tasks or projects.	Mutual benefit, with each party achieving their own goals while aiding others.	A product, service, or outcome that is innovatively achieved through combined expertise and effort.
Examples	A project manager coordinating tasks between different departments to meet project deadlines.	Different organizations sharing resources to host a community event, benefiting from increased outreach without formal partnership agreements.	A team of researchers from different disciplines collaborating to develop a new technology, sharing insights and forging new methodologies.

Natural Limits to Joint Coaction

To enable both shared purpose and mutual trust to happen so that coordination, cooperation, and collaboration can take place, the ability to identify and communicate with other individuals and groups is essential. You recall from Chapter 1 that we discussed the concept of different information technologies and how these enable networks to emerge.

Mark Moffett, in his book *The Human Swarm*, outlines two distinct types of societies: those based on individual recognition and those described as anonymous.[8] The type of society has a profound impact on the pathways of establishing mutual trust and shared purpose, and eventually, the potential of the scale and extent of coordination, cooperation, and collaboration.

In societies based on individual recognition, each member knows all the others, as seen in small, tight-knit groups such as hunting prides or human hunter-gatherer tribes. Here, familiarity is common, and relationships are often cemented by genetic ties. As a result, kinship and social interactions represent the foundation of building reputation and mutual trust and shared challenges are often the foundation of shared goals, objectives, and purpose.

Conversely, in anonymous societies, individuals do not know personally every other member of the community. They rely on common traits for member identification, such as distinctive markers, pheromones, labels, or symbols that distinguish insiders from outsiders. This is usually the case for large groups of individuals coordinating and collaborating, for example, in ant colonies and beehives. This is also the case for large numbers of people who may identify as citizens of a country or members of a certain community without the need to know each other personally.

It is important to remember that instinctive coordination and cooperation observed in nature by species such as honeybees, ants, elephants, and hunting lion prides is still attributed to the presence of shared purpose and mutual trust between the different members of the community. In the natural world, often mutual trust is powered by the fact that individuals in beehives, ants' colonies, elephants' herds, and lions' prides are genetically related to one another.

It is much easier to trust family members. The shared purpose is often shaped by survival and reproduction needs. In a beehive, for example, bees are typically related, and the queen bee, worker bees, and male drones instinctively work to follow their roles within the beehive to ensure the survival of the whole clan.

Dunbar Number

In nature, social structures are generally organized according to either the rules of individual recognition or the principles of an anonymous society. This underlying organization, at least in part, explains why we don't observe lions forming hunting prides consisting of hundreds of individuals or bees and ants forming colonies of merely fifty or 100 members. The scale and structure of these groups are tailored to the specific recognition capabilities and social needs of the species. The only exception to the rule is the human species, where we have the capacity to collaborate effectively in both small and large numbers, transcending both individual recognition and anonymous society principles.

The Dunbar Number, proposed by British anthropologist Robin Dunbar, is a theoretical cognitive limit to the number of individuals with whom a primate can maintain stable social relationships.[9] These are relationships in which an individual knows who each person is and how each person relates to every other person. According to Dunbar, for humans, this number is roughly 150, although it can vary between 100 and 250 individuals. The theory suggests that this limit is a direct result of the size of the neocortex, the part of the brain responsible for conscious thought and language.

This concept originates from Dunbar's studies of primate brain size and social group size. By observing the correlation between neocortex size and group size in primates, he projected the number of sustainable relationships for humans. This evolutionary perspective provides insight into human social organization and the biological constraints on group sizes. The number also signifies the point of transition from individual recognition societies to anonymous societies, which is unique to humans. Other species are either the former or the latter. This indicates a flexibility that no other species possesses, apart from humans, the ability to coordinate, cooperate, and collaborate in both small numbers and large numbers.

This is often attributed to humans' capability of having language, processing abstract thoughts, telling stories, and ultimately constructing intersubjective realities. The mechanisms of inspiring shared purpose and nurturing mutual trust for small and big groups are different.

A Tale of Two Men

Collaborative political leadership, or the lack thereof, can have indelible marks on the lives of millions of people. It also can provide instructive examples of how the presence and the absence of shared purpose and mutual trust can impact collaboration. A very good example of this is the relationship between Mahathir Mohamad (the longest-serving Malaysian premier) and Anwar Ibrahim.

In 1982, Anwar Ibrahim, who was a prominent student leader and an activist, joined the United Malays National Organization (UMNO), which was the party led by Mahathir Mohamad, who himself had become the Malaysian prime minister a year earlier in

1981. A strong relationship between the two leaders emerged, and Anwar was rapidly promoted within the party and the government, serving as a minister of agriculture, education, and finance.

There was a clear growth of mutual trust and the development of shared purpose between these two leaders. This period was marked by strong economic development and industrialization of the Malaysian economy, resulting in robust growth of the Malaysian GDP. Anwar was largely seen as Mahathir's protégé, and the success of the collaborative leadership between the two reached its peak when Anwar was appointed as the deputy prime minister of Malaysia in 1993, positioning him as Mahathir's likely successor.

I arrived in Malaysia in 1997 as the Asian financial crisis was looming large. It was apparent that the two leaders, Mahathir and Anwar, had very different views on how to address the financial crisis. Anwar was in favour of working with the International Monetary Fund (IMF) by initiating austerity measures, curbing government spending, and stopping the mega projects that the country was pursuing. He made it very clear that he did not support any government bailout for Malaysian companies facing bankruptcy. Mahathir, on the other hand, blamed the crisis on currency speculators and wanted to introduce currency controls and tighter regulations of foreign investment in the country.

Both the shared purpose and mutual trust between the two leaders faltered, and tensions were on the rise. In 1998, Anwar was dismissed from his governmental positions and was arrested on accusations of corruption, abuse of power, and sodomy. The trial led to the conviction and imprisonment of Anwar, and I still remember the massive public protests this led to and the Reformasi (Reformation) movement that significantly impacted Malaysian politics.

After Mahathir retired from his position as a prime minister in 2003, the Federal Court of Malaysia overturned Anwar's conviction, and he was released from jail in 2004. Although initially barred from politics, Anwar continued to be an influential opposition figure against Mahathir's successors, particularly Najib Tun Razak. When his disqualification from participating in politics expired, Anwar ran for a parliamentary seat in 2008 and won, becoming officially the opposition leader in the parliament.

In 2009, Prime Minister Najib Razak established the 1Malaysia Development Berhad (1MDB) with the declared intention of promoting economic development and growth in Malaysia. Very quickly, it became embroiled in controversy when investigations revealed that large sums of money were misallocated for personal gain by high-profile individuals, including Prime Minister Najib Razak himself. The scandal gained international attention, as it was linked to luxury real estate, high-profile art purchases, and even the financing of Hollywood films, most notably *The Wolf of Wall Street* (2013). This was one of the largest financial scandals in Malaysia's history.[10]

Both Anwar and Mahathir were avid critics of the 1MDB corruption, demanding an open probe. Amid all of this turmoil, and as Anwar's popularity grew, another sodomy case was brought against him, and he was sentenced to five years' imprisonment in 2014.

While Anwar was in jail, an amazing turn of events took place, which was worthy of a Hollywood blockbuster. Mahathir and Anwar decided to join forces and reconcile to oppose Prime Minister Najib Razak amid the 1MDB corruption scandal. The ability of both leaders to collaborate and find both a sense of shared purpose and mutual trust is proof that the environment to enable collaboration can be engineered in the most difficult of circumstances. The shared purpose that helped them forge this unlikely collaboration was their belief that only by joining forces could they have a chance at ousting Najib. Mutual trust had not been easy to develop, either, taking into account the bitter history the two men had. Anwar agreed that when they succeeded in ousting Najib, Mahathir would form the government with the understanding that he would eventually hand over power to Anwar after securing a royal pardon, releasing the latter from his imprisonment.

The 2018 Malaysian General Election was the most dramatic in the history of the country, seeing the coalition that had ruled the country since independence in 1957 losing power, paving the way for Mahathir to become the prime minister again and for Anwar to be pardoned and released from jail. Almost from day one of Mahathir's second premiership, the question on everybody's mind was, when will Mahathir hand over to Anwar?

As you may expect, there is nothing in this story that goes according to the agreed plot, and the political turmoil in 2020 resulted in Mahathir resigning and Muhyiddin Yasin taking the reins as prime minister.

Finally, in 2022, following a general election, Anwar became the tenth prime minister of Malaysia. This marked a significant milestone in Anwar's political career and a resolution to the long-standing rivalry and collaboration with Mahathir. It is fascinating to see the ups and downs of shared purpose and mutual trust between two leaders and their political base, and how this can impact the prospects of their political collaboration, affecting the lives of millions of people.

As we examine the collaborative spectrum, the story of Mahathir and Anwar can serve as a source of education. Even people who have no reason to trust each other may find a way to forge an alliance, albeit a temporary one.

Part Two

Collaboration from the Bottom Up

Part Two of this book further explores collaboration, demonstrating its presence even amidst the fiercest competitive landscapes. Through a detailed examination of collaboration across diverse forms of life—ranging from bacteria and animals to human societies—this part highlights the prevalence and critical mechanics of collaborative interactions. By presenting a series of examples, it demonstrates not only the widespread nature of collaboration but also deciphers the underlying Collaboration Equation that governs successful collaborative endeavours across these varied instances.

The primary aim of this section is to establish a strong argument for recognizing coordination, cooperation, and collaboration as foundational, rather than merely advantageous organizing principles that orchestrate the dynamics of living systems and human relationships. It underscores the indispensability of shared purpose and mutual trust as the cornerstone elements that enable these organizing principles to manifest effectively.

Through this exploration, this part of the book seeks to elevate our understanding of collaboration from a desirable trait to an essential strategy for thriving in complex environments, showcasing its role as a fundamental driver of progress and innovation—in both the natural world and human affairs.

Chapter 4

The Law of the Jungle

'Nature does not hurry, yet everything is accomplished.'

—Lao Tzu

While phrases such as 'law of the jungle' and 'survival of the fittest' often portray the natural world as a fiercely competitive arena, a closer examination reveals a rich tapestry of collaboration that underpins the survival and evolution of diverse species.

This chapter probes into a variety of cooperative examples across the biological spectrum: from the microscopic cooperation among bacteria to intricate partnerships between insects, animals, and birds. By showcasing these examples, we demonstrate the profound universality of the Collaboration Equation, illustrating how collaborative strategies are employed not just by complex organisms, but also in the seemingly simple interactions of single-cell life forms.

This exploration not only challenges traditional views of natural competition, but also highlights the essential role collaboration plays in the resilience and adaptability of species. Through this lens, we see cooperation to be not just a human attribute, but a fundamental principle of life itself—something integral to the ecological success stories written throughout the natural world.

Many species coordinate and cooperate in highly adaptable and flexible ways—such as hunting whales and lions—but usually, this takes place in limited numbers. Other species can coordinate and collaborate in large numbers, but usually, this cooperation is rigid in scope, like bees and ants.

It is worth mentioning that cooperation is not limited to the *members* of a given species, but it can happen *across* species too. Some natural cooperative examples are described hereafter.

Bacteriacracy

In a 2018 study published in the Proceedings of the National Academy of Sciences of the United States of America (PNAS) accounting for global biomass, researchers Yinon M. Bar-Ona, Rob Phillips, and Ron Milo estimated that bacteria alone constitute about 15 per cent of Earth's biomass.[11] This is significant, considering that all animals represent just about 0.4 per cent and humans about 0.01 per cent. If other microorganisms like fungi, archaea, and protists were included, this percentage would be even higher. Considering the dominance of bacteria, it is a worthy exercise to explore the relationships between individual microorganisms, searching for examples of coordination and cooperation and exploring if the Collaboration Equation and the concepts of shared purpose and mutual trust still hold.

When studying the behaviour of non-human forms of life, critics often caution against anthropomorphism—attributing human characteristics to non-human entities. Indeed, bacteria do not 'intend' to coordinate and cooperate or exhibit trust as humans understand it; their actions are not driven by conscious thought, but by biochemical mechanisms honed for survival.

Yet, this does not diminish the complexity and sophistication of their interactions and the importance of the understanding that can be achieved of how systems work by observing and analysing these interactions.

In the microscopic world of bacteria, a phenomenon known as quorum sensing, where microorganisms communicate and coordinate their actions, offers a striking example of cooperation as it emerges when there are common goals and mutual trust.[12]

Quorum sensing involves bacteria releasing and detecting chemical signals to estimate their population density in the environment they are present in. Once a certain chemical concentration threshold is reached, indicating a corresponding population density, the existing bacteria collectively change behaviour and perform a range of functions such as sporulation, bioluminescence, and biofilm formation, as per the environmental necessities.

The phenomenon of quorum sensing resembles a form of bacterial democracy (bacteriaccy, if I may) in action. This coordinated effort, vital for tasks like nutrient consumption, biofilm formation, or toxin production, can be seen as a result of having survival as a shared purpose, while simultaneously, through trusting the received chemical signals, reaching a consensus for the greater good of the community.

Quorum sensing also transcends the simplistic view of microbes as solitary entities, showcasing how cooperation can emerge even in life's most fundamental forms. It reminds us that mutual benefit and collective action are not solely human traits but are woven deeply into the fabric of life.

Understanding quorum sensing broadens our perspective on social behaviour, cooperation, and communication. It encourages us to appreciate the intricate connections in nature, where even the simplest organisms participate in a dance of mutual reliance and communal decision-making. In a world grappling with collaborative challenges, nature's microscopic cooperative strategies offer profound lessons.

Obviously, both the shared purpose—which is focused on survival and reproduction—and mutual trust—which is chemically defined—are coded in the bacterial genes, rather than intentionally emerging. However, the concept of the need for both shared purpose and mutual trust for successful coordination and cooperation to take place remains valid.

Nature's Ballet

When flying in concert, swarms of bats, locusts, and migratory birds present a mesmerizing spectacle of coordination and collective intelligence that has long captivated scientists and ordinary observers alike.

Bats: As the darkness falls, bats emerge in swarms from their roosts, embarking on their nightly forays. This exodus is not a chaotic frenzy but a meticulously synchronized operation. Relying on echolocation, bats communicate through high-frequency sounds, navigating and foraging with precision. The shared purpose here is survival—locating food while avoiding obstacles and predators. Prioritizing their survival is instinctive, and it creates a sense of a common goal where bats sacrifice their individuality.

Trust is implicit in their echolocation calls, as each bat trusts the echoes returned by its neighbours to accurately represent the external world. This mutual reliance ensures that, despite the seemingly individualistic act of foraging, the swarm moves cohesively, and each bat's success contributes to the collective's.

However, examples of trust breaches have been observed in the wild, when bats, competing for food, 'jam' the signals from other bats[13], making it difficult for them to locate prey and, in the process, compromising their ability to work together.

This breakdown, in a way, proves that trust is an essential component for cooperation to emerge.

It is worth mentioning here that signal jamming is not an exclusive expertise of bats when they want to confuse each other. Some of bats' preys, such as the tiger moth, have developed a jamming secret weapon akin to ultrasonic sonar jamming technology. By emitting signals that jam the bat's sonar, they render them blind, thus saving themselves from predation in the process.

Locust: Locust swarms are often depicted as plagues, yet their formation is a marvel of social coordination driven by a shared purpose: finding food to sustain the swarm.

When locusts swarm, their serotonin levels change, triggering a more gregarious behaviour that facilitates their mass movement. This transformation is underpinned by trust in the collective's direction—a trust that their neighbours' movements toward food sources and away from dangers are correct.

Each locust, by following these cues, reinforces the swarm's direction, creating a powerful and adaptive collective intelligence capable of traversing vast distances in search of sustenance. Trust emerges between different individuals from the same swarm using chemical signalling and pheromones.

Because locusts can decimate vast quantities of crops, people have been interested in exploring ways to combat them. Using pesticides to exterminate locusts can be costly and equally devastating for the environment. Understanding how locusts coordinate and working on disrupting that coordination represents an interesting alternative. In other words, how can we break down the Collaboration Equation of locusts? Research is underway to explore the possibility of breaking the social order in locust societies by disrupting the pheromonal system that regulates the relationships between them, that is, breaking down and undermining the trust that exists between different individuals.

Birds: The V-formation of migratory birds is a testament to the efficiencies achieved through shared purpose and trust. The lead bird takes on the headwinds, while those behind ride in the updraft, periodically rotating to share the energetic burden. This requires immense trust: Each bird relies on the others to maintain formation, pace, and conserve energy for the group over long migrations.

The birds' shared purpose, here, is clear: reaching their destination. Trust emerges not just in aerodynamics, but in the communal knowledge of the route, passed down across generations, with each bird playing its part in the collective memory and effort.

In the examples of coordination and cooperation outlined above, shared purpose emerges as a response to environmental pressures—be it foraging, avoiding predators, or migrating. Mutual trust, on the other hand, is a by-product of consistent, predictable behaviour within the swarm. Whether it's the precision of bats' echolocation, the locusts' alignment towards food sources, or the migratory birds' aerodynamic formation, each individual acts in a way that can be trusted by their peers to contribute to the collective goal.

Natural Organizations

Nature presents us with the most effective and efficient organizations. Ants work together to collect food, honeybees cooperate to make honey and protect the beehive, and lions cooperate to hunt and defend their pride against intruders.

Below is a brief look at some natural cooperative examples seen through the angle of the Collaboration Equation.

Cooperation in Ants: Despite their small size, ants are able to achieve huge feats through their ability to work together. While the shared purpose of survival might be genetically programmed in them, the establishment of mutual trust is an act that ants need to renew repeatedly at every interaction. Ants recognize each other as members of the same colony through a combination of rituals, chemical signals, and pheromones. Each ant colony has a unique set of chemical compounds that rub off the bodies of its members, often referred to as 'colony odour', that help identify nestmates and distinguish them from ants from other colonies.[14]

When an ant encounters another, it uses its antennae to taste and smell these chemicals. If the chemical profile matches that of its colony, the ant will accept it as a nestmate. In contrast, if the chemical signals do not match, the ant may become aggressive or try to repel the intruder.

In addition to chemical cues, rituals enabled by visual and tactile signals can also play a role, especially in species with more complex social interactions. However, chemical communication remains the primary method of recognition among ants.

If two or more ant colonies spread out, and members of different colonies come into contact with each other, all hell breaks loose. As ants realize that they cannot trust the other ants they are encountering as their own, the cooperative behaviour is immediately replaced with an aggressive one.

Cooperation in Honeybees: The cooperation observed in honeybee hives is deeply rooted in their biology, specifically in the division of labour and task allocation among individuals. The hive's primary purpose is reproduction and survival—worker bees, drones, and the queen each play distinct roles in achieving this.

Worker bees forage for food, nurse bees care for the brood, and drones contribute to the mating process. Trust among them is fostered through the consistent execution of roles, and established through the pheromones that ensure that members of the same colony can recognize each other in a pattern broadly similar to an ant colony. Each bee relies on others to perform their duties effectively for the well-being of the entire colony. This mutual dependence creates a cohesive unit where trust is essential for survival.[15]

The overarching goal of the hive requires efficient communication. Bees use pheromones to convey information about the location of food, the presence of the queen, and potential threats to the colony.

Furthermore, in a beehive, bees are typically related genetically. A beehive is organized around a single reproductive female—the queen bee—and her offspring. The majority of the worker bees and male drones in the hive are descendants of the queen. This genetic relatedness enhances the overall cooperation and altruistic behaviour observed in a bee colony. Worker bees, despite being sterile and not passing on their genes directly, share a significant portion of their genetic makeup.

Individual Recognition Based Cooperation

As mentioned in the earlier chapters, there are social animals where trust is built upon genetic relatedness and the individual recognition of members of the group. This creates the space for complex social interactions where hierarchy, alliance-building, and emotions can play a dynamic role in shaping the cooperation between the group members, enabling it to perform a wide range of variety of activities and tasks and to respond flexibly to the challenges it encounters.

The need to remember and recognize individuals within the group exerts a considerable cognitive load on the brain, which, in turn, sets a limit to how big the group can be as proposed by Dunbar.

A pride of lions usually has ten to fifteen members, although it can even go up to thirty. A herd of elephants can vary in size but typically consists of ten to fifty individuals. However, some herds can be larger, sometimes exceeding 100 elephants, particularly in areas with abundant resources. Chimpanzees' troop size can vary widely, but typically ranges from twenty to over 100 individuals.

Individual recognition-based communities are often highly adaptable and complex. Their shared purpose and interest in survival and maintaining order can be established and sustained through continuous negotiation and hierarchy establishment. Mutual trust is built through social grooming, favours reciprocation, cooperative hunting, and shared care for the young. Fostering and preserving mutual trust could be a tricky business, as members of the group may disrupt the social system while seeking higher power, status, and access to more resources like food and mating rights.

Cross-Species Cooperation

One of the most fascinating demonstrations of the Collaboration Equation in decoding cross-species relationships is the link between smaller cleaner fish—such as the cleaner wrasse—and bigger predator fish. Reflecting on a scenario where the latter patiently stands still while the former eats away the parasite from its skin, gills, and even teeth, it is not difficult to deduce the common purpose and interest of the two players. The predator fish gets cleaned, ridding itself of parasites that can harm its health, while the cleaner fish gets a nutritious meal.

Establishing mutual trust in the unforgiving environment of the ocean, nonetheless, is a different ballgame altogether. However, without mutual trust, this transaction that plays a key role in promoting a healthy and balanced ecosystem would have been impossible.

For the fish seeking to be cleaned—such as sharks—building trust with and assuring the cleaner fish starts with the development of a mutual understanding that transcends the typical predator-prey dynamic. This is built on a foundation of clear communication and established routines that prevent them from harming their smaller partners.

Trust begins with recognition. Sharks are able to identify cleaner fish through visual and chemical cues. When a shark approaches a reef cleaning station, it often performs a dance-like display, signalling its intent to be cleaned, rather than to hunt. In return, the cleaner fish approach with a specific swaying motion, indicating their readiness to clean. Cleaner fish tend to inhabit 'cleaning stations' on reefs that act as neutral territories or 'safe zones'. Sharks understand these zones as safe havens where feeding is off-limits. By meeting at these sites, both sharks and cleaner fish reinforce the non-predatory nature of their interaction.

This relationship hinges on the patience and temperament of the shark: something that might seem counterintuitive, given their fearsome reputation. They often hover motionless, with gaping mouths or spread gills, allowing the cleaner fish ample time to complete their task, without the threat of being eaten. Regular and repeated interactions further cement the trust between sharks and cleaner fish. As these encounters accumulate, sharks become accustomed to the benefits provided by cleaner fish, reinforcing the trust placed in these diminutive allies.

In conclusion, while it is obvious that the predator-prey dynamic appears to be prevalent in the natural world, the cooperative dynamics are aplenty as well. The integration of cooperation and competition ensures both high efficiency and synergy, guaranteeing the robustness and long-term sustainability of the natural world.

Coordination and cooperation in the natural world remain underpinned by the availability of a shared purpose and mutual trust. This holds from single-cell organisms to the most complex and within and across species. The Collaboration Equation can explain cooperation in both individual recognition and anonymous society groups.

The next chapters will be dedicated to studying the collaborative phenomena within human groups and societies.

Chapter 5

Human Collaboration

'For together we can stand, divided we fall.'

—Aesop

This chapter examines the complexities of collaborative efforts across the realms of business, technology, and geopolitics.

Through a series of illustrative cases, we explore both triumphant and unsuccessful examples of collaboration, analysed through the framework of the Collaboration Equation. These examples serve to underscore the critical importance of shared purpose and mutual trust as foundational elements that enable effective collaboration. By examining high-profile collaborations that have reshaped industries and even geopolitical landscapes, as well as partnerships that have faltered or failed, this chapter provides readers with an understanding of what drives successful collaboration among individuals and organizations.

This chapter highlights how alignment in goals and values, along with a robust foundation of trust, are not merely beneficial but essential for collaborative ventures to thrive. Furthermore, it equips readers with actionable insights and strategies to foster these key enablers in their own collaborative initiatives: whether in startups, multinational corporations, or international alliances.

As we established in the earlier chapters, humans have become the most powerful and dominant species in the world. Over the past 50,000 years, Homo sapiens emerged from being a marginal species into one that conquered fire, invented writing, explored every corner of the earth, ventured into outer space, and split the atom. While our superior cognitive capacities, ability to communicate through spoken language, and possessing an upright posture were key elements in our success, our civilization was built on another unique capability that sets us apart from all other species—our versatile ability to collaborate with others on large scales to achieve objectives that go beyond our mere survival.

As a matter of fact, the progress of our civilization, and the complexity and impact of the endeavours we were able to undertake, are in direct proportion to the scale of collaboration we were able to muster. The history of the human civilization saw collaboration grow from the level of the family to the levels of tribes, organizations, nations, and eventually, the whole world, where connectivity and globalization are reshaping every aspect of our lives.

As explained earlier, the distinction between coordination, cooperation, and collaboration is more than semantic. It reflects the depth of individuals' and groups' relationships, as well as the potential of collective endeavour, where the outcome is greater than the sum of its parts. In an age where challenges are complex and solutions elusive, collaboration stands as our only plausible pathway to continue to survive and thrive.

This requires a deep understanding of how to build and nurture collaborative coalitions. Individuals and organizations that master the Collaboration Equation will not just endure but flourish, with the potential to leave an indelible mark on the story of human progress.

The Evolution of Human Collaboration

Humans are the most ingenious species that has walked the Earth. Despite not being the strongest, the fastest, or the most prepared to weather the natural elements, humans have managed to dominate the world mainly because of their ability to collaborate with one another.

To put it simply, the only real limitation to what we can achieve is how widely and authentically we can collaborate. The history of humanity can be viewed as the journey to widen the circle and grow the number of individuals in a collaborative endeavour. From small human groups based on family connections and tribes, to the development of the nation-state and multinational corporations, we have been on a quest to integrate more people into the human collaborative project, being at the heart of it our ability to spread our shared purpose and expand mutual trust.

Below is a chronological account of the growth of the size of the collaborative unit:

Family Units (Prehistoric to around 10,000 BCE)

In this era, humans lived within small kin-based groups and were engaged in hunting and gathering activities.[16] The groups' shared purpose focused on the survival of the family unit by providing food and protection, and mutual trust between the members of the group was established through mutual recognition for everyone within the group, as well as genetic relatedness. The productivity, synergy, and value-adding capabilities of these groups were limited, and the skills and talents available were focused on survival.

Tribal Organization (10,000 BCE to 3,000 BCE)

Early tribal societies, like the Sumerians, started to appear in fertile areas such as Mesopotamia.[17] This population growth was simultaneously enabled and driven by the development of agriculture, domesticating plants and animals, and herding livestock. Tending to these large enterprises required the coordination and cooperation of an increasing number of people who share the purpose of safety, security, and aiming for a good harvest. The mutual trust is achieved and maintained through a combination of mutual recognition and societal norms that are agreed upon to encourage working together and punish cheaters, transgressors, and free riders.

Emergence of States (3,000 BCE to 1,000 BCE)

As a result of increasing agricultural productivity in certain parts of the world, a growing number of people started to live in close proximity to each other. Tribes started to consolidate, and early cities, states, and kingdoms emerged in Mesopotamia and ancient Egypt, with kings and pharaohs as central authority figures.

These communities started to cohere around the shared purpose of security and prosperity, with division of labour evolving and members of the community specializing as priests, farmers, soldiers, craftspeople, etc. The world's first empire, the Akkadian Empire of Sargon, was founded in 2334 BCE in the central region of Mesopotamia.[18] Sargon established the empire after conquering the Sumerian city-states, unifying them under his rule. Mutual trust between larger groups of people necessitated the development and establishment of administrative, legal, financial, and religious institutions.

The first known script, Cuneiform, was invented around 3000 BCE in Mesopotamia, specifically in Sumer, which is present-day southern Iraq. Initially, Cuneiform was developed to keep records and evolved from simple pictographs to more abstract symbols used for various administrative and communicative functions. The Code of Hammurabi, which was the first law humanity recorded, was written around 1754 BCE, during the reign of King Hammurabi, the sixth king of Babylon. The concept of money and the first polytheistic religions emerged too.

Formation of Early Nations (1,000 BCE to 500 CE)

The trends of bringing people together with more sophisticated coaction as an organizing principle continued. This gave rise to early city-states like Athens and Sparta in ancient Greece. This was an important development, as Athens's focus on education, philosophy, and cultural refinement gave birth to the concept of democracy as a method for citizens to organize themselves for joint action and the pursuit of the public good.

While Sparta adopted a militaristic and oligarchic bent overall, their approach to women's empowerment was unique: Spartan women had more freedom and rights compared to their Athenian counterparts.[19] They were encouraged to be physically fit and could own and inherit property. This period witnessed the birth of Christianity, along with the emergence of the Roman Empire and the Han Dynasty in China.

Consolidation of Nations (500 CE to 1500 CE)

This period witnessed the consolidation of medieval kingdoms and empires, such as the Roman Empire, which were bent on expanding and unifying its territory. Genghis

Khan and his successors established the Mongol Empire, the largest contiguous empire in history, stretching from Europe to Asia, facilitating trade and cultural exchange along the Silk Road. While Christianity continued to spread, Islam was born in Arabia.

Religion continued to play a growing role in shaping the political, economic, cultural, and social discourse. The consolidation of power by monarchs in countries like England, France, and Spain led to the formation of centralized nation-states. This also led to territorial conflicts such as the Hundred Years' War (1337–1453), which was a prolonged conflict between England and France over territorial claims, significantly impacting both nations.

Modern Nation-States (1500 CE to present)

The modern nation-states continued to coalesce, and their borders took shape, allowing different political, social, cultural, and economic systems to emerge. The unification of Italy took place in 1861 and Germany in 1871 after the Franco-Prussian War. Many nations in Asia, Africa, and South America became independent too. This era tested the limits of collaboration, as it featured two World Wars and one Cold War, and as I write, multiple conflicts are taking place globally, with others threatening to erupt. At the same time, initiatives such as the European Union (EU) were able to be delivered as a supranational organization beyond the traditional nation-state model.

The table below illustrates the history of human organizational growth and evolution, highlighting the overarching trend toward collaboration and unity. However, this history is also marked by setbacks, failures, and lessons that have yet to be fully learned.

Period	Collaboration Basis	Shared Purpose	Mutual Trust	Economy/ Financial Development	Religious Development	Information and Literacy Development	Legal Development
Prehistoric–10,000 BCE	Family Units	Survival	Kin-based and Mutual Recognition	Barter System	Animism and Shamanism	Oral Tradition	Tribal and Clan Systems
10,000–3,000 BCE	Tribes	Survival	Kin-based, Mutual Recognition, and Tribal Norms	Barter System	Fertility Cults and Mother Goddesses	Oral Tradition	Tribal and Clan Systems
3000–1000 BCE	Kings (strong leaders) dominated groups	Safety, Security, and Division of Labour	Mutual Recognition, Society Norms, Authority of the Central Figure	Early money Mesopotamia: Barley, Silver, Temples as Early Banks Egypt: Grain and Metal Rings China: Cowrie Shells	Polytheism and belief in after life. Hinduism Emergence of Judaism and Monotheism	Early Writing Systems Mesopotamia: Cuneiform Egypt: Hieroglyphs China: Early Chinese Writing	Written Legal Codes, e.g. Code of Hammurabi

Period	Collaboration Basis	Shared Purpose	Mutual Trust	Economy/ Financial Development	Religious Development	Information and Literacy Development	Legal Development
1000 BCE–500 CE	Early Nations	Safety, Security, and Division of Labour	Society Norms, Law	Coinage	Buddhism Christianity	Alphabets	Early Laws
500–1500 CE	Consolidated Nations	Safety, Security, and Division of Labour	Society Norms, Law	Bills of Exchange	Islam	Paper and Printing in China and the Islamic World The Printing Press	. Feudal Laws . Religious Laws: Catholic and Sharia Law . Signing of the Magna Carta
1500 CE–Present	Modern Nation States	National Interest	Society Norms, Institutions, Law	Banking System Digital Currency	Religious tolerance	Mass Media Information & Communication Technology AI	Magna Carta Civil Law

While earlier human societies started with collaboration within families and tribes that were genetically related for purposes concerned with survival, such as hunting, gathering, producing food, and fending against danger, humans also possess the potential and capacity to build alliances and work with others who are not related to them for longer-term mutual gain, such as establishing trading routes, performing scientific research, or even waging wars. Many of the significant undertakings that we engage in require a large number of people of different skills, talents, and backgrounds to collaborate. The story of human civilization can be seen as a series of milestones, where we successfully collaborated or failed to do so, often with consequential outcomes.

It is important to note that collaboration in itself is a value-neutral tool. People can unite for both benevolent and malevolent objectives, which is why it is important to cultivate leaders and leadership mindsets that favour the development of a positive, true higher purpose. As more people come together to create more value and harness more resources, the potential for exploitation, injustice, and aggression increases as well. This is why building legal and governance structures, institutions, and culture to maintain collaboration in the net positive territory is very necessary. The essence lies in the fact that effective collaboration within teams or groups empowers them to achieve feats beyond the capacity of any lone individual. Ten people skilled at different construction specializations can, over time, build ten houses, while any one of them will struggle to build one house on their own.

The Tragedy of the Commons

Imagine a green communal pasture open to multiple herders with their livestock grazing. It makes sense for each herder to maximize their benefits by putting as many livestock as they can on the pasture. If every herder thought in a similar self-centred way, the pasture could end up being overgrazed, resulting in all herds declining, and everybody losing. This situation is described as the 'Tragedy of the Commons,' a term coined by ecologist Garrett Hardin in 1968 to illuminate the dangers of individual self-interest in shared resource environments.[20]

As we navigate the complex web of our globally connected world, the lessons of the tragedy of the commons are more relevant than ever. Today, our commons are not just pastures, but oceans, air, forests, and even the digital landscape. The relentless pursuit of short-term gains has led to overfishing, deforestation, air pollution, and data breaches.

It is important that we develop a more collaborative approach to using our global commons in a way that does not compromise the long-term longevity of our resources so that others, including future generations, are not deprived of the opportunity to enjoy and benefit from them.

Market Forces and Collaboration

In his seminal work, *The Wealth of Nations*, published in 1776, Adam Smith, the Scottish economist and philosopher, established the foundation of classical economics and capitalist theory. He also laid the foundation for our understanding of the mechanisms of the tensions between competitive and collaborative dynamics and how, through that, markets emerge.

Summarized in Smith's statement that '. . . the wealth of nations is built on the division of labour,' is the potential for unlocking value that can be created when we focus on what we do best, while trusting others will collaborate with us and do their part so the shared purpose is delivered.

In a world where the quest for short-term goals is trapping our corporate and political leaders into believing that competition is the most obvious and safest choice of action, it is refreshing to adopt a leadership style that helps us avoid the tragedy of the commons and embrace collaboration as a strategic choice.

The Purpose-Trust Matrix

It is obvious that collaboration is a choice that we need to make repeatedly. Humans are highly complex creatures, and they can be self-interested and have the capacity for aggression and manipulation. They are simultaneously capable of great acts of selflessness, kindness, love, and wisdom. Whenever the interests, values, or narratives of people or groups collide or contradict, the potential for conflict may loom large; however, there will always be room to find common ground for collaboration.

Understanding the art and science of building collaborative coalitions through the Collaboration Equation is key to empowering us to be on a trajectory of avoiding conflict and enabling harmony.

When there is a lack of shared purpose and/or mutual trust, collaboration fails to take place; the result can be cynicism, confusion, or flat-out conflict. The different combinations of shared purpose and mutual trust are shown diagrammatically below.

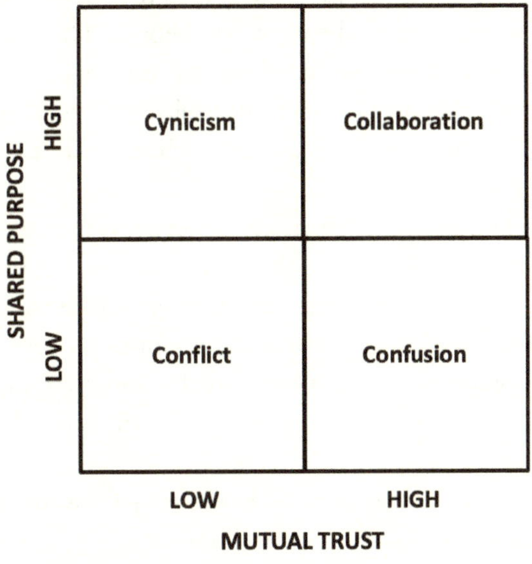

Fig. 1 – The Purpose-Trust Matrix

High Shared Purpose-Low Mutual Trust

During the Covid-19 pandemic era, which peaked in 2020–2021, the economy came to a halt. Most of the world went into a lockdown mode, where schools, universities, malls, offices, and borders were closed. A race started to discover a vaccine, and research centres, pharmaceutical companies, and drug-approving authorities went into overdrive to get it ready, slow the progress of the pandemic, and open the economy again.

While everyone had the shared purpose of keeping themselves and their families and communities healthy, some individuals harboured deep doubts and a lack of trust while assessing the intentions of the governments, media, and pharmaceutical companies when it comes to rolling out mandatory vaccination programmes, enforcing lockdowns, or even requiring the wearing of surgical masks in public places.

Despite the presence of a shared purpose, the lack of mutual trust between the anti-vaxxers and the establishment resulted in deep cynicism, causing a refusal to take the vaccine and igniting a variety of rumours and conspiracy theories. The way the media and the authorities responded to the anti-vaxxers, with pure ridicule rather than trying to respectfully address their concerns, did not help improve the situation when it came to fostering mutual trust.

A similar, and probably more consequential, situation prevails in the area of addressing the climate emergency. Parties, including states, who agree on the urgent nature of the situation and the need for immediate action to reduce emissions often fall short of collaborating on this worthy goal when they do not have the mutual trust that their counterparts will carry their side of the bargain.

This is an area that we will examine again in the book, as it represents an existential threat to humanity.

Low Shared Purpose-High Mutual Trust

When individuals trust each other but lack agreement on a shared purpose, vision, or goals, it is rather difficult for them to muster the commitment and resources for collaboration to take place. Even if the parties involved are willing to allocate resources, the lack of a clear shared purpose will ensure that the results are far from adequate, and confusion reigns.

So, while the situation may remain peaceful, and the parties can coexist and even have cordial relationships—at least for a while—confusion, complacency, and lack of action are the most likely outcomes.

When the iPhone was first released in 2007, Nokia's share of the global smartphone market was over 50 per cent. With fierce competition from Apple and Samsung, Nokia saw its smartphone market share sharply decline to just over 27 per cent in 2010.[21] Marred by a lack of innovation and the ability to compete in a shifting market landscape, Nokia appointed Stephen Elop, a former executive of Microsoft, as its CEO in September 2010. Elop realized that Nokia was struggling to adapt to a rapidly changing market and authored the now-famous 'burning platform' memo in which he likened Nokia to a person standing on a burning oil platform with two options: stay there and try to extinguish it, or jump into the unknown only to hope for the best.[22]

With this assessment in mind, Elop relied on his strong ties with Microsoft to reach a strategic partnership with the software giant that he announced in February 2011. Through this partnership, Nokia committed to adopting the Microsoft operating system for all its phones, practically abandoning its own, Symbian, and stopping the development of the MeeGo operating system. This was aimed at helping both companies to compete against Apple and Android operating systems, and was largely empowered by the mutual trust and loyalty that both Nokia and Microsoft enjoyed.

Although the deal sounded logical on the surface, as Nokia aimed at leveraging the expertise of Microsoft in software development, industry critics warned that this partnership might limit Nokia's ability to differentiate itself in a competitive market. Unfortunately, the deal's objectives were not achieved, as Nokia's software transition proved to be challenging. Furthermore, as industry experts had predicted, the limitations of the Microsoft software imposed on Nokia's hardware resulted in losing key advantages the latter had enjoyed. All of this resulted in delays and gaps in product lineup, allowing competitors the opportunity to further cement their market position.

On reflection, it is now clear that the Nokia-Microsoft partnership lacked a market-relevant shared purpose. While Nokia aimed at protecting and growing back its market share, the partnership prevented it from exploring opportunities in the burgeoning Android market, which eventually became the industry's dominant operating system.

When Microsoft announced the acquisition of Nokia's Devices and Services Division in September 2013, Nokia's share of the smartphone market was a mere 3 per cent. The Nokia mobile phone business continued to struggle and was, eventually, phased out entirely.

In this example, it is apparent that although trust and loyalty existed, a truly shared and well-articulated purpose was lacking. The purpose that Nokia could have aspired for is to keep making a difference in its customers' lives, while paying close attention to the fact that the needs and desires of these customers have shifted. Spending more time on its articulation and development of shared purpose could have resulted in a realization that Microsoft was not the right partner in the first place. Alternatively, it could also have resulted in Nokia and Microsoft joining forces to build a new operating system that leveraged off Nokia's hardware advantages or even developing an open-source operating system to compete with Android.

The case of Nokia-Microsoft is not unique. According to most studies, 70–90 per cent of mergers and acquisitions fail to achieve their objectives to create the expected value.[23] While the studies have outlined many reasons for this observation, the lack of attention, time, and effort dedicated to articulating, communicating, and realizing a shared purpose between partners is a common theme.

This is not a book about mergers and acquisitions, and those contemplating an M&A venture should consider detailed due diligence work before proceeding. What it argues, however, is the importance of evaluating the possibility of discovering or even inventing a shared sense of purpose for both merged entities. This shared purpose should be anchored in the positive impact the two merging organizations can have on their customers' lives—or even the world.

This shared purpose goes beyond the business hygiene factors, such as reducing cost, improving efficiency, and increasing productivity. Investing time in articulating and agreeing to a shared purpose makes the development of a hardwired implementation agreement, which inevitably includes doing difficult, painful, and unpopular things, much easier. Utilizing the Collaboration Equation as part of the due diligence process could be an instructive undertaking.

Low Shared Purpose-Low Mutual Trust

When both shared purpose and mutual trust are in short supply, conflict becomes more likely, unless people find some pathways to disengagement. When parties occupy the same geographical locations or market positions, disengagement can be very challenging.

In 2011, Apple and Samsung engaged in a multi-jurisdiction legal war, accusing each other of infringing on intellectual property rights and copying design and functionality features. While each aimed to dominate the competitive smartphone market, their strategies differed markedly. Apple was known for prioritizing product design and emphasizing its unique user experience, while Samsung was trying to retain its market position with a disruptive new competitor. The series of bitter and costly lawsuits in multiple countries highlighted the anaemic trust situation.

Clearly, the objective should be to work on avoiding conflict and maximizing the potential of collaboration by inspiring a shared purpose and nurturing mutual trust. It is also necessary to note that situations when either shared purpose or mutual trust are scarce are relatively unstable, and they could deteriorate into conflict if no disengagement pathways are available or avenues to build shared purpose and mutual trust are not identified. Movement from conflict, cynicism, or confusion to collaboration is possible and requires skilled and committed leadership.

In the rest of this book, we will further discuss different examples to elucidate strategies that can be implemented to achieve sustainable and lasting collaboration. Once a collaborative state is reached, it is not to be taken for granted, as maintaining the conditions to keep the collaboration healthy and productive would be one of the leaders' key objectives.

Trust Lost and Found

Uber is one of the most disruptive companies in the world. Its success transformed how entrepreneurs saw the world, starting a whole new class of businesses, and even earning its own new dictionary entry: uberization.

Becoming the largest taxi company in the world, without owning any cars, was one of the feats that Uber achieved by leveraging technology and the access capacity that private cars and drivers have. Moreover, the company has been working on automating the customers' rides by using self-driving cars. Recognizing Google's work in the development of self-driving vehicles, Uber acquired Otto, a company founded by former Google engineer Anthony Levandowski in 2016.

Soon after the sale, Google's self-driving division, Waymo, filed a lawsuit against Uber, accusing it of using trade secrets and privileged technical information that were stolen by Levandowski before leaving the company. Despite Uber firing Levandowski after he was accused of trade secrets theft, Waymo claimed that Uber's top executives were aware of the alleged 'theft', further deepening the trust crisis and straining the relationships.[24]

After a long and bitter legal battle, the trial ended abruptly in 2018, only five days after it began, when the parties decided to settle. This agreement entailed that Uber pledges not to use any of Waymo's intellectual property and also pay a penalty of $ 245 million. Two years later, in 2020, Uber indicated that it was moving entirely out of the autonomous vehicles business when it sold its self-driving division to Aurora Innovations.

While both Uber and Google shared a deep sense of purpose and commitment to delivering self-driving vehicles, they shared no mutual trust. This type of interaction, which is rife with cynicism, doubt, and suspicion, is highly unstable and can slide into conflict easily—which is what happened in this case.

In a surprising turn of events, Uber and Waymo seemed to finally decide to put their differences aside and combine their effort to address long-haul autonomous trucking. 'Rising shipping demand coupled with a growing shortage of drivers has brought the logistics industry to an inflexion point, and the need for an autonomous trucking solution like Waymo Via has never been more apparent. To help accelerate this autonomous future, we're partnering with Uber Freight to connect our technology with their platform and deploy autonomous trucks across their network,' announced a Waymo Via statement in June 2022.[25]

Charlie Jatt, head of Commercialization for Trucking at Waymo Via, went on to say, 'Uber Freight's network of shippers, carriers, and marketplace technology is a great match for the Waymo Driver. Through this partnership, we can empower carriers to fully utilise their investments in the Waymo Via solution through Uber Freight and create a great experience for shippers while keeping our focus on developing the core Driver technology. We're really excited to see how this partnership can impact the logistics industry and solve critical challenges over the next decade and beyond.'

Clearly, the deep sense of shared purpose represented a sufficient foundation for the two rivals to come together and build mutual trust, enabling their journey of collaboration to start anew. This demonstrates how dynamic human interactions are, and that while rivalry and conflict are possible, the opposite is equally achievable. The need for leaders who can build mutual trust and inspire shared purpose has never been as acute in all domains of human existence.

As humanity's collaborative project unfolds, the need to bring more of us into it is obvious, but not inevitable. This will require leadership and intentional focus that recognize collaboration as the only viable way forward. Humans are the only species that deal with two competing factors: their awareness of their mortality and the limited lifespan they have on one hand, and their desire to leave a positive legacy on the other. Leaders can and should leverage these defining traits to bring the best out of us.

The following parts of the book focus on the kind of necessary leadership skills, mindsets, and attitudes for solving the Collaboration Equation and help us build the sustainable, equitable, and enjoyable world we all desire.

Part Three

Collaborative Leadership

We have, by now, established the importance of the simultaneous presence of both shared purpose and mutual trust for optimal human interaction to take place. Mergers and acquisitions that make perfect business sense on paper could fail due to a lack of a shared sense of purpose between different stakeholders. Issues such as public health and environmental challenges do enjoy a wide agreement on their importance, and many share the purpose of improving them. However, often, the lack of time and effort dedicated to fostering mutual trust between different parties involved results in the intractable lack of success experienced in these ventures.

While intuitively, one may think that inspiring shared purpose and mutual trust are key leadership skills, there is very little evidence that current leadership development frameworks do truly prioritize and inculcate these essential skills. This is part of a bigger leadership training and development failure recorded in the literature that HR directors are too familiar with. A *Harvard Business Review* study reported that 'American companies spend enormous amounts of money on employee training and education—$160 billion in the United States and close to $356 billion globally in 2015 alone—but they are not getting a good return on their investment.[26] For the most part, the learning doesn't lead to better organizational performance because people soon revert to their old ways of doing things.'

While many agree that building shared purpose and mutual trust is essential for the success of business deals and change programmes, seldom do we see that projects' Gantt Charts or budgets allocate time or resources for these. Often, they are mentioned as an afterthought or included in reports as standard boilerplate components next to the sections on vision, mission, and values.

Now, more than ever, the world needs true leaders who can positively shape the business and societal narrative and help us rise to the occasion and the challenges we face. This style of leadership is required at all levels and in all sectors. As our world continues to be defined by the paradoxes of tremendous economic growth and increasing productivity on the one hand, and rampant inequality and ecological degradation on the other, leadership that prioritizes, initiates, and maintains human collaboration is essential.

One may feel compelled to reflect on the state of leadership and ask the question: Does the world suffer from a crisis of leadership? 86 per cent of the 1,767 experts who responded to a 2015 World Economic Forum Survey on the Global Agenda think so.[27] Should we be surprised by this? While the headline survey result may be shocking, the apparent failure of leadership to deal with the existential challenges faced in today's world might be behind this perception. Challenges that start with climate change, and do not end with global inequality, geopolitical instability, and economic and health crises are making the world more volatile, uncertain, complex, and ambiguous (VUCA). These are tough issues for leaders at every level to deal with.

Interestingly though, this lack of faith in leaders is happening just as a global recognition of the importance of leadership is consolidating. Business schools and universities are making leadership a staple part of their curriculum and educational outcomes, while organizations are investing more than ever in leadership development, and the leadership section at the bookstores is growing daily.

The crisis of leadership seems to emanate, at least in part, from the contradictions between what markets currently reward leaders for and what the world needs. Let us examine three of the dimensions where these contradictions are more profound.

1. **Timescale:** While many of the challenges we face require very long-term thinking, short-termism is rampant. Leaders can be under pressure to deliver quick results or pay a hefty price.
2. **The sphere of focus:** Despite all the rhetoric, many organizations measure results with an internal focus on their individual success rather than the success of the entire ecosystem. This influences the decisions leaders make.
3. **Competition versus collaboration:** While no single individual, organization, or even country will ever be able to address the biggest challenges of our time, such as climate change or inequality, alone, we still see nationalism, populism, tariff wars, and even outright war happening around us. Leaders often find it difficult to balance the fine line between competing and the need to work together for the common good.

Clearly, we need a new breed of leaders who can deliver immediate results without sacrificing the long-term viability of their organizations, sectors, and even the world. These leaders need to possess an ecosystem mindset and be capable of finding commonalities, inspiring shared purpose, and building consensus and mutual trust with competing and disagreeing parties while driving the agendas and interests of their institutions and communities.

These leaders will need to master a number of attributes, values, and skills, including having a deep sense of higher purpose and faith in the possibility of building trust, being self-aware, and having the effectiveness and soft skills to be able to deliver a positive impact to their constituencies and the wider world. We call these purpose-driven leaders, as having a clear sense of purpose at the individual and organizational levels can go a long way in empowering them to both do well and do good.

To stand a chance at addressing the challenges of our time, we need to transform the leadership that we teach, learn, and practice into a purpose-driven one. Redefining our educational systems and how we develop, reward, and recognize our leaders will be how we achieve this, and in doing so, we will avert the leadership crisis that so many people think we are facing today.

John W. Gardner, the former United States Secretary of Health, Education, and Welfare, once said:

> Leaders have a significant role in creating the state of mind that is the society. They can serve as symbols of the moral unity of the society. They can express the values that hold the society together. Most importantly, they can conceive and articulate goals that lift people out of their petty preoccupations, carry them above the conflicts that tear a society apart, and unite them in the pursuit of objectives worthy of their best efforts.[28]

Put simply, what Gardner said is that true leaders have the opportunity and the responsibility to play a key role in inspiring a shared sense of purpose and building mutual trust that will shape the collective, collaborative spirit necessary for us to survive our challenges and achieve our full potential.

For leaders to be able to foster authentic and sustainable shared purpose and mutual trust within and between individuals, organizations, communities and even nations, they will need to create new realms and realities where a deeper connection is possible. This may sound naïve or too simplistic, yet it is the most practical thing to pursue. With the technological, environmental, social, and geopolitical disruptions we face, this may indeed be the only viable option we have.

Leaders will need to transform the nature of the social contract between people from the transactional domain that focuses on utility and interests to a covenantal domain where transformation happens. This was eloquently explained by Rabbi Jonathan Sacks: 'A contract is about interests. A covenant is about identity. It is about you and me coming together to form an "us". That is why contracts benefit, but covenants transform.'[29]

Achieving this transformation will necessitate redefining how we see ourselves and others. It requires reigniting and propagating faith in humanity and the innate uniqueness, potential, and goodness in all of us. This means that we choose to start with trust and accept that we may be disappointed from time to time as a small price that we are willing to pay for a bigger reward. Remember: This is not a sign of naïvety or weakness, but a manifestation of a principle that has been mathematically demonstrated through the prisoner's dilemma. It also means that we will work hard on discovering and articulating our higher purpose, for only when we are driven by purpose can we inspire a sense of shared purpose.

Leaders will need to inculcate understanding and empathy within themselves first and within their spheres of influence second. They will require the development of a recognition that the 8 billion people on the planet are all unique, the fact that our minds create our realities and stories which are different from one another and that despite all of our differences, we all share the foundational needs of feeling safe, being seen, and feeling validated through the acceptance of others. This will be the biggest leadership challenge and its greatest opportunity.

The creation of a flourishing human community is not inevitable. Competitive and combative dynamics are still strong and fuelled by mistrust, misinformation, and a lack of articulated shared higher purpose. However, a major source of hope is that deep inside people, there lies a recognition that the only way forward is together. I am talking here about the grand challenges of our time, such as environmental degradation, the increasing tendency to have more pandemics, and the disruptions (and potentials) created by technology.

This part of the book highlights the critical roles that leaders play in cultivating a sense of shared purpose and fostering an organizational culture marked by safety, inclusivity, and deep-seated mutual trust. The chapters contained herein provide practical techniques to accomplish these objectives, enriched with real-life examples, drawn from a broad spectrum of industries and cultural settings, illustrating the universal applicability and effectiveness of these methods.

Chapter 6

Inspiring a Shared Sense of Purpose

> 'Purpose is a stable and generalised intention to accomplish something that is at once meaningful to the self and consequential to the world beyond the self.'
>
> —William Damon

While visiting NASA in 1962, President John F. Kennedy was reported to have struck up a conversation with a janitor there. When JFK asked the janitor what he was doing, he replied, 'Mr President, I am helping put a man on the moon.'

The janitor's main job was, no doubt, keeping the place clean. Still, when everyone in an organization shares a higher purpose and is aligned with the overall mission, deep collaboration can take place. No wonder NASA could achieve such great feats, which are still impressive even today, with technology that is nowhere near as good as what we have now.

This chapter outlines the fundamentals of purpose and provides methods and techniques that leaders can use to discover and articulate both personal and organizational purpose. It also guides how to strategically mobilize these insights to create substantial impact by building purpose-driven collaborative alliances between the resources of multiple individuals and organizations. Drawing on my experiences and successful interventions, the content goes beyond theoretical discussions to offer proven strategies and real-world applications.

The Case for True Purpose

Humans have always known the importance of having a clear sense of purpose and the awareness of what brings meaning to our lives. As Mark Twain once said: 'The two most important days in your life are the day you were born and the day you find out why.' Philosophical, spiritual, and human development practices have always recognized the importance of purpose for the good life. German philosopher Friedrich Nietzsche believed that the primary objective of philosophy is to guide us in becoming our true selves, driven by a yearning to discover our purpose.

But some distinction is equally important.

There are two types of purpose: true purpose, which is innately good, emanates from within, and generally has a positive impact on the world; and false purpose, usually manipulated, is often driven from outside (the latest fads or being part of a group, among others), and doesn't have a positive impact on the world. The former requires discipline to discover and mobilize, while the latter can exist without all this. Unfortunately, when shared, both purposes can be the basis of collaboration. That is why the role of leadership to drive positive value-adding collaboration is paramount.

Viktor Frankl, the Austrian neurologist, psychiatrist, and Holocaust survivor, demonstrated that having a sense of purpose can even help in surviving the concentration camps. During World War II, he and his family were captured by the Nazis and sent to various concentration camps, including Auschwitz. Despite enduring the horrors of the Holocaust, he managed to survive by finding a profound sense of purpose and meaning.

While imprisoned, Frankl realized that the will to find meaning in one's life, even in the dire circumstances, was a powerful force, noting that those who gave up hope and their sense of purpose were more likely to succumb to the conditions of the camps. He mentally and emotionally disconnected himself from the immediate suffering and focused on a future beyond the camp, where he could share the insights he gained from his experiences. After the war, Viktor Frankl wrote about all this in his famous book, *Man's Search for Meaning*, wherein he described his philosophy of logotherapy (logos means 'meaning' or 'reason' in Greek), which emphasizes the importance of finding meaning in all forms of existence, even in the face of suffering.[30]

More recently, the work of William Damon, a Stanford professor, established the significance of having a sense of purpose for youth for success, well-being, and overall positive development. However, it pointed towards a deficit of purpose as his research pointed out that 'only about one in five young people in the 12–22 year age range express a clear vision of where they want to go, what they want to accomplish in life, and why.'[31]

The work of Professor Damon, along with our earlier observation about failure of mergers and acquisitions, are but a few reminders that while the concept of purpose is simple and intuitive, discovering it requires commitment, hard work, and soul-searching. Ensuring that searching for purpose and pursuing it is part of mainstream human activities demands the development of intentional purpose-driven leadership, which we are making the case for in this book.

Purpose and Passion

Morten Hansen, a management professor at the University of California, Berkeley, performed research that focused on understanding the relationship between passion, purpose, and performance. Within the context of jobs, passion can be defined as excitement towards our work, while purpose is the sense that our work has a broader meaning and that it positively contributes to others.

But Hansen was curious as to which has more impact on job performance.

He studied the performance of a group of employees that varied in their level of passion and sense of purpose. Those who have both a high sense of purpose and high levels of passion were the absolute stars of their organizations and were ranked by their superiors, at the eightieth percentile on average. On the other end, those with a lower sense of purpose and passion exhibited inferior performance and were rated, on average, at the tenth percentile. Neither of these are surprising.

When individuals lack meaning and are unenthusiastic about their jobs, it is rather difficult to overachieve. The question now is: If employees are strong only in one attribute, passion, or purpose, which group will perform better? Results showed that those with a low sense of purpose and high levels of passion were rated at the twentieth percentile only. The real surprise was those with a high sense of purpose were able to exhibit solid performance, rated at the sixty-fourth percentile, even though they had a lower passion. The findings are clear: purpose trumps passion, when it comes to performance.[32]

Level	**High Purpose**	**Low Purpose**
High Passion	80th Percentile	20th Percentile
Low Passion	64th Percentile	10th Percentile

Passion is often an individual trait. It invigorates, but has the potential to isolate too, especially when team members do not develop it equally. On the other hand, it is easier to subscribe to a shared purpose beyond oneself—like putting a man on the moon. This can bring a group of people closer together and facilitate deep collaboration.

The Economics of Higher Purpose

The importance of shared purpose for business is an area of active exploration by both academics and practitioners. Robert Quinn, the organizational scholar and co-author of *The Economics of Higher Purpose*, outlined the importance of shared purpose for organizations and how becoming a purpose-driven organization is the pathway to better collaboration, business success, career satisfaction for employees, and deeper engagement with customers.[33]

A 2020 McKinsey Survey exposed an interesting 'purpose gap' between executives and upper management staff.[34] 85 per cent of executives agree they can live their purpose in their day-to-day work, compared to 85 per cent of frontline managers and employees who either were unsure or disagreed that they could live their purpose at work. This represents an important area for leaders to work on and improve, as bridging this gap in shared purpose can translate into a direct improvement in collaboration within the organization, leading to higher productivity, creativity, and goodwill.

Clearly, the world needs more purpose-driven leadership. This leadership leap is rquired in all sectors, including policy-making, education, and business.

Purpose-Driven Leadership

As we repeatedly mentioned the need for purpose-driven leadership as a precursor to enabling collaboration in various human activities, it is appropriate to introduce the concept of a purpose-driven leadership, where the role of leaders is seen as building, enhancing, growing, and preserving five primary types of capital: human, social, emotional, natural, and economic.

Purpose-driven leaders deploy these five capitals in an integrated fashion so that they complement, enhance, and leverage each other for more effective and impactful results. As organizations perform their strategic planning, resource allocation, and goal-setting functions, and as team members set their key performance indicators (KPIs), it will be empowering to consider the utilization and creation of these capitals as the background to all these processes.

A short description of these five capitals is given herewith:

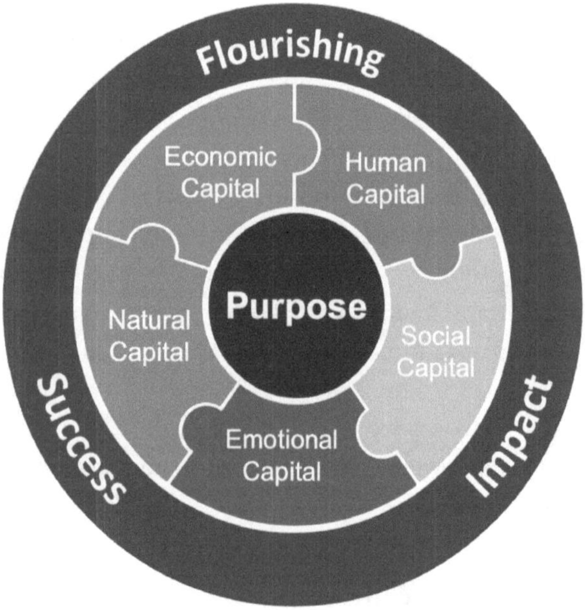

Fig. 2 – Purpose-Driven Leadership Model

1. Human capital refers to the knowledge, skills, and capabilities that a team or an organization has access to or would like to develop, promote, and deliver. Purpose-driven leadership prioritizes the development of human capital so that it creates more success, impact, and flourishing. This implies strategic investment to develop and upskill people to deliver organizational objectives, while pursuing the higher purpose and the people associated with it.
2. Social capital accounts for the positive relationships and networks that a team or an organization have access to, or would like to nurture and develop, in order to simultaneously deliver on both the higher purpose and the business objectives. Social capital can be highly potent as it serves as a multiplier of all other types of capital.
3. Emotional capital is the ability to assess and positively influence emotions to motivate and inspire others to align business objectives with a worthy higher purpose and create an emotional commitment to delivering that. It also refers to the connection that customers may have with a brand, service, or product. Often, the lack of emotional capital is the bottleneck to delivering on the organizational strategy.
4. Natural capital refers to our environment and the natural resources we all share and how the presence and operation of a team and organization help not only preserve, but also enhance and improve this capital that we hold in trust for our future generations. Strategies must outline how they will actively enhance and improve the environment in which they operate and we all live. Holding the higher moral ground in this realm is the right thing to do on multiple levels, including making clear business sense by potentially reducing the cost of operation in the long term, as well as building goodwill and brand trust.

5. Economic capital is the financial resources that a team or organization has access to and how they can be used to create more value and help further the mobilization of purpose into positive impact. Economic capital represents the bloodline of an organization and directly affects its ability to honour its obligations, realize its objectives, and deliver on its purpose. Being skilled in the management of this capital is a prerequisite for the successful leadership of organizations large and small.

Viewing the potential for partnership and collaboration, business decision-making, and goal-setting processes through the lens of the above five capitals and leveraging them can help develop strategies that not only deploy resources but also inspire people to go on the journey of becoming a purpose-driven team, business, and organization.

Finding Personal Purpose

If we are not sure what our individual purpose is, it is difficult for us to authentically subscribe to a shared purpose with others. In my book *Driven By Purpose*, I describe the process I'd developed for finding both personal and organizational purpose in detail. The outcome of it is a succinct Impact Statement.[35]

Following this process, I have personally facilitated Impact Statement discovery workshops for thousands around the world, as young as fourteen and as old as seventy. Many participants were university students, but some were CEOs and world champions in their fields. I also facilitated the process of discovering and articulating institutional impact statements for corporations, non-profit organizations, schools, and universities.

Here is an attempt to provide a summary of this process.

The Impact Statement has three parts: the 'I Am Statement', the 'Purpose Statement', and the 'Actions Statement'. It is worth mentioning that we made participating in the workshop a requirement for all staff and new students at my university to reflect on how they want to make the world a better place through their work, talents and the programme of study they choose. Coming up with an Impact Statement is never easy, and it takes a lot of one-to-one interactions with our Impact Coaches.

However, we found that the effort and time invested in writing an Impact Statement at the beginning of a university student's first semester pays multiple dividends. Students who are aware of why they started studying a certain subject are more likely to stay the course when the going gets tough.

When we ask students why they joined our Actuarial Science programme, which is one of the most demanding programmes in the university, they often say that they love mathematics and that having a degree in actuarial science will secure them a good job. After completing the Impact Statement exercise, students are clearer about their true north. One of them wrote, 'I am a math lover. My purpose is to use my mastery of math to reduce complexity for others when they need it the most. I am an actuary.' How is that for an Impact Statement?

The three parts of the Impact Statement are described below:

1. **I Am Statement**

   This represents the superpower of the individual, the one thing that makes them different. Articulating the I Am Statement requires a deep self-awareness and involves an exercise of Core Values discovery and a reflection on the individual's life journey with a focus on peak moments.

   Participants in an Impact Statement workshop reflect on their lives and review moments when they were at their best or most challenged through the lens of their core values.

They ask themselves: At this key moment in my life, what core value was I honouring or not honouring? What feelings and emotions did I have? What did I learn about myself as a result of this situation?

Through this exercise, some common threads start to appear, pointing towards the superpower and the I am Statement.

Participants are encouraged to share their core values, peak moments, and I Am Statements with their friends and families to validate their discoveries with those who know them best.

2. **Purpose Statement**
This statement describes the purpose that brings a deep sense of meaning and fulfilment to the life of an individual. One of the most effective ways of discovering purpose is the Japanese concept of *ikigai*. In the Japanese language, ikigai translates to 'reason for being,' with 'iki' signifying 'life' and 'kai' connoting 'meaning or results.' Ikigai encapsulates the idea of having a meaningful direction or a sense of purpose in life. Psychologist Michiko Kumano describes it as 'entailing actions of devoting oneself to pursuits one enjoys and is associated with feelings of accomplishment and fulfilment.'[36]

Purpose and ikigai are usually at the intersection of four areas in our lives: What we love doing, what we are good at, what the world needs, and what we can be paid for. Making four lists of ten items each for these four areas and searching for similarities and intersections can give a strong hint towards our sense of purpose.

Fig. 3 – Purpose and Ikigai

3. **Actions Statement**

This part of the Impact Statement focuses on the plans and actions an individual will have to develop to mobilize their purpose into a positive impact on the world. Impact Statement workshop participants are encouraged to create action plans and goals that are specific, measurable, attainable, relevant, and timely to mobilise their purpose into a positive impact on the world.

The structure of an Impact Statement is shown diagrammatically in the figure below.

Fig. 4 – Impact Statement Structure

We are all unique. Our uniqueness stems from the fact that we are all different in our genetic make-up, life experiences, and mindsets. This diversity needs to be harnessed and leveraged as we collaborate to create value and address the challenges we face. The Impact Statement process is designed to elucidate this diversity, and usually results in statements anchored in the individual's strengths, values, and sense of meaning. Finding purpose is paradoxical: We all get its importance at a visceral level, but somehow, many choose to avoid the effort to engage with this part of our personal and professional development.

This is reflected in the questions frequently posed to those who advocate for purpose:

Q. Am I too young/old to articulate my purpose?

A: It is never too early or too late to start discovering and articulating your true purpose. Now, more than ever, this is becoming a necessity.

Q. Will articulating a well-defined purpose prevent me from exploring other things in life?

A: On the contrary, the true purpose is an enabler, not a limiter. Formulating and declaring your purpose will also send a signal to those of similar interest to join you and collaborate with you.

Q. Should purpose be heroic or larger than life?

A: No. Your true purpose can be as large or as focused as it suits you.

Q. Will my purpose change as I go through life?

A: While true purpose has stability to it, the way you articulate your purpose will evolve over time as your self-knowledge improves.

Q. Can my purpose be framed in an aspirational way?

A: Of course, an aspirational true purpose can encourage us to live up to its higher standards.

Q. Will I one day just discover my true purpose spontaneously? Or is intentional work necessary?

A: It is necessary to intentionally work on discovering and committing to paper your true purpose. A structured Impact Statement workshop, under the tutelage of an experienced Impact Coach, is a very effective way to achieve that.

To demonstrate the structure of an Impact Statement, below are two examples:

- I am a builder of relationships. My purpose is to use the trust that I have developed to help create employment opportunities for others. I am helping the workforce of tomorrow to navigate the fourth Industrial Revolution today.
- I am a storyteller. My purpose is to inspire others to tell empowering stories about themselves and the world we live in. I dedicate my life to supporting youth to be their best as they identify their impact, harness their talent, and become purposeful individuals.

Finding Institutional Shared Purpose

As illustrated by the Collaboration Equation, articulating a shared purpose is key to harnessing the power of collaboration within teams, groups, and organizations. There is a growing recognition that having a well-defined sense of purpose is not only meaningful but also economically and commercially advantageous. Businesses and organizations articulating, embedding, and genuinely pursuing a clear and authentic higher purpose frequently experience enhanced customer loyalty and increased staff engagement. Purpose serves as a genuine driving force and a motivational factor for team members, not to mention its capacity to attract support and collaboration from partners and customers.

The Porter Novelli purpose tracker study[37] showed that a 93 per cent of employees surveyed assert that companies must, more than ever, prioritize purpose. This signifies a collective understanding among employees that business goes beyond mere profit-making. Notably, 88 per cent employees contend that it is no longer sufficient for companies to solely pursue financial gains; they must also contribute positively to society.

As businesses pivot toward this evolved perspective on impact, employees recognize their role as essential stakeholders—something businesses must consider. In fact, 95 per cent of employees believe that businesses should benefit all stakeholders, not exclusively shareholders.

At a time when short-termism is widespread, purpose-driven organizations are in a much better position to make long-term decisions and investments and effectively articulate and justify those decisions to their stakeholders. This can be a clear advantage as many of the challenges, and indeed the opportunities we encounter today, demand long-term thinking to address and realize them.

That is why many leaders, after articulating their Impact Statements, start exploring the possibility of developing the same for their teams. Just like individuals, teams and organizations can benefit from articulating their shared purpose.

The process of articulating an institutional Impact Statement is done by a team that represents different stakeholders of the organization. A company that produces consumer goods, for example, can have members of its leadership team, staff, customers, distributors, and shareholders join the team.

The process follows a similar sequence to the personal Impact Statement crafting and has the three sections described below:

1. **'We Are' Statement**
   This represents a unique capability of the organization, the one thing that differentiates it from other similar organizations. Articulating it involves an exercise of Core Values discovery and a reflection on the organization's life journey, exploring the peak moments and milestones in this journey and how these were shaped by the core values.

   When reflecting on peak moments, often, the participants will converge on situations when they are truly proud of their teams or organizations, even if these took place prior to some of them being associated with the organization.
2. **Purpose Statement**
   It describes the purpose of the organization. Just like the personal ikigai, it is usually the intersection of four areas: What the community of the organization loves doing, what the people at the organization are good at, and what resources are available to it, what the world needs, and what functions the organization fulfils.
3. **Actions Statement**
   This part of the Impact Statement focuses on the strategies, plans, and actions the organization will develop to mobilise its purpose and have a positive impact on the world.

As Heriot-Watt University embarks on crafting its Strategy2035 for the next ten years, we've decided to initiate this journey by defining an Impact Statement for the institution. We observed that many universities have vision and mission statements that often resemble one another. Conversely, an Impact Statement allows us to convey our distinctive heritage, values, purpose, and the impact we aspire to have on the world.

The process involved having three teams representing our constituencies, campuses, and stakeholders, including students, academic staff, professional services staff, and governors. Each team went through the Impact Statement workshop in order to validate the authenticity of the work undertaken.

Below is the institutional Impact Statement that our community agreed upon:

'We are future shapers. Our purpose is to develop leaders to build an equitable, sustainable, and enriching society. Our community will leverage its global presence and focused expertise to provide applied learning and research to transform lives and address real-world challenges.'

Collaboration in Purpose-Driven Organizations

Organizations that can leverage shared purpose and capitalize on mutual trust are able to produce phenomenal results, while maintaining high levels of engagement, loyalty, and advocacy among their employees, stakeholders, customers, and beneficiaries. This is a direct dividend of the deeper levels of collaboration these organizations are capable of harnessing.

Take, for instance, Alice Smith: a private school in Malaysia. It realized the need for the creation of a shared purpose for their community so that they could prepare their students not only for the next stage in their studies journey but also to get them ready for life. The school embarked on a transformational journey to articulate the purpose of their community and help all its members—including students, teachers, parents, and governors—to have their personal Impact Statements.

I had the honour of working with the school's leadership on this project.

As the process of having more teachers, students, and parents document their purpose progressed, the school began to notice signs of deeper alignment among members of their community with the shared purpose they articulated. I received this feedback from one of their teachers:

'I want to express my appreciation for the way you challenged my thinking and pushed its boundaries. Your perspectives have given me a new lens through which to view my own path. As a teacher, I think I have been guilty of turning up to work, working hard, and loving my job without really questioning my purpose or the impact I am hoping to make. I was happy for my students to get good grades, enjoy my lessons, and get positive parental feedback. But now, I'm inspired to be a more purpose-driven teacher, and for my students to have more clarity about their own purpose. As a leader, I am now considering purpose-driven Impact Statements for members of my team.'

A quick look at organizations that are characterized by extraordinary performance makes it clear that most of them have purpose-driven leaders and compelling shared purpose that guide their communities to collaborate and push the limits. This is true for Space X, Google, Open AI and others.

Shared Purpose Among Opposing Parties

Collaboration is not only a phenomenon that is desired within organizations and teams. Often, the collaboration that is required to achieve the more consequential objectives needs to happen between different, sometimes opposing, parties and nations.

This is true for objectives such as achieving sustainable development goals, addressing climate change, or delivering world peace.

Carving a shared purpose for parties and nations that are ideologically diametrical and with different cultures and interests is an art that purpose-driven leaders need to master, as without a long-term positive shared purpose, our entire way of life and the potential for sustainable progress will be at jeopardy.

Our current track record in building shared purpose across the national, ideological, and organizational borders to address the grand challenges is patchy. This will need to change.

More examples and discussion about this will be provided in the coming chapters.

Chapter 7

Nurturing Mutual Trust

> 'Is commercial credit not based primarily upon money or property?'
>
> 'No, Sir. The first thing is character. Because a man I don't trust could not get money from me on all the bonds in Christendom.'
>
> —J.P. Morgan
> Testimony before the
> Bank and Currency Committee
> House of Representatives
> Washington, D.C., 19 December 1912

We are innately trusting beings, and trust is essential for our existence. If you are a coffee lover like me, you trust the coffee shop not to use expired milk to make your favourite latte. Otherwise, you will require proof that the ingredients in your coffee will not badly affect your health before you consume it. The process of verifying everything that goes into the making of a cup of coffee can be very complicated, costly, and slow. It can result in us deciding not to buy it altogether.

This example can be extended to almost all aspects of our lives. We trust the supermarkets not to tamper with the expiry dates on the goods we buy; we trust that airlines to have trained their pilots and maintain their planes; and we trust our friends to keep secrets.

Even when we use legal contracts to safeguard our interests, we trust in the institutions that will enforce these contracts if a contract breach takes place. Of course, in all these cases, we are taking risks by trusting others, and from time to time, we are in for disappointment.

Trust is an important part of our lives at the personal, social, organizational, political, and geopolitical levels. It is known for reducing the transactional cost in all these settings. High-trust relationships, societies, and organizations are more healthy, productive, and successful. High trust is often associated with high GDP for nations, as trust in the system and mutual trust between individuals and organizations enable collaboration, facilitate transactions, increase the flow of credit, and speed up arriving at deals and agreements.[38]

The topic of trust has been widely studied by researchers from diverse fields spanning psychology, sociology, computer science, political science, and economics, and the literature on trust is rich and deep. While this book is not about trust per se, as the topic has many books dedicated to it, it is, however, about how trust contributes to enabling collaboration and facilitating co-action.

Just like the case for the need for a shared purpose, we live now in a time when unprecedented levels of trust are urgently needed to facilitate the required levels of collaboration to address our current challenges and realize our potential opportunities. And unfortunately, the state of trust in the world is not near what it needs to be.

Trust is associated with having positive expectations of people and situations. Semantically, 'trust' functions as both a noun and a verb. As a noun, the Oxford Online Dictionary defines trust:

> A firm belief in the reliability, truth, or ability of someone or something; confidence or faith in a person or thing, or in an attribute of a person or thing.

Hence, trust is a self-assuredness or confidence that gives us a feeling of security. It is a form of expecting, and depending on, the reliability of others. While this reliability may be built upon previous experience and observation, ultimately, it is predicated upon our expectations and assumptions and may be withheld when needed the most, as it is in the hands of someone else.

As a verb, the Oxford Online Dictionary describes trust as:

> To have faith or confidence in a person, quality, or thing; to rely on.

This way, we can experience trust as a process between people. At the beginning of a relationship, trust can start as a belief about the other, which can be based on perceptions, assumptions, or promises made. As a track record is established, trust can become a quality of the relationship. So, trust is both a state and an act, intertwined with each other. In both cases, trust is associated with being vulnerable to the other party in the relationship, as we trust their goodwill and their intentions.

As we write this, two major wars are ongoing in Ukraine and Gaza, with tens of thousands of people killed thus far. The levels of mistrust in the world seem to be so high, that it may appear too naïve to advocate for revolutionary mutual trust. However, this advocacy is not merely wishful thinking; rather, it stems from a realization that this historic moment will mandate the emergence of fresh leadership paradigms required to enable the rise of mutual trust as a survival necessity.

This chapter explores the vital role of mutual trust in fostering effective collaboration. It delves into the foundations of building and sustaining trust within teams and organizations, emphasizing inclusivity, transparent communication, consistent actions, and shared values. Practical strategies and real-world examples illustrate how leaders and team members can cultivate an environment where trust thrives, thereby enhancing cooperation and achieving common goals more efficiently.

Readers will learn to identify barriers to trust, implement trust-building practices, and recognize the profound impact of trust on collaborative success.

Elements of Trust

Just like other important things in life, such as love, respect, and happiness, trust cannot be bought or sold, but we all would love to have more of it. We know that it takes time, intention, and effort to cultivate, and can be compromised easily. Because of how essential it is to success and the good life, it is important to understand its elements so that we can have a better chance at cultivating it.

Let us explore an example.

Imagine that you have a nasty leak in your bathroom's plumbing. This stubborn leakage is threatening to damage your living room walls and beyond. You are looking for a 'trusted' plumber to save the day.

What traits would one want to see in this plumber?

Let me try to outline them for you.

1. You want a plumber who is competent in doing the job well. They need to have the experience, skills, and capabilities to diagnose the situation, discover the source of the leak, and fix it. You are not interested in hiring someone who is incompetent, and who may do a subpar job, or even create bigger issues.

2. You want a responsible and reliable plumber. They need to respect the timing of the project and be committed to starting the job on time and completing it on time. The last thing you need is a plumber who collects a deposit, cuts the water supply, digs your walls, and stops taking your calls.
3. You want an honest plumber who will balance their interest in making a decent profit with your interest in receiving a good service and a thorough job. You expect them not to take shortcuts and use substandard parts, while charging you a fair price.
4. You want a respectful and courteous plumber who will treat you and your house with respect. You want to deal with someone who will respect your privacy and personal information.

The above example used in assessing a trusted plumber is instructive, and it can be used as a template for many human interactions when trust is an essential requirement. Distilling the elements of building mutual trust, particularly in the professional collaborative setting, they can be simply put as follows:

1. **Competence:** The ability, skill, or knowledge to do something successfully and efficiently or to deliver an expectation satisfactorily. It encompasses the traits, qualifications, and capabilities that enable an individual or an organization to perform tasks, functions, or expectations properly and adequately.
2. **Reliability:** The consistency, dependability, and predictability of an individual or an organization to perform and deliver as expected over time. It indicates the ability to produce good and consistent results or outcomes under similar conditions repeatedly.

3. **Balance:** The fairmindedness of an individual or an organization that is manifested by acknowledging the needs and interests of others while satisfying their own needs and pursuing their own interests. This is sustained by the confidence that an individual or an organization has the right motivations through their track record and also through the presence of governance, legal, and professional checks and balances. Examples of that are the expectation that your dentist will only suggest procedures that you need to improve your health rather than lining their pocket.
4. **Security:** A feeling of safety derived from the faith in the integrity and professionalism of an individual or an organization will be built on a consistent and visible track record of acting empathetically and professionally, and also the existence of governance, legal, and professional structures and practices that assure the respect of personal data and privacy and guarantee against other types of malpractice.

This discretion and empathy create an atmosphere of openness that empowers risk-taking. An example of that is believing that our lawyers will act in our interest and will not reveal our confidential information to third parties.

These four components are consistent with the trust models available in the literature. For example, in their book *The Trusted Advisor,* authors David Maister, Charles Green, and Robert Galford describe being trustworthy with an equation where trustworthiness is the product of credibility, reliability, and intimacy divided by self-orientation.[39] The ABCD model of trust, proposed in the book *Trust Works*, introduces trust as the result of being able, believable, connected, and dependable.[40] Ashley Reichheld and Amelia Dunlop analyse trust as being the product of capability, reliability, transparency, and humanity in their book *The Four Factors of Trust.*[41]

While different authors adopt slightly different terminology when describing the elements of trust, we can characterize its overarching domains as expertise, assurance, fairmindedness, and safety.

The table below compares the four elements that we adopt in this chapter to the different components of the trust models mentioned briefly above.

Comparison of Different Trust Models

Source	**Expertise**	**Assurance**	**Fairmindedness**	**Safety**
The Collaboration Equation	Competence	Reliability	Balance	Security
The Trusted Advisor	Credibility	Reliability	Self-Orientation	Intimacy
Trust Works	Able	Believable Dependable	Connected	Connected
The Four Factors of Trust	Capability	Reliability	Transparency	Humanity

Recognizing that trust takes place within relationships between people, it is enlightening to use these four elements as a framework to diagnose, grow, and cultivate mutual trust. Nurturing trust requires careful attention to all its four elements.

It is important to note here that while this book advocates for the importance of mutual trust as one of two keys to effective collaboration, it does not promote gullibility. We do not call for simply trusting every stranger we meet, any claim made by an organization, or anything we hear or read. Lasting trust that takes into account the four elements outlined earlier and encourages critical thinking is the way to go.

Importance of Trust

Trust implies a willingness to be vulnerable to the whims of others but having the faith that, at least most of the time, we will not be taken advantage of or harmed. This perspective needs to be taken from a well-informed rather than a naïve position. Hence, assessing people and organizations along the four elements of trust we identified above is essential. When trustworthiness and the willingness to trust prevail, indicating the abundance of trustworthy individuals and institutions, the cost of interacting and transacting with others drops precipitately as the need for verifying, monitoring, and enforcing can drop too. This relative ease of interacting and exchanging has a sizable impact on individuals, communities, and economies, including the ease of getting people to work together and collaborate.

Exploring the importance of trust for economic development is not new, as it has captured economists' imaginations for decades. The winner of the 1972 Nobel Prize in Economics, Kenneth Arrow, wrote an article the same year titled 'Gifts and Exchanges,' in which he observed that 'virtually every commercial transaction has within itself an element of trust, certainly any transaction conducted over a period of time.'

Additionally, according to the World Values Survey, a 10 per cent rise in trust correlated with a 0.8 per cent increase in economic growth.[42] In a 2013 study by Algan and Cahuc, which explored the connection between trust and growth using more detailed data and economic analysis, identified a causal relationship. It suggested that trust does indeed drive economic growth, and not just correlate with it.[43]

The State of Trust in the World

To study the global state of trust, the Edelman Trust Barometer has been running since 2004. For its latest 2024 report, the global public relations and communication firm surveyed over 32,000 people in twenty-eight countries. The survey calculated the Trust Index as the average percentage of trust in NGOs, businesses, governments, and media. For both the 2023 and 2024 editions, developing countries such as China, India, UAE, and Indonesia appear to be leading on the Trust Index. On the other hand, developed countries such as Japan, the US, Germany, and France seem to rank at the bottom of the Trust Index, with the UK now among the least-trusting countries.[44]

Another interesting finding of the 2024 survey is that, globally, governments are seen as far less competent and ethical than businesses. This represents a unique opportunity for businesses and business leaders to build more trust with communities and stakeholders, particularly as the same survey showed that businesses are more trusted to integrate innovation into society ahead of NGOs and governments.

While business remained the most trusted institution overall, the survey revealed that NGOs were distrusted in twelve countries, business and media in fifteen countries, and governments in seventeen out of twenty-eight countries where the survey was conducted.

Clearly, there is a crisis of trust in our world marked by polarization, conflicts, and outright wars. Viewing this through a glass-half-full lens, it presents a historic opportunity for leaders to shine and steer events and mindsets towards a more conducive, productive, sustainable, and collaborative direction.

This can be done by applying the Collaboration Equation and nurturing mutual trust and shared purpose.

Building and Nurturing Trust

In the previous chapter, we argued that inspiring a shared purpose begins with discovering the individual's sense of purpose. Similarly, building mutual trust starts with trusting oneself and having self-confidence before progressing to trusting others in relationships, trusting the society, and ultimately trusting the political system in a country, then building trust between nations in the geopolitical system.

While it is not inevitable that trust prevails throughout the continuum just described, it is essential to aspire to realize this continuous trust field, as this is the only way to have sustainable trust. At all these levels, building trust requires enhancing the four elements of trust: competence, reliability, balance, and security.

Self-trust is an essential foundation for success and happiness. And while it does not mean that you trust yourself to know everything or have all the answers, it is, however, a realization that you can rely on and depend on yourself in a manner that will enable you to be kind and respectful to yourself, regardless of the outcome. Author Barbra Myerhoff said: 'A self is made, not given.' A fundamental way to nurture oneself is to develop self-trust and self-confidence.

Guided by the four elements of trust, you can build your self-trust by doing the following:

1. **Competence—Build your strengths:** To enhance your competence and capabilities in any field or situation, you need to keep learning and practising and be prepared. Whether you are getting ready for an important meeting, job interview, business meeting or exam, the bedrock of building your capability is to work hard on your preparation.
2. **Reliability—Develop your self-management capabilities:** Inculcating self-discipline will strengthen your reliability.

3. **Balance—Develop self-awareness:** Being transparent with yourself and clear about your strengths and areas for development is essential. You need to know who you are, what your gifts are, and also your limitations that you need support with.
4. **Security—Practise self-care and self-acceptance:** It is important to be kind to yourself and take care of yourself.

Trust in Countries' Products

Countries are composed of diverse groups of people, interconnected systems, and cultural heritages. In order to gain foreign currencies, they need to trade with other countries. Some countries possess commodities they can exchange for foreign currency, while others need to rely on trading products and services.

Unlike commodities, products and services are sold on their quality and reliability. While it is not advised to generalize while describing a country, one cannot help but recognize that countries sometimes have an overall reputation or a collective perception when it comes to what is expected of their systems and even the things produced by them.

For example, when encountering a product that carries the stamp 'Made in Japan', more often than not, it's associated with high quality. Interestingly, the products of Japan in the 1940s and 1950s were not associated with high quality but rather seen as cheap and poorly made, particularly in Western markets. In the early years after World War II, Japan was rebuilding its economy and manufacturing capabilities, leading to a flood of inexpensive consumer goods that were often viewed as inferior when compared to those from the US and Europe. The phrase 'Made in Japan' was sometimes synonymous with shoddy workmanship.

As a number of Japanese companies, such as Sony and Honda, realized that real sustained growth could only be achieved through producing high-quality products and the creation of highly trusted brands, a transformation was afoot. This transformation was anchored in building the four elements of trust: competence, reliability, balance, and security.

Through a commitment to investing in capacity building, innovation, and developing new technologies, Japanese firms were able to enhance their competence and capabilities for designing and manufacturing products that customers desire at prices they can afford. Sony, for example, introduced the first commercially successful transistor radio, the TR-55, allowing for portable music access and paving the way for the portable electronics revolution. It went on to invent the first home video cassette recorder, transforming how people consumed media at home.

The commitment to innovation and introducing new products would not go a long way if these products did not last long and performed well. Here comes the role of the dedication to quality control and the relentless obsession with masterful workmanship that the Japanese came to be known for. This cemented the reputation of their products for reliability. Frameworks such as the Toyota Production System, for example, are renowned for their focus on efficiency, quality, and continuous improvement, emphasizing principles of 'just-in-time' production—making things only when needed, along with automation with a human touch. This management system enabled not only Toyota but Japanese cars, in general, to be among the most reliable in the world. Other manufacturing sectors around the world are adopting the Toyota Production System as well.

Japanese firms also demonstrated their clear intent to understand the needs of their customers and address them in a way that exceeds the customers' expectations. This fair-minded and balanced approach to achieving business success is a key element for building mutual trust with consumers. Over the years, this clear commitment to quality and unwavering investment in innovation became a characteristic of the Japanese industry and resulted in faith in the Japanese system, giving consumers a sense of security and peace of mind when purchasing a Japanese product.

This progressive and sustained growth in competence, reliability, balance, and security culminated in a change in the perception of Japanese products in general, where many people now view the 'Made in Japan' phrase as a stamp of high quality, safety, and good workmanship.

As mentioned in the Edelman Trust Barometer Survey:

> Trust defines an organization's license to operate, lead and succeed. Trust is the foundation that allows an organization to take responsible risk, and, if it makes mistakes, to rebound from them. For a business, especially, lasting trust is the strongest insurance against competitive disruption, the antidote to consumer indifference, and the best path to continued growth. Without trust, credibility is lost and reputation can be threatened.

Trust in the Making

It is fascinating to explore the evolution of global consumers' perception of the quality of Japanese products, as this transformation seems to follow a recognizable pattern that appears to be replicating in other countries that are on their own intentional journeys to global recognition and acceptance.

Initially, global consumers tend to be open to purchase and gradually develop trust in products considered to be low-risk, such as low-cost consumer electronics, where the affordability, benefits, and reliability can be easily assessed, and the risk associated with them is limited and manageable. After all, if you buy a cheap Sony transistor radio, and it stops working after a few weeks, it is not the end of the world. However, if it stands the test of time, the story will take another turn, transforming your initial perception into a narrative of reliability, appreciation, and trustworthiness, likely leading you to recommend Sony products and consider them for larger purchases in the future, such as televisions or audio systems. Your experience could shift from mere consumer apathy to brand loyalty, illustrating how the longevity and performnce of a seemingly simple product can impact overall brand reputation and customer confidence in a company's offerings.

Over time, as people's experience with multiple Japanese brands was positive, the trust premium and favourable perception started to encompass the phrase 'Made in Japan', not only a specific brand. This enabled the trust to expand to more significant products, moving from electronics to items such as automobiles. Accumulated positive experiences with products people use opened the door to trusting items they ingest, such as food and beverages. Accepting food and beverage products made in a certain country is an indication of higher trust, as the risk taken is higher, and it is associated with health and wellbeing.

Eventually, this trust extends to brands of cosmetics and pharmaceutical products. This is the ultimate vote of approval, as these products can have long-term side effects if they are not produced, processed, and tested to the highest quality standards. This gradual progression reveals how initial confidence can pave the way for broader acceptance and trust across diverse product categories, highlighting a dynamic interplay between consumer experiences, brand reputation, and perceived quality. Understanding this trajectory in the light of the four elements of trust sheds light on consumer behaviour and offers valuable insights for businesses aiming to cultivate trust in their offerings within an increasingly competitive global market.

Japan's journey of trust-building can thus be summarized below:

1. Post-World War II (1940s to 1950s)

After World War II, Japan's economy was devastated. The government and businesses focused on building rapid capacity to both satisfy the immediate local needs and provide some exports to attract foreign currency. Many of the goods produced during this time were of low quality, and products like toys or household items were often seen as cheap and inferior.

Japan's GDP per capita in 1950 was $2,805.

2. The Rapid Industrialization of the 1960s

To strengthen competence, improve reliability, build trust, and enhance the image of Japanese products, Japanese industries adopted Quality Control techniques such as Total Quality Management (TQM) and Just-In-Time (JIT) production. These techniques matched the Japanese nature well-known for discipline, and also capitalized on the innate pride in precision and good workmanship that characterized the Japanese people. The earlier fruits of these efforts were the boom in consumer electronics as products such as radios and televisions began to improve in quality, leading to increased foreign sales and positive reviews.

By 1969, Japan's GDP per capita rose to $11,953, more than fourfold growth in a decade.

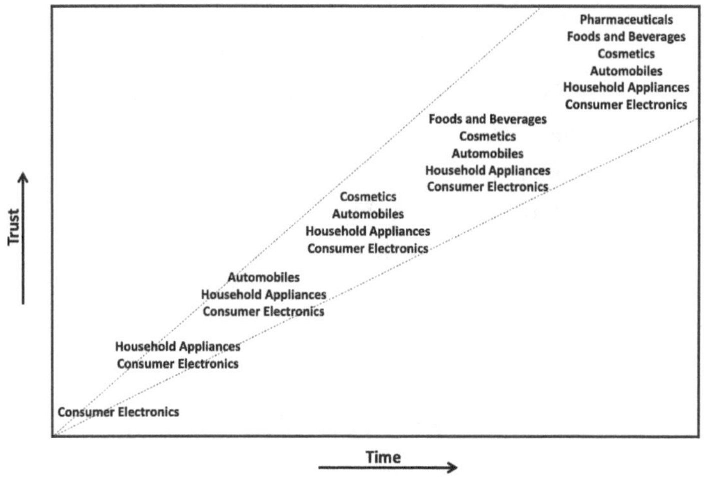

Fig. 5 – Potential of Trust Growth in a Country's Products Over Time

3. The Rising Reputation in the 1970s

As Japanese manufacturers adopted advanced technologies and management practices, the quality of products such as cars, electronics, and appliances improved significantly. Brands like Sony, Toyota, and Honda began gaining international recognition, and consumers started associating 'Made in Japan' with innovative and high-quality goods. Japanese manufacturers started to be seen as serious consumer-centred businesses, and Japanese products and after-sale services began to be associated with quality and peace of mind.

This was reflected in the GDP per capita growth, which reached $19,874 in 1979.

4. Establishing Japan's Leadership in the 1980s

The global competitiveness of Japan cemented its status as a leader in technology and manufacturing. The automotive industry, in particular, saw vehicles that were efficient, reliable, and cost-effective, challenging firms in the US and Europe. This was the era when Japanese culture, values, and lifestyle began to influence global trends, further enhancing the appeal of Japanese products.

With a focus on high-precision innovation in high-growth areas and benefiting from the accumulated trust in Japanese products, the Japanese pharmaceutical industry began to emerge as a major global player in this decade, capturing an increasing share of the worldwide market, reaching 11 per cent by 1989.[45]

The GDP per capita continued to grow, reaching $ 27,335 in 1989.

5. The Challenges and Resilience Decade (1990s)

Despite the economic stagnation in the second half of this decade, the reputation of many Japanese companies remained strong based on the foundation that was built over the earlier decades. Despite the financial challenges, Japanese companies persisted in innovating. For instance, advancements in technology, such as video games, robotics, and digital media, kept Japan relevant in global markets. The GDP per capita reached $37,560 in 1996, and remained the same until the end of the decade.

By the mid-1990s, Japan was not just part of the global pharmaceutical landscape—it was helping define it. With a global share of 18.5 per cent, the country had become the world's second-largest pharmaceutical market. This position was underpinned by a combination of domestic innovation, improving global reputation, and stable, predictable pricing frameworks.

It is clear that commitment to building competence through enhancing capability and reliability, as well as having the right intent demonstrated through acting and communicating transparently and humanely, will result in enhancing trust in the system of a country. This will often be accompanied by real economic advancement.

Exploring the patterns of growth in trust in Korea and China, similar trends can be detected.

The Korean Story

The Korean economy was ravaged by war at the beginning of the Twentieth Century. The country was under Japanese occupation from 1910 until the end of World War II in 1945. This occupation severely impacted local industries and perceptions of Korean products. After Japan's defeat in 1945 and the subsequent division of Korea into the North and South, the South faced immense challenges in rebuilding its economy and infrastructure. The war devastated the South Korean economy, leading to reliance on foreign aid and imports. During this time, domestic products struggled to gain trust, as the focus was on basic survival rather than quality consumer goods. The South Korean GDP per capita in 1953 was a mere $1,112, growing to $1,256 in 1960.

The South Korean government implemented a series of five-year economic plans focusing on industrialization, export-driven growth, and technology investment. Large family-owned conglomerates like Samsung, Hyundai, and LG began to emerge. These companies focused on producing consumer goods, electronics, and automobiles, gradually improving their quality and reputation. Initiatives such as quality control and the adoption of modern manufacturing techniques contributed to improvements in product quality. The government incentivized export-oriented industries and established quality standards, further fostering better production practices.

This was accompanied by a noticeable GDP per capita growth rising from $2,211 in 1970 to $5,812 in 1980.

All that accumulated planning, government coordination, and investment in quality started to bear fruit in the 1980s and 1990s when Korean products, particularly in industries like electronics and then automobiles, began to gain international attention. Brands like Samsung and Hyundai started competing on the global stage. This was accompanied by the spread of Korean culture, such as K-pop, dramas, fashion, skincare products, and cuisine, which helped enhance the image of Korean products, promoting a sense of pride and trust among consumers. The South Korean GDP per capita reached a height of $24,834 in the year 2000.

In the 2000s, Korean companies invested heavily in research and development, producing high-quality and technologically advanced products such as smartphones and televisions, making brands like Samsung and LG recognizable for producing high-quality electronics, and Hyundai became known for reliable vehicles. This helped shift public perception from viewing Korean products as low-cost alternatives to being synonymous with quality and innovation. This success culminated in witnessing South

Korea's GDP per capita exceeding that of Japan in 2017, 2018, and 2019, when it was $42,219 compared to $39,704 for Japan.

The journey of South Korea from the backwaters into becoming a global powerhouse of technological and cultural innovation went hand-in-hand with the growth of trust in Korean products. This multi-faceted journey was marked by significant historical events, economic development, and cultural influences. The transformation of major corporations, government support for industrialization, and a focus on quality and innovation have collectively contributed to the positive perception of Korean products on the global stage.

Awakening the Chinese Dragon

For most of the twentieth century, China faced political instability, foreign invasions, and internal strife. The economy was fragmented, and modern manufacturing was limited. During this period, Chinese products were often seen as inferior due to poor manufacturing processes and a lack of technological advancements, particularly in comparison to Western products.

After the establishment of the People's Republic of China in 1949, the government implemented a centrally planned economy focused on self-sufficiency. Many consumer goods produced during this time were of low quality due to limited resources, outdated technology, and emphasis on quantity rather than quality. Trust in Chinese products was generally low.

In 1978, the Chinese government, under the leadership of Deng Xiaoping, initiated significant economic reforms that moved the country towards a market-oriented economy. This included opening up to foreign investment and technology. The introduction of modern manufacturing techniques and management approaches, such as Total Quality Management, began to reshape the production landscape. Throughout this period, the economic growth was very limited. The GDP per capita was a meagre $963 in 1952, growing to only $1,677 in 1979.

In the 1980s and 1990s, Special Economic Zones (SEZs) were established to attract foreign investment and technology. This led to a rapid increase in exports of Chinese goods. While some products began to improve, many low-cost consumer goods continued to be produced, leading to mixed perceptions regarding quality. However, companies began to gain recognition in various sectors, such as textiles and electronics. Notable growth in GDP per capita was experienced in this period, from $1,678 in 1980 to $3,931 in 1999.

In the 2000s, Chinese manufacturers intensified their investment in advanced technologies and research and development, leading to significant improvements in product quality. Companies like Huawei, Lenovo, and Haier emerged, becoming globally recognized for their quality and innovation. The continuous effort to build trust with the West resulted in China's accession to the World Trade Organization (WTO) in 2001, which further integrated the country into the global economy, increasing its credibility and market access.

In 2015, China launched the 'Made in China 2025' initiative, which aimed to elevate Chinese manufacturing by focusing on high-tech industries, innovation, and quality. As Chinese products began to be associated with higher quality, the perception of 'Made in China' shifted from low-cost to competitive and reliable. Chinese firms expanded into various sectors, including renewable energy, telecommunications, and technology, contributing to enhanced reputations. The Chinese focus on new technologies such as solar panels and electric vehicles is bearing fruit as the country is emerging as a global leader in these areas. The growth it witnessed in the 2000s was phenomenal. The GDP per capita grew from $4,200 in 2000 to $ 14,129 in 2019. According to a World Bank report, China was able to lift 800 million of its citizens out of extreme poverty between 1982–2022.[46]

Today, many Chinese brands are viewed as leaders in certain technology and consumer goods sectors. Brands like BYD, Xiaomi and Alibaba have gained significant consumer trust, both domestically and internationally. Despite these advancements, challenges such as concerns over intellectual property, quality control in certain industries, and geopolitical tensions can sometimes impact trust in Chinese products. Efforts to address issues of quality control and safety have been made to strengthen consumer confidence.

The stories of how Japan, South Korea, and China transformed the trust in the outcomes of their economies are instructional because of their similar patterns of the payoff of relentless commitment to quality, innovation, and the building of human connections. The three nations started gaining trust for their low-risk products, such as consumer appliances, and moved up the value chain to more expensive products, where safety and reliability are key requirements, such as automobiles.

In the cases of Japan and South Korea, the trust reached the pharmaceutical and cosmetics industries, which are considered highly personal and require a higher level of confidence to use and consume. In my assessment, trust in Chinese products has yet to go beyond the food and beverage barrier. A major setback occurred in 2008 when the Chinese melamine crisis took place as it was discovered that melamine, a toxic chemical, had been illegally added to milk and infant formula in China. Melamine was used to falsely enhance the protein content of these products, making them appear more nutritious than they were. Hundreds of thousands of babies fell ill, and six died as a result.[47] Although the Chinese government implemented stricter regulations on food safety and launched investigations, the incident had a major impact on the trust in products made in China.

The growing trust has its clear economic dividend, as when the outputs of an economy become trusted and desired, growth will follow. This is intertwined with cultural influences that are shaping the youth culture and their views of the world.

The graph below shows the growth of GDP per capita for Japan, South Korea, and China between 1950 and 2019.

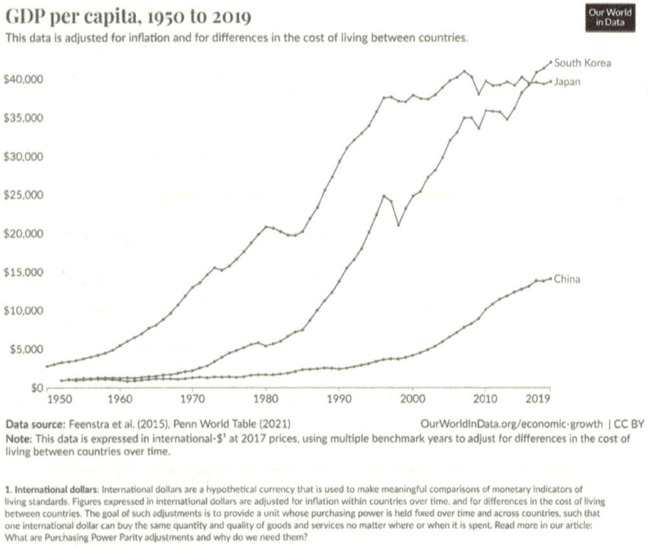

Fig. 6 – The Growth of GDP per Capita for Japan, South Korea, and China from 1950 to 2019.[48]

Maintaining and cultivating trust in this century will not be a straightforward matter. Nations, governments, and corporations will need to demonstrate their competence, reliability, and ability to address global challenges such as climate change and inequity and exhibit a deeper and more genuine commitment to balance and transparency.

Trust in Crisis: The Johnson & Johnson Tylenol Case

It is clear that when it comes to consumer trust, trusting in pharmaceutical products represents one of its ultimate forms.

People would ingest chemicals they know very little about, based on trusting the manufacturers of drugs and the medical establishment.

This spans the four elements of trust:

1. **Competence:** Consumers believe that the manufacturers have the expertise, competence, and infrastructure to create, test, and manufacture these drugs.
2. **Reliability:** They also trust that the drugs they are taking have been approved by the necessary authorities and are made by adopting reliable manufacturing and quality assurance processes so that each batch of the drug is consistent and contains the exact amount of active ingredients necessary for treating their conditions and not resulting in any negative side effects.
3. **Balance:** Consumers also feel assured that pharmaceutical companies will prioritize public health, not only the business imperatives. Companies are expected, for example, to withdraw a drug if they suspect that it may harm some of the patients.
4. **Security:** Consumers expect that in case of any mishap within the company, there will not be a cover-up, and the management will be transparent with the public and cooperative with the authorities who may be investigating the matter.

Consumers may not be consciously aware of the dynamic of the above four elements every time they make a purchase decision or every time they ingest a tablet, but the dynamic is real, and at any moment when one of the elements of trust is compromised, the whole situation will come to the fore undermining the overall trust.

Pharmaceutical companies operate at the highest levels of trust, which manifests in the brand recognition of a company and the products it manufactures. This process of trust-building is sophisticated, long-term, and fragile, but it can be highly rewarding, particularly when the company owns several bestselling drugs.

In 1982, one such blockbuster drug, Tylenol, accounted for 17 per cent of Johnson & Johnson's net annual revenue. However, a crisis struck when, in September 1982, seven people died from ingesting cyanide-laced capsules of extra-strong Tylenol. Tylenol capsules had been laced with the fatal chemical, with containers resealed and placed back on the shelves at multiple outlets. To this day, the motive or identity of the perpetrators are yet to be discovered. As one could imagine, its immediate aftermath shook consumers' confidence in the product—and the company itself.

We shall now examine the Johnson & Johnson Tylenol crisis, exploring how trust can be lost and found. Through the framework of competence, reliability, balance, and security, we will analyse the company's response to the crisis and how its commitment to these elements helped it rebuild consumer faith.

Johnson & Johnson's leadership, under Chairman James Burke, recognized the critical need to address these trust issues head-on. Their response serves as a robust example of how trust can be rebuilt through deliberate and strategic actions aligned with the four elements of trust. The leaders of the company immediately understood the need to prioritize addressing the Balance and Security elements.

1. **Demonstrating Balance**

   Johnson & Johnson took the unprecedented step of recalling 31 million bottles of Tylenol capsules from store shelves, prioritizing consumer safety over profits. This signalled that the company was serious about its ethical responsibilities. The company's leaders realized that they had only one chance to get this right.

They did not opt, for example, to run a media campaign to ascertain that the tampering was limited and that the products on the shelves were safe to use. This could have saved the company millions, if at all it worked. In all likelihood, consumers wouldn't have believed it, and such an incremental approach would have ended up compromising the confidence in how serious the company was about the interests of its customers.

2. **Reaffirming Security**
   The company decided from day one that it would assume a totally transparent approach to handling the crisis. Journalists were invited to sit in and observe leadership team meetings where the crisis and the response to it were discussed. This reassured the public that the company is committed to reaching the bottom of this and that consumer concerns are at the centre of everything that the company will do. Through transparent communication, Johnson & Johnson engaged with the public in a manner that acknowledged consumer fears and addressed their concerns. Burke's forthrightness during media briefings allowed the company to demonstrate a balance between corporate interests and consumer safety. By prioritizing consumer wellbeing, the company fostered a sense of partnership with its customers.

To regain the consumers' confidence in their competence and the reliability of their products, Johnson and Johnson promptly reintroduced the product in a safer tablet form, ensuring that future offerings met stringent safety standards. By taking steps to enhance product safety, Johnson & Johnson reestablished reliability and reinforced consumers' confidence in their commitment to quality.[49]

By investing over $100 million into the recall and relaunch, Johnson & Johnson provided a safe space for consumers to express their concerns. The extensive media campaign surrounding the relaunch, focusing on tamper-proof packaging and safety assurances, helped reassure the public that their vulnerability would be taken seriously and addressed proactively.

The trust-rebuilding effort was successful.

Within just two months after the crisis, Tylenol's market share rebounded from a drastic decline to 30 per cent of the $1.2 billion analgesic market. The bold actions taken during the crisis not only safeguarded Johnson & Johnson's reputation but also underscored the company's capacity for responsible leadership in times of adversity.

Investors observed the positive trajectory, with Johnson & Johnson's stock recovering significantly after the initial panic, illustrating that consumers were willing to restore their trust in the brand following its transparent and decisive response. Over the decades, the company transitioned from being primarily known for consumer products to becoming a foremost player in pharmaceuticals and medical devices, solidifying its reliability for both consumers and investors.

The case of Johnson & Johnson's Tylenol crisis serves as a profound illustration of how trust lost can be regained. By aligning its actions with the four elements of trust—demonstrating competence, reaffirming reliability, achieving balance in interests, and creating security—the company not only weathered an unprecedented crisis but emerged stronger and more resilient than before. The leadership response showcased the potential of well-considered strategies to restore faith in a brand and reinforced the notion that trust is essential for sustained success in any market. The lessons learned from this episode continue to resonate with leaders seeking to navigate trust-related challenges in their own organizations.

Responsible Gambling and Collaboration

Gambling in Singapore was legalized briefly in 1923, when the island republic was a British colony. After only three years, the practice was criminalized, as it led to multiple societal issues and gambling addiction among the population. Gambling remained illegal, and when the topic of establishing a casino in Singapore was brought up in the 1990s, Lee Kuan Yew, the founder of the country, was reported to say, 'Over my dead body.'[50] While he understood the financial potential of the casinos' contribution to the Singaporean economy, he was concerned about their negative societal effects.

The lack of legal gambling outlets did not deter Singaporeans from finding creative ways to satisfy their cravings. They resorted to gambling on cruise ships sailing international waters, or even travelling to Hong Kong or Malaysia to spend their money at the casinos there.

As Singapore faced economic challenges, and the government sought ways to boost tourism and the economy, the context changed. By the mid-2000s, after extensive deliberation and with the recognition of potential benefits, the Singapore government decided to develop integrated resorts that included casinos. The initial governmental resistance gave way to support—provided there were stringent regulations and measures in place to mitigate gambling-related harm.

As legalizing gambling remained hotly debated, the Singaporean Ministry of Social and Family Development established the Responsible Gambling Forum in 2013, comprised of industry and community leaders. Its purpose was to enable the representatives of the gambling industry and the populace, particularly those who had opposed it, to try and come to some middle ground and develop ways to promote responsible gambling.

The forum was chaired by Dr Patrick Liew, chairman of a grassroots organization, and Mr Tan Soo Nan, the chief executive of Singapore Pools. When I interviewed him, Dr Liew recalled the days when he was chairing the forum with pride and satisfaction. 'I had to bring two parties, the gambling industry representatives and the activists who opposed gambling, to see eye to eye,' he said. 'In the first meeting, all I was able to achieve was to get them to introduce themselves to each other—that was it. This was no small achievement,' he added.

'People from different religions have a lot to disagree about. However, they all agreed on their aversion to gambling. Imagine Christian, Muslim, Buddhist, and Taoist religious leaders arguing the moral angle on the one hand, and the industry representatives arguing the economic and job creation case on the other,' Dr Liew continued. 'We had to shift the paradigm and find a common purpose. I told both parties that if they do not work together, bad things can happen. People will not only lose their money, but they could even take their own lives. There is a better way, for sure. Slowly, the two sides agreed that they could see the safety of people as a common goal, a shared purpose, so to speak.'

But trust was another matter altogether.

'It required the industry to really be empathetic and prove that they are not in it simply for the money. They invested heavily in research to identify signs of excessive gambling and addiction, and agreed to safety measures, such as the moment someone exhibits these signs, the casino staff will stop them and escort them to counselling' he explained. 'Slowly but surely, the religious leaders realized that the gambling industry representatives are true professionals, and that they're in the business for the long run. They were interested in a balanced win-win situation, as they pursued their interests while caring for the interests of their clients, who were looking for a thrill dose without ruining their lives or their families.'

But what did running the Responsible Gambling Forum feel like?

'We were solving the Collaboration Equation without being aware of it. We were in the business of establishing shared purpose and kindling mutual trust,' Dr Liew concluded.

Mutual Trust

This chapter examined the four elements of trust in various contexts. For collaboration to take root, mutual trust is essential. We can establish mutual trust by actively and intentionally making ourselves and our organizations trustworthy, thus enhancing our standing on the four elements of trust. This effort can be furthered by initiating our trust in the other party, of course, after assessing their corresponding position on the same four elements of trust.

Leaders can utilize the four-element trust model described here to foster trust in themselves and their organizations. They can also use this model to diagnose situations they encounter and assist those under their care in developing and nurturing trust over time.

The trust model is also beneficial in responding to crises when trust has been shattered. It provides a framework for planning, action, and investment to regain trust.

Part Four

The Future of Collaboration

This part of the book examines the pivotal role that collaboration will play in shaping a sustainable, equitable, and enjoyable future. It emphasises how adopting a collaborative mindset is essential to addressing the world's most pressing challenges and seizing its greatest opportunities.

Through a blend of theoretical insights and practical examples, the chapters herein discuss how enhanced collaboration across borders, disciplines, and cultures can lead to innovative solutions that benefit all of humanity. The growing importance of developing shared purpose and mutual trust will continue to shape the future and provide us with hope to restore the health of our planet, reap the benefits of our technology, reinvent our business philosophy, find peaceful ways to resolve our conflicts, negotiate better deals, and even reinvent our work.

We will explore how fostering global partnerships and collective action can transform societies, drive sustainable development, and create a world where equity and peace are at the forefront. This future-focused analysis is aimed at inspiring hope and equipping individuals and leaders with the tools to actively participate in and shape a collaboratively empowered tomorrow.

Chapter 8

Saving Our World

> 'Sustainable development is the development that meets the needs of the present without compromising the ability of future generations to meet their own needs.'
>
> —Gro Harlem Brundtland
> Our Common Future: The World
> Commission on Environment and
> Development UN Report, October 1987

What would you have done differently if you were told in 2014 that the Covid-19 pandemic was going to happen in 2019? Would you have prepared yourself or your business to pivot digitally? Or would you have bought shares in surgical gloves, food delivery, and vaccine companies?

My guess is you would have done *none* of that.

In December 2014, Barack Obama, while trying to convince the American Congress to invest in building capacity to deal with future pandemics, said:

> There may and likely will come a time in which we have an airborne disease that is deadly, and in order for us to deal with that effectively, we have to put in place an infrastructure, not

> just here at home but globally, that allows us to see it quickly, isolate it quickly, respond to it quickly, so that if and when a new strain of flu like the Spanish flu crops up five years from now or a decade from now, we've made the investment and we're further along to be able to catch it.[51]

Sadly, he failed to mobilize the Congress to approve the necessary investment.

Three months later, in a TED talk in March 2015, Microsoft co-founder Bill Gates said: 'If anything kills over 10 million people in the next few decades, it's most likely to be a highly infectious virus rather than a war.'[52]

A virus 'like the Spanish flu of 1918,' Gates added, 'would spread throughout the world very, very quickly. And you can see over 30 million people died from that epidemic. So, this is a serious problem. We should be concerned.'

Both Gates and Obama were fully aware of how unprepared the world was to deal with a pandemic. Their views were based on the experience of confronting Ebola in Western Africa in 2014.

With all this advance warning, why did the world fail to adequately prepare for the pandemic? I would suggest that preparing for a pandemic is not the only thing that existing leadership structures and mindsets are incapable of addressing. The world's current policymaking, business, finance, and education frameworks are inadequate to respond to many of the existential challenges we face—such as economic fragility, demographic changes, climate crisis, and geopolitical struggles.

In this chapter, we will outline the gap between the nature and scale of the global challenges we face, and the collaborative capacities and system-thinking capabilities we possess to address these challenges at the individual, organizational, and societal levels. The aim is to make the case for the needed change in order for us to be truly fit for the future ahead. While in the past few decades, the shocks that the natural, social, political, and financial systems encountered exposed the inadequacy of our existing tools, policies and mindset to effectively and promptly respond, I believe that endless opportunities exist to construct an alternative system.

We focus here on the pressing issues of the worsening planetary health and environmental degradation. These phenomena are universally acknowledged, and the urgency to mitigate them is broadly recognized. However, despite numerous Conferences of the Parties (COP) meetings and commitments made at global forums, effective collaboration and collective action remain elusive. This chapter seeks to unveil the complexities behind this inertia, examining the underlying reasons why global initiatives often falter.

We will explore the disparities in international priorities, the challenges of conflicting political and economic interests, and the barriers posed by national sovereignty that collectively hinder unified global responses. Drawing on insights from environmental science, policy analysis, and international relations, we will dissect these multifaceted challenges and propose a collaborative framework designed to overcome them.

By illustrating successful models of collaboration and drawing lessons from past failures, we aim to chart a practical, collaborative path toward sustainable environmental stewardship.

Finally, a way forward that leverages the power of multi-stakeholder partnerships, integrating government, the private sector, civil society, and local communities, will be proposed.

The Price of Success

The staggering scientific and technological human advancements we described earlier in the book coincided with substantial economic progress, witnessing global gross domestic product (GDP) surge from $1.92 trillion in 1870 to approximately $101 trillion in 2022. The human population also experienced significant growth, expanding from 1.3 billion in 1870 to surpass 7.8 billion in 2022. However, this progress was accompanied by escalating environmental pollution, exemplified by the rise in atmospheric carbon dioxide concentration from 287 PPM (parts per million) in 1870 to 417 PPM in 2022.[53]

According to the Science Information for Climate-Smart Nation website, the current level of atmospheric carbon dioxide is the highest the Earth has experienced in the past 800,000 years. The last time such high levels were experienced was 3 million years ago, during the Mid-Pliocene Warm Period. Back then, the temperature was 2°C to 3°C higher than the temperatures of the pre-industrial era, and the sea level was 15 to 20 meters higher than today. While the Earth system is very complex, and our models may not be able to accurately fully describe the environmental dynamics, these data should get us to stop and think.[54]

When I interviewed Prof. Mercedes Maroto-Valer, the Champion and Director of the UK's Industrial Decarbonisation Research and Innovation Centre, she described our condition as follows:

> The impending environmental implosion is similar to a meteor that is hurling in space towards us. The collision could happen in ten or twenty years, but it will happen. Individuals and leaders of organizations and nations can, for a while, ignore this meteor and focus on the pressing matters of the present, but that will change nothing; future generations will suffer the consequences of the current inaction. True collaborative leadership is needed so that all of us do our parts and make the sacrifices associated with allocating the resources necessary to address the environmental challenges as they are truly existential.

Failing to Respond

A well-trained Judo player can, with almost magical ease, topple an opponent who weighs more than them. They do this by predicting the trajectory of their opponents' body movements and positioning themselves so that they use the opponent's weight as leverage against them. This metaphor can be very insightful as even with deteriorating environmental trends, having the right mindset can enable us to emerge on the positive side. Organizations and governments, and even some individuals, closely study global trends that operate through our world yet fail to respond in a manner that ensures sustainable success, so why is that? This is because the current mindset within business and leadership is not set up to enable us to be that Judo player.

There are a few reasons for this, among them:

1. Effectively addressing global challenges requires competing parties to have a shared purpose, trust each other, and work selflessly in a collaborative manner. For example, if only some of us do our part for the environment while others go on creating negative ecological externalities, no positive progress will be made.
2. The observed trend or the perceived risk may not materialize within the predicted timescale. In this case, any investment to mitigate the risk or benefit from the trend may be perceived as a loss. The opportunity cost, in this case, may be too high for the concerned parties to bear.
3. Change is difficult by nature. It is not easy to convince individuals and organizations to change the ways that they are comfortable with to gain something or mitigate a risk that will materialize in the future. This is why, inherently, it is challenging to save for retirement, go on a diet, or exercise for better health.
4. When faced with a trend that seems unstoppable, such as climate change, organizations and people can have a sense of paralysis, as it is difficult for them to see that anything they do will make any difference.

So, what kind of changes do we need to make to be able to address these challenges and respond to the trends we are observing? Otto Scharmer speaks of a shift from an 'Ego-system' to an 'Ecosystem' mentality.[55] An ego-system mentality is structured in a self-centred and competitive manner to maximise the shareholder's value and seldom pays attention to the externalities it produces.

On the other hand, an ecosystem mindset is collaborative, values all stakeholders and is interested in the community's wellbeing. It adopts a transparent approach to recording transactions and calculating all costs.

'What's really needed is a deeper shift in consciousness so that we begin to care and act, not just for ourselves and other stakeholders but in the interests of the entire ecosystem in which economic activities take place,' Scharmer wrote.

For most of our history, our economic activities have had a relatively limited impact on the health of the planet. Since the first industrial revolution, the effect of human activities on the planet has rapidly accelerated. This was the time that our political, economic, and business theories were formed on the basis of fierce competition. This gave us tremendous, albeit not inclusive, economic growth. It also gave us slavery, war, colonization, and multiple environmental perils.

The only sustainable way ahead for us is to transform our business activities into the era of the 'Purpose and Trust Economy', where the ability to connect with oneself and others and exhibit self-awareness, respect, and empathy will be the sign of delivering true and unrivalled value. Acting from our higher purpose and building mutual trust with others will enable us to address the obstacles to action outlined above. This will require that we rewrite our playbook in education, human resources management, marketing, engineering and governance. It is the responsibility of the leaders among us to support our people, especially our youth, to succeed and thrive in such a different environment.

The table below shows how a purpose-driven leadership approach can provide antidotes to reasons for inaction compared to a traditional leadership approach.

Reasons for Inaction	**Traditional Leadership**	**Purpose-Driven Leadership**
The risk may not materialize	Investment is a loss. Players avoid opportunity cost.	Investment will further support the purpose anyway.
Change is difficult	Inertia tends to maintain the status quo.	Purpose is a strong motivator for action.
Paralysis due to size of the challenge	Our actions will not make a difference.	Our actions will make a difference.
Everyone needs to do their part for the intervention to be effective.	Competitiveness and lack of trust are obstacles facing collective action.	Trust and shared sense of purpose will enable collective action.

Sustainable Development

For the past century, development has largely been seen as an economic phenomenon largely measured by GDP growth. However, the shortcomings of this approach are increasingly becoming apparent. This focus on measuring progress and development exclusively through economic indicators resulted in encouraging consumption and the abuse of natural resources to satisfy this growth appetite, resulting not only in the depletion of finite resources, such as raw materials and energy sources, but also in the dumping of toxic waste beyond the capability of the environment to process.

In 2022, Andrew Fanning and his colleagues published their work that studied the ability of different countries to satisfy their residents' needs as measured by eleven social indicators linked to the UN Sustainable Development Goals within the planetary boundaries, measured by six environmental indicators. Their empirical study showed that currently, no country achieves the required social thresholds without transgressing multiple biophysical boundaries, as demonstrated by the figure below.[56]

There is a growing realization that a paradigm shift is needed, as this unsustainable approach to development is not only leading to environmental degradation but also exacerbating inequality and geopolitical tensions. The interconnectedness of our world means that open burning to clear agricultural land in one country can cause a massive degradation in the quality of air in another country, and a war in one continent can create a refugee crisis in another. The sad fact is that the poorer people, who consume the least, pollute the least, and hence contribute the least to the environmental woes, often bear the brunt of climate change.

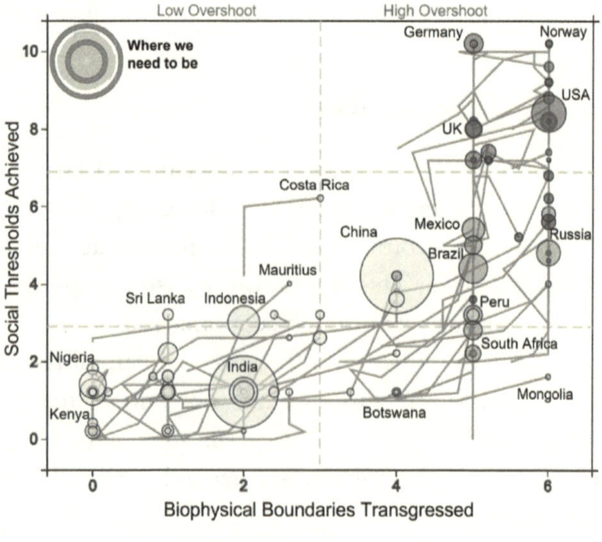

Fig. 7 – Number of Social Thresholds Achieved versus Number of Biophysical Boundaries Transgressed by Countries Over Time, 1992–2015.[57]

Amid all the uncertainties, complexities, and challenges that we experience, the principles that stand out as guiding essentials for creating a sustainable future are:

1. **Prioritizing collaboration:** The only way we can address the challenges we face is through building the shared purpose and the mutual trust necessary for coaction to take root.
2. **Focusing on future generations' interests:** Lester Brown said, 'We have not inherited this earth from our forefathers, we have borrowed it from our children.' This is so eloquently true that it needs to be a key guiding principle. Whatever we do, we need to prioritize the maintenance of the health of our planet so that our children, grandchildren, and generations beyond them can enjoy it too.
3. **Recognizing interconnectedness:** A system-thinking approach that considers the people, culture, and ecosystem is essential for providing any long-term credible solutions for the challenges we face.
4. **Adopting holistic measurement:** Progress needs to be redefined and its scope to be widened to include, besides the GDP, concepts such as peace, happiness, embracing local wisdom, flourishing, wellbeing, and planetary health.
5. **Strengthening and modernizing governance:** Institutions matter, and we need political, legal, and governance structures that truly prioritize sustainability and build collaborative opportunities to provide real solutions to the world's challenges.
6. **Unlocking the business value in sustainability:** Often, operating sustainably is seen as a business burden. This way of thinking needs to change. Besides being the right thing to do, operating sustainably means using

fewer materials and less energy, and as the cost of these keeps on increasing, sustainability becomes a business imperative. Furthermore, new business areas, such as climate financing, represent fresh opportunities for meaningful investment and business growth.

7. **Reforming education systems:** Education needs to recognize that the development process begins with developing the individual, assisting them to know their superpowers, discover their purpose, and mobilize that purpose into a positive impact on the world.

The Collaboration Premium

A report by the International Energy Agency titled, 'Net Zero by 2050 A Roadmap for the Global Energy Sector', emphasized the importance of international collaboration to bring emissions down.[57]

It asserts that it isn't simply a matter of all governments seeking to bring their national emissions to net zero, but finding ways to fix global challenges through coordinated actions. 'Governments must work together in an effective and mutually beneficial manner to implement coherent measures that cross borders. This includes carefully managing domestic job creation and local commercial advantages with the collective global need for clean energy technology deployment,' it said. 'Accelerating innovation, developing international standards and coordinating to scale up clean technologies needs to be done in a way that links national markets. Cooperation must recognise differences in the stages of development of different countries and the varying situations of different parts of society.'

The report estimates that if we fail to have the sufficient international collaboration necessary to achieve net zero by 2050, we could delay this goal by four decades. So, clearly, international collaboration is a fundamental enabler in our journey towards sustainability. This is another area where the Collaboration Equation needs to be applied.

The Paris Agreement

Our best scientific data is conclusive that human emissions of greenhouse gases are the primary drivers of climate change. Carbon dioxide, along with other greenhouse gases such as methane and nitrous oxide, is released through various activities, including the burning of fossil fuels, the production of materials like steel, cement, and plastics, and the agricultural processes. Reducing these emissions and even actively removing some of the greenhouse gases that have been emitted is crucial if we are to mitigate the impacts of climate change. To make a meaningful difference, transitioning our energy systems, industrial practices, and food production methods to more sustainable and renewable sources is essential.

The challenge of reducing emissions is more complex than just a blanket reduction of what goes into the atmosphere. Issues such as energy poverty, low living standards, and inadequate nutrition that affect billions of people worldwide need to be simultaneously considered and effectively addressed. The pursuit of a cleaner, more sustainable future must go hand-in-hand with efforts to improve the quality of life for all people. When discussing emission reduction targets, developing countries often make the argument that developed nations had two centuries of polluting head start, a period in which they built their infrastructure and accumulated wealth and should be responsible for a higher proportion of the global emission reduction targets.

Fortunately, technological advances hold the potential to address both climate change and human welfare. In recent decades, the costs of solar panels, wind energy, and battery storage have dropped significantly, increasingly out-competing fossil fuel alternatives. This progress suggests that we will, potentially, be able to provide affordable, clean energy to everyone, transforming how we power our lives and economies.

However, for this transformation to succeed, political change is also essential. We need to create systems and policies that support rapid decarbonization and encourage the adoption of sustainable technologies.

While emissions continue to rise globally, there is hope: several countries have effectively reduced their greenhouse gas emissions over the past few decades. With the right investment in affordable low-carbon technologies, other nations can achieve similar success, improving their living standards without following the high-carbon pathways that wealthier countries have historically taken. The journey toward sustainability is not only feasible but also an opportunity to create a brighter future for all.

The figures below show the current situation of our emissions.

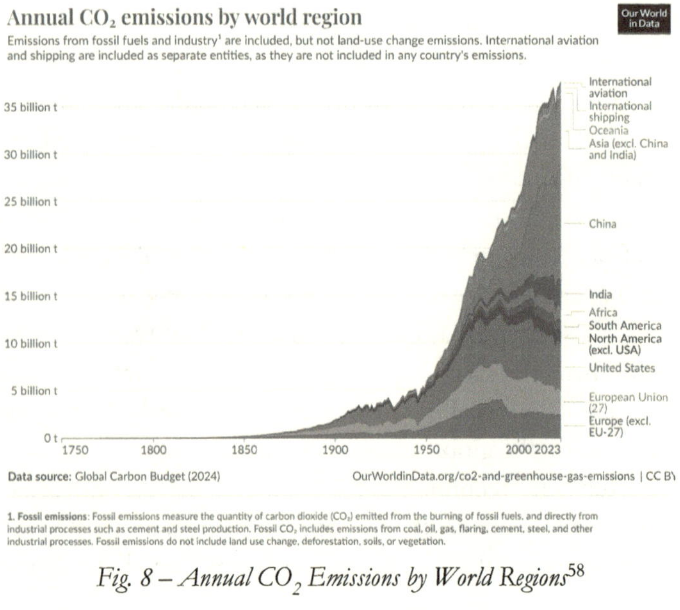

Fig. 8 – Annual CO_2 Emissions by World Regions[58]

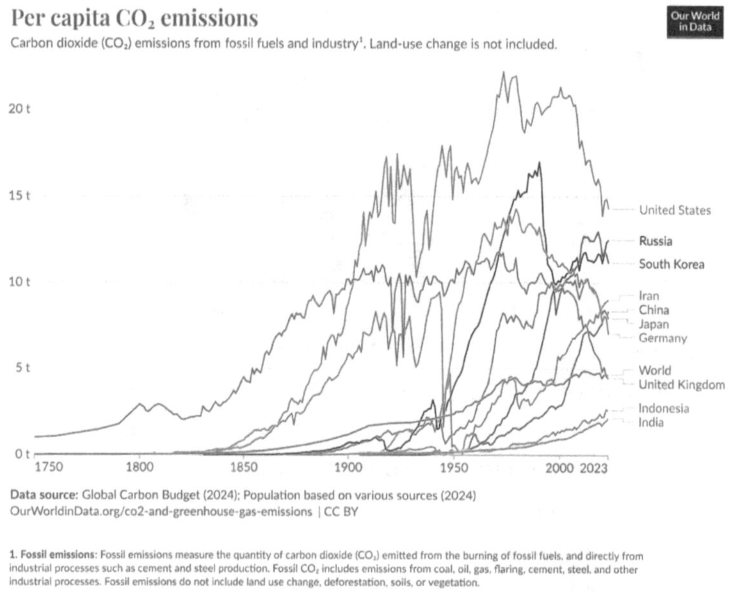

Fig. 9 – Per Capita CO_2 Emissions for Selected Countries and the World

As we have repeatedly iterated, the emission challenge can only be addressed collaboratively. The Paris Agreement, adopted on 12 December 2015 during the 21st Conference of the Parties (COP21) in Paris, represents a historic global effort to combat climate change. Its central aim is to limit global warming to well below 2°C above pre-industrial levels, with an aspiration to limit the temperature increase to 1.5°C.

The Paris Agreement is unique in its framework, which encourages countries to pledge their targets voluntarily, known as Nationally Determined Contributions (NDCs). Each country assesses its own responsibilities and ambitions in light of national circumstances and capabilities. The agreement advocates for mutual trust and emphasizes transparency and accountability, requiring nations to report on their progress and update their NDCs every five years.

Signing the agreement was just the beginning. The real work started when countries were to deliver their voluntarily set reduction targets. The U.S., for example, signed the agreement under President Barack Obama in April 2016 and formally joined in September 2016. In June 2017, President Donald Trump announced his intention to withdraw the U.S. from the agreement, which was completed on 4 November 2020. However, on 20 January 2021, President Joe Biden signed an executive order to rejoin the Paris Agreement, and the U.S. officially re-entered on 19 February 2021. Issues related to building trust in the geopolitical field are fraught with challenges. How can we, for example, convince governments that have deep disagreements, conflicts, or even outright war to trust each other and collaborate in climate matters?

Interestingly, we do have some precedents to learn from. The International Space Station[59] (ISS) is a collaborative space initiative between five space agencies: the American, Russian, European, Japanese, and Canadian. It is the largest space station ever built and maintained in low Earth orbit to perform space research in microgravity conditions.

Since its launch in 1998, the space station has represented what is truly possible, not only in the scientific and technological realms, but also in the field of international geopolitical collaboration. The levels of shared purpose, mutual trust, technical integration, political will, and financial commitment needed for this project are literally a matter of life and death, at least for the inhabitants of the space station.

Following the war in Ukraine in February 2022, almost all the political, economic, and scientific ties and partnerships between Russia and the West stopped. The only one left standing is the work on the International Space Station. This is mainly due to the high level of integration at the hardware, technical, and human levels. In fact, the ISS is made of two integrated modules:

the Russian Orbital Segment and the US Orbital Segment. The necessary operational software and technologies are provided and maintained by all participant agencies, particularly the US and the Russian.

Finally, astronauts from both parties have been on joint training programmes for over two decades, and it is not feasible to unentangle the human capabilities needed to keep the station up and running. For these ISS partners, it seems obvious that they have the shared purpose of keeping a highly valuable project going, and mutual trust appears to be forged in the fire as astronauts are trusting their lives to each other and the systems keep the project on. Collaboration, then, comes as a natural outcome.

Writing these words, I could not help but see the similarities between the ISS and Spaceship Earth, a concept popularized by R. Buckminster Fuller, the American architect, systems theorist, and futurist, who portrayed Earth as a shared vessel with limited resources that we all depend on for our survival.[60] Of course, the timescales are different; if the five space agencies stop collaborating, the disastrous consequences will be immediate, while Spaceship Earth may take a much longer time before we reach an irreversible catastrophe as a result of our lack of collaboration. But once we expand our time horizon to our children and their children, the view should be clear, and the differences diminish.

It is essential that leaders and politicians adopt this expansive viewpoint, build collaborative partnerships with other nations and leaders, and educate their constituencies so that planetary health issues become essential political campaign matters.

Some of the arguments for this long-term thinking necessary to foster the conditions for voters to support sustainability-focused policies are given below:

1. Just like the human body, the health of the planet is holistic. Any investment in, or sacrifice for, improving the

planetary health will pay dividends for all of us. By the same token, neglecting our part in taking care of it will make us and our children pay the price.

2. Environmental crises will lead to a larger humanitarian and potential refugee crises. If people, somewhere, face severe drought that creates famine, excessive rising sea levels that submerge their lands, or toxic air pollution, they will have no choice but to migrate elsewhere to stay alive. If we want people to flourish in their home countries and not be forced to migrate under environmental pressures, better than building walls, we can invest in improving the climate conditions for all of us.
3. Developing environmentally friendly and sustainable technologies and practices can be exercised in a way that makes business and economic sense. It can be the foundation for the growth of new industries and the creation of more jobs. For example, politicians can campaign to make their nations a centre for excellence in green financing or green manufacturing, with all the jobs and economic development this will bring along.

Collaboration Towards a Circular Economy

Many would have a drawer full of old mobile phones, tablets, and similar electronic devices. People keep these devices because it is either difficult to recycle them or because we still have personal data, photos, and videos in them.

Now, imagine if the responsibility of recycling these electronic devices at the end of their life was legally assigned to those who manufacture them. What impact would that have on the way these devices are designed, manufactured, and distributed?

In 2004, the Extended Producer Responsibility (EPR) Act legislated by the European Union made it the responsibility of producers to collect and deal with automobiles and electronic equipment at the end of their life cycle. This act represents the world's first comprehensive legislation to regulate waste and toxicity, and it is already inspiring other jurisdictions to adopt similar laws.

The fact that the European Union is a profitable market will mean major producers outside the continent will change their practices to meet these requirements, so that they can maintain this market access. So, change will be afoot.

There is an interesting story behind the enacting of this law that is rooted in the public-private collaborative space. The story is cited in a book by Peter Senge and his co-authors.[61] It all started with BMW deciding to transform the recycling of its old automobiles into a strategic opportunity. The company's management was convinced that building a recycling facility to recover used components and materials from its cars sold in Germany was economically viable, aligned with the growing societal expectations for high environmental standards, and politically attractive as it would create 1,500 job opportunities.

The leader of this initiative was Horst-Henning Wolf. When he crunched the numbers with his team, he realized that their plan in its current format would not work. The company then planned a centralized recycling facility where old BMW cars from all over Germany would be sent for processing. When factoring in the cost of transporting cars and the carbon dioxide emitted in the process, both the environmental and economic cases faltered. The alternative that Wolf favoured was a network of smaller recycling centres, where less energy is utilized and ensuring that only high-value materials and used components are shipped around. The only drawback was that the cost of such a network of recycling centres was beyond what BMW could afford.

After convincing key stakeholders within BMW of the validity of his feasibility study and economic analysis, Wolf went on a quest to convince other competing automakers, such as Mercedes-Benz, Audi, and Volkswagen, to partner with them in building the recycling network. The harbingers of the concept of EPR were already there, and the principle has been debated since the 1980s, when environmental concerns started to gain more momentum.

Wolf spared no time or effort in working to convince his fellow automakers to realize that they had the shared purpose of being on the right side of the environmental equation, and also being on the front foot when it came to formulating the legislation. They all favoured legislation that would encourage innovation, while facilitating the creation of new business value rather than stifling it. If legislation was coming their way, they may as well position themselves to be included and consulted in writing it.

The commitment that Wolf and BMW dedicated to this project, and the soundness of his environmental, political, and economic analysis helped in building trust between the competing automakers. The shared purpose and mutual trust made collaboration between the automakers possible and were also extended to the EU's bureaucrats and lawmakers, as the automakers proved that their stand is not only a matter of compliance. They demonstrated their competence, reliability, balance, and commitment to security—the four elements of trust.

The success in collaboration in the case of EPR is both inspiring and instructive. Collaborating across boundaries, whether cultural, corporate, or national, is not easy. However, when it comes to the environment, we know that Mother Nature does not recognize boundaries. We will need to work out the pathways to enable collaboration; this will be the space where leadership will be tested.

The Role of Universities

Around the world, trust in institutions is not where we would like it to be. Unfortunately, this did not spare the higher education sector and universities. There is a growing sentiment that questions the return on investment in higher education. While this is not entirely unfounded, and universities need to reform and evolve, one should be careful before passing judgment on an entire sector that could potentially be a source of solace.

At a time when geopolitical polarization is rampant, universities are among the few institutions left where researchers and scholars on the opposite side of the ideological spectrum can still interact, debate, and collaborate. The personal relationships that students and scientists from all over the world build, while studying and researching together, represent a hugely valuable asset that can provide a foundation for building trust and reaffirming the shared purpose of healing our planet.

While we still need more collaborative leadership in the area of environmental sustainability, the examples of government-to-government (International Space Station) and business-to-business and government-to-business (Extended Producer Responsibility) collaborations are a source of encouragement.

Chapter 9

Transcending Ourselves

'The cave you fear to enter holds the treasure you seek.'

—Joseph Campbell

Having been born in Baghdad, Iraq, meant that I was surrounded by history, which was in its air, water, and soil. Mesopotamia, as it was formerly known, was where humanity invented the wheel, writing, and law. One of the earliest Mesopotamian and human literary masterpieces that I grew up listening to and was fascinated by was the Epic of Gilgamesh.[62] It chronicled the adventures of the King of Uruk, who embarked on the journey to understand the essence of life and mortality.

The epic, which represents the first documented human attempt to achieve immortality, begins as below:

> He who has seen everything, I will make known to the lands.
> I will teach about him, who experienced all things alike:
> Anu granted him the totality of knowledge of all.
> He saw the Secret, discovered the Hidden,
> he brought information of (the time) before the Flood.
> He went on a distant journey, pushing himself to exhaustion,
> but then was brought to peace.

The text follows Gilgamesh, a powerful and charismatic ruler, who, despite his earthly successes, was haunted by an inner void. The death of his close companion, Enkidu, acted as a catalyst, shattering his illusion of invincibility and plunging him into an existential crisis. He thus began a quest for immortality, which eluded him no matter how hard he tried.

Gilgamesh's narrative arc—from a tyrannical ruler defined by power, authority, and physical strength to a seeker of eternal truths—mirrors the universal and collective human journey. Since the time of Gilgamesh, our view of who we are has evolved from being defined by our strengths and what we can physically do, to our comprehension and how much we know, and ultimately by our wisdom and the positive impact that we can have on the world beyond ourselves.

This evolution was largely intertwined with and enabled by the technologies we developed. From the invention of writing to the development of AI, it appears to be true that while we shape our technologies, these technologies end up shaping us.

Beyond harnessing the power of AI, there is now a rapid move to pursue Artificial General Intelligence (AGI), which refers to a type of AI that can understand, learn, and apply knowledge across a wide range of tasks, mimicking human cognitive abilities. Unlike narrow AI, which is designed to perform specific tasks (like language translation or playing chess), AGI is characterized by its general capabilities, allowing it to solve unfamiliar challenges, learn from experience, and adapt to new situations in a way similar to humans.

While the race for AI dominance is ongoing, another one, for achieving Quantum Computing supremacy, is brewing, where the volume and speed of data processing will be at unprecedented levels. When AI reaches the level of AGI and has access to quantum computing capabilities and massive data-collecting capacities, the possibilities will be endless, and the implications will go beyond the mere technical.

When AGI begins to routinely resemble and surpass the human cognitive capacity, questions about the nature of consciousness and what makes humans special will move from the theoretical, ethical, and philosophical realms to the social, legal, and computer science realms. Humanity will have to confront the Gilgamesh questions of who we truly are on an extraordinary scale.

In this chapter, we will examine the necessary levels of collaboration required to enable us to harness the disruptive technologies of AGI, Quantum Computing, and others as a force for good, avoiding the dangerous pitfalls that could accompany their deployment.

We will emphasize the crucial roles of a collaborative mindset, shared purpose, and mutual trust in developing and deploying AI technologies responsibly. This chapter will address the ethical considerations and collaborative frameworks necessary to ensure AI is used safely and beneficially. This is hoped to serve as a call to action, urging collective vigilance and collaboration to steer AI towards outcomes that enhance global wellbeing and progress, and it brings to light lessons we learned from our failure to collaborate at the inception of nuclear technology.

AI and Our Last Chance at Collaboration

Within the teams that worked on the Manhattan Project, a group of scientists grappled with the ethical ramifications of the atomic age. Led by physicist James Franck, they penned the Franck Report,[63] a plea for collaboration and shared responsibility in the development and use of nuclear energy. As the world recoiled from the devastation brought on Hiroshima and Nagasaki, this report emerged as an early warning urging nations to transcend political and ideological differences for the sake of global security.

The Franck Report was completed and submitted to the US government in June 1945, a mere two months before the nuclear attacks on Japan. It called for the US not to attack Japan, and instead, opt to demonstrate the destructive power of atomic bombs through a nuclear bomb test. The authors hoped that this test would encourage Japan to surrender, saving the world from a true human catastrophe.

The report affirmed that:

> Nuclear bombs cannot possibly remain a secret weapon at the exclusive disposal of this country for more than a few years. The scientific facts on which their construction is based are well known to scientists of other countries.

As such, the authors advocated for the sharing of nuclear technology and know-how with other nations. The underlying principle was simple yet profound: as the US openly shares the technology, it will give the rest of the world the confidence that it does not intend to use its destructive power against them. That mutual trust would have provided the space for the emergence of a shared purpose of using atomic energy peacefully, enabling more nations to collaborate, which could have averted the nuclear arms race that ensued almost immediately after the attack on Japan.

Needless to say, politicians chose to ignore the recommendations of the Franck report. The prospect of having the nuclear upper hand proved to be seductive. Amid today's complex geopolitical landscape, where nuclear capabilities continue to be a source of global concern, revisiting the Franck Report's ethos becomes increasingly relevant, for it foresaw the dangers of a world fragmented by competing nuclear arsenals, urging nations to come together to prevent an uncontrollable proliferation of these weapons.

The thinking behind the Franck Report was not entirely in vain, as in its aftermath, attempts were made to establish international control through organizations like the United Nations Atomic Energy Commission. However, the subsequent Cold War era witnessed a different trajectory, marked by intense rivalries and a race to acquire even more destructive nuclear capabilities.

As we rush deeper into the era of AI, the spectre of unintended consequences looms large. The parallels between AI and the advent of nuclear technology are striking, inviting reflection on the lessons learned from history and the imperative for a collaborative approach as the exponential growth of AI capabilities raises critical questions about ethics, accountability, and the potential weaponization of intelligent systems.

If history is our guide, it's essential to heed the warnings embedded in the Franck Report and proactively address the ethical dimensions of AI.

The crux of the matter lies in the urgency to establish a collaborative framework akin to the one proposed by the Franck Report—one that encourages transparency, shared purpose, and international collaboration in AI development. The stakes are high, and the unchecked proliferation, without a unifying global vision, could result in unintended consequences, from biased algorithms to massive disinformation and the creation of autonomous lethal weapons.

While the comparison between nuclear weapons and AI might seem exaggerative, the impact and potential of the latter may even exceed that of the former. The core issue, however, remains the same: the need for responsible stewardship of powerful technologies. The Franck Report's failure to prevent a nuclear arms race serves as a stark lesson on the importance of global collaboration in navigating the ethical complexities of emerging technologies.

Artificial Intelligence has the potential to shape the destiny of nations and the course of humanity. The urgency to act is palpable. Initiating a modern-day equivalent of the Franck Report—one that encourages nations to collaborate on the ethical, equitable, and human-centric development and deployment of AI—is not just a prudent course of action; it's an ethical, practical, and strategic imperative.

Such an initiative could involve the establishment of international agreements, ethical guidelines, and collaborative research efforts to ensure that AI serves humanity's collective interests rather than becoming a tool for division and conflict. It requires the commitment of governments, industry leaders, and the scientific community to prioritise a future where AI benefits society as a whole.

While we navigate the uncharted territories of the Age of AI, the question is not whether we can afford to act early to lay down the legal, governance, and societal infrastructure so that we can safely and collaboratively develop this technology but whether we can afford not to. The lessons from the Franck Report remind us that the responsibility and the capability to shape the future lies in our hands, and the time to act is now.

The 2024 Edelman Trust Barometer,[44] cited earlier, revealed a mixed picture when it comes to how people perceive AI as a force for improving their future. They clearly can see its potential for good, but at the same time, worry about its possible negative side effects.

The two collaborative challenges in this space are:

1. How can governments, corporations, educational institutions, and individuals collaborate to make sure that AI remains a technology subservient to humans and mitigate the potential for weaponizing it within geopolitical or corporate conflicts?
2. How can we safely use AI in ways that enhance our human value and strengthen our ties rather than undermine trust between us and reduce our relevance?
3. How can we ensure the sustainable and equitable deployment of AI in light of its huge resource

requirements, including high energy and fresh water demands of data centres?

Being in a position to have positive responses to these questions requires that we transcend our current mental models and realize that we have unlocked a new technology that is creating new potentials that we could only dream of in the past.

Keeping AI Safe and in the Open

In an interview with the BBC in December 2014, the late Stephen Hawking said:

> The development of full artificial intelligence could spell the end of the human race. It would take off on its own and re-design itself at an ever-increasing rate. Humans, who are limited by slow biological evolution, couldn't compete and would be superseded.[64]

Nine years after this interview, alarmed by AI's dizzying development, multiple scientists and corporate leaders wrote an open letter urging caution and recommending a pause for AI development in a move reminiscent of the Franck Report. These included Apple co-founder Steve Wozniak and Elon Musk, as well as researchers from Alphabet-owned DeepMind and experts in machine learning, such as Yoshua Bengio and Stuart Russell.

The open letter starts with 'AI systems with human-competitive intelligence can pose profound risks to society and humanity, as shown by extensive research and acknowledged by top AI labs.[65]

As stated in the widely endorsed Asilomar AI Principles, advanced AI could represent a profound change in the history of life on Earth and should be planned for and managed with commensurate care and resources.'

The letter goes on to ascert that, 'Unfortunately, this level of planning and management is not happening, even though recent months have seen AI labs locked in an out-of-control race to develop and deploy ever more powerful digital minds that no one—not even their creators—can understand, predict, or reliably control.'

It then moves on to outline the risk of AGI stating that, 'Contemporary AI systems are now becoming human-competitive at general tasks, and we must ask ourselves: Should we let machines flood our information channels with propaganda and untruth? Should we automate away all the jobs, including the fulfilling ones? Should we develop nonhuman minds that might eventually outnumber, outsmart, obsolete and replace us? Should we risk loss of control of our civilization? Such decisions must not be delegated to unelected tech leaders. Powerful AI systems should be developed only once we are confident that their effects will be positive and their risks will be manageable.'

While concerns regarding AI, as with any emerging technology, are not new, the endorsement of such concerns by figures like Stephen Hawking lends them additional gravity. However, just like the case of the Franck Report, thus far, none of the key players in AI development have heeded the request of the open letter to have a six-month pause on training systems more powerful than GPT-4.

The concern about the weaponization of AI is real and goes beyond the use to enhance physical weapons. Psychological warfare has always been an integral part of wars and conflicts to undermine the enemy's self-confidence and weaken them to give up without a fight.

Imagine a chatbot masquerading as a social media application that gives life advice, while simultaneously targeting the youth of the enemy to spread misinformation or convince them to engage in self-harm. This would be a dream weapon for unhinged psychological warfare proponents.

Unscrupulous business opponents, or even mischievous individuals, can adopt similar approaches to create chaos or gain unfair advantages over a corporate competitor. They can, for example, use AI to flood the internet with content that undermines customer confidence in a product or a service delivered by their competitors.

For instance, following false reports that Ethereum's founder, Vitalik Buterin, had died in a car crash, the company's market value reportedly plummeted by $4 billion.

To create and sustain a sense of shared purpose and mutual trust between nations and corporations to enable collaboration in the area of safe development and deployment of AI, the following may be adopted:

1. **Build International Institutions**
   To ensure the responsible use of nuclear power and to promote its peaceful application, the UN established the International Atomic Energy Agency. A similar body is necessary to regulate all aspects of AI development and deployment, which can help enhance trust between different parties and ensure that the interests of smaller countries are being considered while bigger decisions are made.
2. **Establish Legal Responsibility and Accountability**
   In the early 1990s, the internet was in its early beginnings. It was largely unregulated and rife with questionable content, such as a significant amount of pornography that was accessible to users of all ages, including impressionable children. This situation raised alarms among certain US lawmakers concerned about the potential impacts of such unrestricted access.

In response to these concerns, in 1995, legislators proposed the Communications Decency Act (CDA), a bipartisan effort intended to extend existing laws on obscene and indecent communications via telephone services to the burgeoning digital landscape. This extension seemed a logical step, as the internet back then was transmitted over phone lines. A key provision of this legislation aimed to hold websites and online platforms accountable for any indecent or obscene material posted by their users.

Amid this legislative backdrop, a notable legal battle unfolded between Stratton Oakmont and Prodigy, two companies that played prominent roles in the evolving internet narrative. Stratton Oakmont, later made infamous by the movie *The Wolf of Wall Street*, was a brokerage firm that filed a lawsuit against Prodigy, a pioneering internet service provider of the time. The dispute arose after an anonymous user posted allegations on a Prodigy bulletin board, accusing Stratton Oakmont's president of fraudulent activities. The court ultimately ruled in favour of Stratton Oakmont, citing Prodigy's moderation of content as evidence of editorial control.

Concerned that the Communications Decency Act might stifle the Internet's growth and innovation, Representatives Ron Wyden and Chris Cox introduced Section 230 as an amendment. This stipulated that 'interactive computer services' would not be held liable for user-generated content, even if they engaged in some degree of moderation of that content. This critical provision sought to encourage responsible content management while safeguarding the nascent internet industry's dynamic expansion.

Section 230 of the Communications Decency Act is the key legislative foundation that absolves social media platforms and other internet-based applications from prosecution over content generated by their users. Three decades after the introduction of Section 230, social media and internet communication applications wield massive power over shaping social and political narratives—not through generating the content, but rather, through their algorithms that are designed to maximize users' engagement, which is measured by the time spent on the platform as well as actions such as subscribing to a channel, liking a post or content, and sharing it with friends.

Through increasing user engagement, internet platforms collect more data on their users, sell more advertisements, and thus grow richer and more influential. In the pursuit of the gold dust of user engagement, social media algorithms discovered that what generates clicks and user engagement is usually content that is sensational, hateful, controversial, and not necessarily true or useful.

As human brains are not wired to deal with such an onslaught of information, algorithms are now customizing our personal feeds and serving us largely what they think we will engage with and share with our friends. This has a huge impact on increasing polarization and sowing division rather than promoting truth and harmony.

A Pew Research Centre report titled 'The Future of Truth and Misinformation Online' affirmed that:

> Experts are evenly split on whether the coming decade will see a reduction in false and misleading narratives online. Those forecasting improvements place their hopes in technological fixes and in societal solutions. Others think the dark side of human nature is aided more than stifled by technology.[66]

With more powerful AI, the algorithms are expected to gain exponentially higher abilities to capture our attention and create user engagement. It is time now to review the legislations that govern how information is shared with the potential of making the algorithm owners responsible for the actions of their algorithms and the consequences of these actions. As the AI-generated content, including videos of people that are indistinguishable from real ones, a key requirement is to outlaw the impersonation of people by AI.

3. **Fair Distribution of the Benefits**

As we stand on the brink of a digital revolution, it is crucial to recognize the roots of AI's power: the vast training data derived from the collective knowledge, experiences, and content generated by humanity over millennia. AI, in many respects, is not merely a product of technology; it reflects our shared human endeavour.

Given this context, we must ensure that its benefits are equitably shared by all—not just a privileged few. The extraordinary value it creates should serve as a foundation for fostering global progress and addressing pressing challenges that confront humankind today. One compelling idea is to establish a global development fund financed through a designated percentage of taxes levied on the value generated by AI. This fund would be administered by an independent global body dedicated to investing in initiatives that have far-reaching implications for humanity, such as:

Addressing global challenges: The world faces numerous interconnected issues, including climate change, pervasive poverty, and conflicts that threaten international stability. A global fund could channel resources into impactful projects aimed at tackling these challenges.

For example, investment in renewable energy initiatives can help mitigate the effects of climate change, while funds could support sustainable agriculture and education programmes in impoverished regions, ultimately reducing global poverty.

Promoting equity and inclusion: As AI continues to evolve and create wealth, there is a growing concern that the benefits will disproportionately favour richer nations and corporations. By establishing this global fund, we can ensure that a portion of the value generated by AI is reinvested into marginalized or overlooked communities. This inclusive approach not only fosters social equity, but also empowers individuals around the world to participate in shaping their own futures.

Sustaining peace and stability: Promoting world peace is inherently tied to addressing the root causes of conflict. A global development fund can be instrumental in financing initiatives that foster dialogue, understanding, and collaboration between nations.

Projects focusing on education, community-building, and conflict resolution can help create a more peaceful world, reducing the likelihood of conflicts that stem from inequality and resource scarcity.

Investing in future generations: The potential of AI is only beginning to be realized, and its landscape will continue to evolve. By establishing this global fund, we create a mechanism for future generations to benefit from the wealth generated by AI. Investments can be directed towards research, education, and innovation that prioritize human flourishing, sustainability, and ethical considerations, ensuring that the transformative power of AI contributes positively to society in the long term.

For this global development fund to be effective, it must be governed by an independent and transparent body that operates with accountability and inclusivity. Stakeholders from various sectors—including governments, non-profits, academia, and the private sector—should be engaged in decision-making processes to ensure diverse perspectives are considered. Clear criteria for funding projects based on their potential impact, sustainability, and alignment with global priorities will be essential to achieving the fund's objectives.

4. **Sustainable and Equitable Use of World Resources** AI Data Centres are power and fresh water hungry establishments. It is essential to make sure that their operations do not happen at the expense of vulnerable communities that are struggling with access to these resources.

Impact of AGI on Trust and Collaboration

As the provost of Heriot-Watt University Malaysia, my job is not just about running the university and ensuring that our education, research, and community experiences are top-notch. I am also responsible for managing the stakeholders' relations, chief among these stakeholders are our alumni in Asia.

Recently, I was hosting an alumni dinner in Singapore, and as usual, the alumni department invited the 2000 or so alumni that we have in the country. While checking the list of attendees, I noticed some of our more senior alumni hadn't responded. So, I decided to send each one of them a personalized email, letting them know how much I was looking forward to meeting them.

One of them, who was a president at a multinational corporation, wrote back, thanking me for my email and requesting further information about the evening before committing herself to attend. I shared the programme, and eventually, she attended, and we had a truly wonderful time.

While chatting with her, she mentioned she graduated with an MBA from Edinburgh Business School, Heriot-Watt University, twenty-four years ago. She told me that every year, like clockwork, the alumni department would send her two to three invitations to various university events. 'I never responded to any of these,' she said. 'But your personalized email intrigued me, so I decided to check out this professor who wrote to me out of nowhere.'

She revealed another secret: Even though my email intrigued her, she was still not sure that engaging with me was worth her time. 'My reply to your first email was with Microsoft Copilot,' she told me. No wonder the language sounded a little strange. However, my response to her, or rather to Microsoft Copilot's email, sealed the deal, and she decided to spend a few hours with us at the alumni dinner.

In the 2013 film *Her,* written and directed by Spike Jonze, the main plot revolves around a character named Ted, who develops a romantic relationship with an AI virtual assistant named Samantha. One time, while chatting with her, he asks how many people she was simultaneously engaging with. The answer shocked him: It was 8,316!

As AI becomes even more powerful in representing and imitating humans, for Ted, the alumna who received emails from our university, and for humans at the receiving end of communication plans, the question will increasingly be: Am I dealing with another human being who is dedicated to this conversation, or am I dealing with a piece of technology that is engaging with many thousands of people pretending to be a human?

Paradoxically, a stronger AI seems to be nudging us to work harder on bringing our humanity to the fore, which may not be a bad thing.

As more technologies, and particularly AI, get woven into our lives, building trust and maintaining personal connections begin to require a whole new set of approaches and skills. This will continue to have far-reaching implications for establishing mutual trust. People will always value being treated as individuals rather than an entry in a database, and while some may hail AI as the technology that will enable us to personalize the customer experience, we need to be extremely careful not to see AI as a way of replacing the highly coveted human connections.

Trust among people has always rested on whether we know who we are dealing with. Historically, dealings depended on the reputation of individuals. As the sizes of the networks we operate within grew, the issue of establishing who we are dealing with became more complex, but we were always able to develop techniques to do that. We invented documents, credentials, and passwords that enabled a bank teller at a branch to establish the identity of the customer at the counter and accept a withdrawal from their account.

As large portions of our dealings and interactions moved online, cryptology evolved even further to prevent the impersonation of individuals, which can lead not only to monetary loss but also to reputation damage and security violations. With the advent of AI and the endless possibilities of abuse in impersonating humans convincingly, the risks are never higher.

The big questions, as we allow AI, and later AGI, to take a bigger space in different corners of our lives and businesses, are:

1. How can we be sure that we are dealing with real humans?
2. How can we make sure that AI will continue to enhance the value humans create rather than diminish it and create human redundancy?

In summary, below are some of the suggestions that experts are advocating for and exploring:

1. The building and enabling of strong and well-funded global institutions that will continue to monitor the rollout of AI and AGI.
2. Legislating laws that ban and incriminate the impersonation of humans by AI.
3. Extending legal liabilities for the damage done by algorithms through their promotion of certain online content to those who own the companies that own the algorithms.

Trust in a Technology Disrupted World

While traditional AI models existed for a while and were designed to typically analyse and classify data, generative AI has the ability to produce original content, including text, images, audio, and other media formats, based on input data and learned patterns. AGI, often referred to as 'strong AI' or 'full AI', is AI's theoretical form that possesses the ability to understand, learn, and apply intelligence across a wide range of tasks at a level comparable to, or even surpassing, that of a human being. Unlike narrow AI, which is designed to perform specific tasks, AGI would be capable of generalizing knowledge and skills, enabling it to perform any intellectual task that a human can do.

Although these developments have massive potential for good, particularly through increasing productivity and extending our ability to fight diseases and address environmental challenges, there is also the negative potential. Issues such as deepfakes, where AI can produce videos and audio that convincingly impersonate human individuals, can undermine trust and make the potential of destroying relationships and destabilizing social peace a real prospect. Another challenge is keeping AI aligned with the best interests of humanity while its power continues to increase.

Countries, primarily the US and China, as well as corporations developing AI, are engaged in a relentless race for AI dominance. As AI is developing at this speed, testing and the inclusion of safety guardrails may be sacrificed, as these would delay the progress. No party seems to be able to slow down the process for fear of losing the race. Paradoxically, those in charge of developing AI seem to trust the safety of the AI algorithms they are rapidly building and releasing more than they trust their human competitors. Building trust with competitors will continue to be an active area of development for leaders, particularly in the context of keeping AI safe.

When it comes to the potential of misuse, imagine a realistic video showing a loved one in a compromising situation, a major world leader endorsing a controversial policy, a powerful CEO admitting wrong business doing, or a celebrity spewing racist comments. These can have profound negative effects. Of course, deepfakes can also be used in less public affairs, such as scamming, fraud, and convincing people to part with their money or cybersecurity credentials.

In order to be ready to lead in such a world, we will need to be more self-aware, more knowledgeable of the technology and its capabilities and limitations, and simply more human.

Below are some of the things that we need to do more of:

1. **Be more human:**
   In the age when our machines are so capable, we need to take our humanity more seriously. To ensure that trust prevails, we need to prioritize the maximum possible transparency, promote deep human connections, and emphasize ethics and values. Whenever possible, individuals, organizations,

and even states need to put more effort into allocating real human attention, not only automation, to delivering essential tasks.

At a time when we potentially can have abundance in almost everything, the ultimate limiting factor is our time and attention. It would be ideal if we could use AI to deliver whatever it can do, particularly in the cognitive workspace and use precious human time and attention to focus on building relationships and making other humans feel special and valued.

2. **Be confident**

   If you or your organization are the subject of a deepfake assault, trust your core values. Remaining transparent is probably the only way out. This area is still firming up, and as we progress, I am sure there will be social norms developing around it. It is also highly likely that the legislative dimensions will be responding by, for example, demanding that makers and owners of algorithms and tools used to produce deepfakes be responsible and accountable in one way or another.

   With all the preparation in the world, a crisis may still hit, so the need to be crisis-ready and prepared to address the situation when you, your team, or your organization is hit by such an attack is paramount. This readiness can be established through building protocols to deal with the crisis and running drills and simulations to train the team to handle the situation.

3. **Be more critical**

   Now that generative AI can perform many intellectual and cognitive tasks to a considerable level of speed and competency, it will be, by default, capable of confabulating fiction that might be indistinguishable from fact. This results in the need for relentless verification, cross-referencing, and rigorous fact-checking.

Whether the fabrication created by AI is created on purpose or not, AI is not infallible—just ask Peter LoDuca. As a lawyer, he learned this the hard way when he was representing a client suing Avianca Airlines in New York federal court, claiming injuries from being hit by a cart during a 2019 flight. LoDuca decided to use ChatGPT to help him with his legal research and ended up citing eight prior cases, all of which turned out to be fabricated by the software. This ended up not only being embarrassing, but highly damaging for the case.

This phenomenon, when generative AI produces what appears to be factual and relevant information that is totally confabulated, is called hallucination. AI researchers are still working on mitigating this. The bottom line is that part of the unique value that humans will be expected to add, in a world that is continuously shaped by technology, is the ability to discern fact from misinformation, disinformation, and fiction that might be generated by AI.

4. **Be more technology literate**
   AI technology will keep on evolving, and we all need to adopt a lifelong learning mindset when it comes to being aware of what technology is capable of doing, as well as its limitations. Technology literacy will increasingly become a necessity for personal and professional success.

The Tower of Babel

The mythological history of our species is filled with stories of old civilizations that possessed advanced technologies, yet at the peak of their power, these civilizations collapsed and disappeared.

The Tower of Babel and Atlantis are but two of these mythical stories with narratives that talk about humans becoming too powerful, selfish, and arrogant—traits that eventually bring the demise of their civilizations. While mythology is not a source for us to write our policy playbooks, myths are a profound reflection of our deepest fears and highest hopes. These stories seem to be reminders for all of us of the need to transcend our selfishness and reach deep down to our wisdom, compassion, and love.

The technological revolution our civilization is experiencing now is unprecedented. We are approaching a peak of our power, knowledge, and wealth. Our only way forward is to prioritize collaboration, shared purpose, and mutual trust to ensure that we can live in peace and deliver the vision of a flourishing humankind. While this is a hopeful way to look at the world, it is not naïve. It is the most pragmatic way, and this thinking is supported by our biology, psychology, and the history of our successes and failures.

We have all the tools and resources to solve the Collaboration Equation; what is next is up to us.

Chapter 10

Saving Our Businesses

> 'Business is a very beautiful mechanism to solve challenges, but we never use it for that purpose. We only use it to make money. It satisfies our selfish interest but not our collective interest.'
>
> —Muhammad Yunus

> What does it mean to say that the corporate executive has a 'social responsibility' in his capacity as businessman? If this statement is not pure rhetoric, it must mean that he is to act in some way that is not in the interest of his employers. For example, that he is to refrain from increasing the price of the product in order to contribute to the social objective of preventing inflation, even though a price increase would be in the best interests of the corporation. Or that he is to make expenditures on reducing pollution beyond the amount that is in the best interests of the corporation or that is required by law in order to contribute to the social objective of improving the environment.

The above is an excerpt from a 1970 article by Milton Friedman titled 'A Friedman Doctrine—The Social Responsibility of Business is to Increase its Profits.'[67] The Nobel Prize winning economist, crystalized, intellectualized, and legitimized the ethos of an era in which business focused on profit.

It goes on to reaffirm:

> In each of these cases, the corporate executive would be spending someone else's money for a general social interest. Insofar as his actions in accord with his 'social responsibility' reduce returns to stockholders, he is spending their money. Insofar as his actions raise the price to customers, he is spending the customers' money. Insofar as his actions lower the wages of some employees, he is spending their money.

This inspired generations of business owners and executives to behave in a way that maximizes the shareholders' value, deprioritizing the need to collaborate with other stakeholders to ensure that the wider needs of people and the planet are addressed too.

Trading, exchanging, and doing business are among the innate differentiating features of humans from other living beings. Since the dawn of time, people have bartered, bought, and sold goods and services from one another. Millennia of progress were enabled by this proclivity, and the accumulated advancements and wealth contributed to more sophistication in the nature and ways of doing business. Innovations like the invention of money, the creation of financial institutions, the formulation of the market economy, and capitalism created unprecedented levels of added value.

However, this progress, coupled with a worldview epitomized by thought leaders like Milton Friedman, simultaneously contributed towards environmental degradation, inequality, and other challenges. Interestingly, despite all of that, business remains the most trusted institution, at least when compared to governments and NGOs, as shown in the 2024 Trust Barometer. This may not be a very high bar to surpass, but one should not be cynical about these results, as they are a clear indication that people still see business and free enterprise as indispensable in supporting the human condition.

However, it is apparent that there is still a need to reform and transform them to remain fit for addressing future challenges and realizing future opportunities.

A Time for Business

At a time when politics are becoming a highly toxic affair, and geopolitics are fraught with conflicts, the business mechanisms may provide the necessary hope by being the platform for us to collaborate and work together. While governments traditionally hold the mantle of responsibility for public welfare, an emerging perspective increasingly argues that businesses, driven by market forces and innovation, are better positioned to serve as vehicles for the global public good.

Businesses operate in a competitive environment, compelling them to be efficient and agile. Unlike government bureaucracies that can be slow and encumbered by red tape, businesses are motivated to maximize resources, streamline operations, and adapt quickly to changing circumstances. This responsiveness allows them to create impactful solutions that address urgent global challenges. For instance, companies like Tesla have accelerated the transition to renewable energy not through mandates but by pioneering electric vehicles that capture consumer interest and drive change.

While in a democratic environment, politicians are elected for a certain duration, and their constituencies can evaluate their performance at the end of the term and either reward them with re-election or boot them out, customers of a business usually have the same opportunity every time they make a purchase decision. Although the choosing and purchasing processes can be a very complex combination of economic, psychological, and cognitive behaviours, they represent a responsive dynamic to shape the businesses that we are customers of.

This rapid feedback mechanism could be used to ensure that businesses that are supposed to serve us would be, in a way, a mirror of our true selves. So, the more customers align their purchasing decisions and their sense of higher purpose with the necessity and aspiration of creating a sustainable, equitable, and peaceful world, the more businesses will align their practices and policies towards the delivery of these goals. With the global reach of businesses, the power of this collaborative cycle is not to be underestimated.

These reforms and transformations will need to be accompanied by reforms and transformations in the traditional metrics of business success. Business has always been driven by profit. This is not inherently bad in and of itself.

As the saying goes, without profit, there is no capital in capitalism. However, the simplistic formula of measuring costs and revenues fails to capture the full spectrum of impacts that businesses can have on society, the environment, and the economy. The future of business lies in understanding and optimizing the true cost and total value that businesses generate.

A New Way of Thinking

Commenting on studying human behaviour, sociologist William Bruce Cameron said: 'Not everything that can be counted counts, and not everything that counts can be counted.'[68]

This is very true when evaluating business impact too. As a matter of fact, sticking to the classic yardstick of financial metrics could result in using the free market competitive mechanisms to drive out businesses that are attempting to have a positive impact on the world while pursuing their corporate objectives. In the absence of strict and clear regulations, it is cheaper to use non-sustainable and polluting resources and to squeeze the workforce by paying them the least amount possible.

To save the soul of business and ensure that we can use its institutions and mechanisms to contribute towards addressing the grand challenges we have, such as climate change, inequality, and pandemics, as well as realizing our opportunities, such as the safe and inclusive deployment of AI, a new economic theory will be needed. We need economic thinking that recognizes that prosperity is ultimately the product of collaboration rather than only fierce competition, that public good is created mainly through reciprocity rather than mere self-interest, and that true growth happens when people grow not only capital.

The true cost of doing business extends beyond the visible expenses captured in traditional financial statements, such as capital cost, supply cost, and wages, which form the foundation of financial planning and operational management. Relying solely on these provides an incomplete picture of a business's true impact. The true cost of doing business includes the damage that business activities can result in through the supply chain, labour practices, and environmental impact. These hidden costs often manifest as negative externalities, such as resource depletion, pollution, and exploitative labour practices. Addressing these is not just a moral imperative but a strategic necessity. Integrating true cost accounting practices allows businesses to see the full scope of their operations and make more informed decisions that benefit all stakeholders. By choosing to intentionally internalise these hidden costs, businesses can identify inefficiencies, mitigate risks, and build a more resilient and sustainable value model.

While profit remains a fundamental indicator of business health, it's crucial to realise that mere profit as it appears on the bottom line of a profit and loss financial statement does not tell the whole story. To correct for this, Colin Mayer suggests adding what he calls a 'Just Profit' increment, something that goes beyond the bottom line, integrating ethical considerations, fair labour practices, and sustainable sourcing.[69] The just profit increment represents the additional value created by aligning business operations with broader societal goals.

To save capitalism and to use its highly effective mechanisms to address the grand challenges rather than aggravating them, a new type of sustainable and holistic capitalism is necessary. This coming together requires redefining our mindsets and the stories we tell at multiple levels. It demands that we create a deeper shared purpose and unprecedented levels of mutual trust, so that we can utilize the business mechanisms to unlock the collaborative potentials that are needed to ensure that the inclusive progress of humanity continues as we reap the dividends of the latest technological advancements.

The Path Forward

For most of our history, we lived in a 'stuff economy' era where value, wealth and power were mainly measured by physical possession. Those who owned land, buildings, and large factories were in control. The past few decades represented the climax of the 'knowledge economy', where information, knowledge, and cognitive capabilities corresponded to value creation, power, and wealth more than at any other time. It is the era where companies such as Google or Facebook, with relatively little physical possession, could rival behemoths such as General Electric in market value. We are now moving into the era of the 'purpose and trust economy', where the ability to connect with oneself and others and exhibit self-awareness, respect, and empathy will be the sign of delivering true and unrivalled value. Knowledge will gain a huge value when underpinned by a deep and compelling sense of purpose and is deployed within trusting networks and partnerships.

This era will require that we rewrite our playbook in education, policy-making, human resources management, marketing, engineering and governance. It is the responsibility of the leaders among us to support our people, especially the youth, to succeed and thrive in such a different environment. I believe that the starting point is an education system that embraces the role of developing not only technically competitive individuals but also purpose-driven, trust-building, and emotionally intelligent leaders. Businesses also need to integrate concepts such as purpose, values, and trust into their models. To truly align business practices with the creation of total value, companies must embrace a holistic approach to value creation.

This involves:

1. **Redefining profit:** Moving beyond financial gain to include ethical, social, and environmental considerations.
2. **Transparent reporting:** Adopting comprehensive reporting frameworks that capture true costs and total value created by the business.
3. **Stakeholder engagement:** Involving employees, customers, suppliers, and communities in decision-making processes to ensure diverse perspectives and shared benefits.
4. **Innovation and collaboration:** Fostering a culture of innovation that prioritizes sustainable solutions and collaborative efforts.

As we navigate the complexities of the twenty-first century, businesses have a unique opportunity to redefine success. The shift from profit-centric to value-centric business models is not just a trend but a necessity for long-term success and societal well-being.

Business-Technology Synergy

One of the global challenges that can only be addressed when business objectives are aligned with societal aspirations is the reduction of global carbon dioxide emissions. Ultimately, when we arrive at an adoption scale where the required change makes business sense, the market mechanisms will align themselves fully to deliver the solution.

The International Energy Agency report cited earlier shows how the annual carbon dioxide emissions savings in the Net Zero pathway, relative to 2020, will most likely be achieved through a combination of behavioural change, technologies on the market, and technologies under development. In all of these, there is a role for individuals, businesses, policymakers, and governments to play.

These roles of different players are briefly outlined in the table below.

Businesses can play a key role in this green transition by embracing the available technologies and working towards increasing the scale of adoption in order for the scale to grow to a sufficient level that will lead to reducing the cost and mitigating the risk, leading to mainstreaming these solutions. It is encouraging to see from the International Energy Agency report that approximately 50 per cent of the transition requires the adoption of technologies and solutions that are already available in the market. This is the space where collaborative business practices, like the case of the EU automakers we discussed earlier, can be deployed. This can be supported by individuals and policymakers through personal choices and policy instruments that are aimed at accelerating the arrival at the critical adoption scale that will make the transition a logical business imperative. Increasingly, businesses will be expected to play the role of building coalitions that are based on shared purpose and mutual trust.

	Individuals	Businesses	Policymakers
Behavioural Change	Accept the pain and sacrifice of changing habits of consumption	Create products and services to reduce the pain of adopting new behaviours and habits	Support the change by investing in alternatives and ifrastructures that smoothen the change process
Technologies on the Market	Vote with their feet for products adopting new more effective green technologies	Invest in pilot projects to facilitate mainstreaming the technologies, reducing the cost and derisking adoption	Support adoption through tax incentives, mandating emission reductions, and other policy levers
Technologies Under Development	Vote for politicians that will support investment in developing new technologies	Invest in the development of new technologies and enter private-public partnerships.	Fund the development of new technologies through sovereign funds

One example where the synergy between business and technology can be leveraged to lead the way is the area of reducing emissions associated with air travel through the adoption of sustainable aviation fuel (SAF).

Aviation is a critical component of globalization, which necessitates sustainable growth to mitigate its environmental impact. Despite the drop in air travel due to the Covid-19 pandemic, by March 2023, global air traffic had nearly returned to pre-pandemic levels, causing carbon dioxide emissions from aviation to reach around 80 per cent of 2019 levels in 2022. Addressing aviation's environmental impact requires diverse strategies: novel aircraft designs, operational improvements, and new infrastructure. Sustainable Aviation Fuel (SAF) is considered pivotal in achieving decarbonization goals, especially for early reduction targets by 2030.

Sustainable aviation fuel is a biofuel that has similar properties to hydrocarbon-based jet fuels with a much smaller carbon footprint, which means that airlines can use it to reduce their emissions without any modifications to the engines of their aeroplanes. Sources of biomass to produce sustainable aviation fuel include dedicated energy crops, algae, fats, oils, greases, agricultural and forestry residues, wood mill and municipal waste, and wet wastes such as manures and wastewater treatment sludge.

Current SAF production falls substantially short of what is needed to make a difference in the emission of the aviation sector. A 1500-fold increase of SAF by 2050 is required for SAF to become a serious greening contributor. As is the case with any new source of renewable energy, SAF is currently expensive. On average, it is three times more costly than conventional jet fuel and making it part of the energy mix will require that the scale of using it increases to a level that will enable the cost of processing and producing it to drop. This can only be done with substantial and long-term levels of investment.

This situation perfectly demonstrates the role that business can play in mainstreaming a technology that is already on the market. The path from proof-of-concept to wide adoption of a technology is neither straightforward nor inevitable. A clear shared purpose, mutual trust, and establishing multiple collaborative pathways in a fiercely competitive sector such as aviation are fundamental for this transition to take place. While a policy solution to this challenge may sound like a straightforward option, as the government can mandate the use of SAF, the increase in cost could have a devastating impact on demand for air travel, causing far-reaching negative consequences on trade and multiple economic sectors, such as tourism. A business approach supported by gentle policy carrots (like tax incentives) rather than sticks remains the favoured option.

To spark the business initiation of solutions for the adoption challenges outlined above, a recent paper published by the Journal of Energy and Environmental Science proposed the establishment of 'green flight paths' between key international aviation markets as pathways for incentivizing 100 per cent SAF use on specific routes, like London to Dubai, as a model for wider aviation sector adoption.

This initiative supports a just transition, targeting regions where emissions from long-haul travel are concentrated and where economic benefits could be maximized, while de-risking the massive investments needed for SAF production and distribution infrastructures. Coupling green flight pathways with broader industrial decarbonization plans allows a coordinated approach to be adopted.[70]

We can see that business, enterprise, and entrepreneurial mindset have a great role to play in helping humanity address the thorny issues of our time. To qualify for this, an alternative economic theory that appreciates the role of purpose, trust, and collaboration is necessary. The following principles can be the foundation of this transition of thinking.

1. The foundation of prosperity is collaboration, not only competition. Of course, competition has its place, but collaboration remains a fundamental way to unlock greater value, widening the economic pie for everyone.
2. The purpose of business needs to be seen as not maximizing the shareholders' value, but instead, the improvement of the wellbeing of all stakeholders associated with or touched by the business and its activities. Paradoxically, this will lead to taking care of the sustainable and long-term interests of shareholders anyway.
3. Trust is a key element in doing sustainable business. Business leaders need to prioritize building mutual trust with all stakeholders, including their competitors, by genuinely addressing the four elements of trust, pursuing the interests of all, and doing social and environmental good rather than focusing on mere compliance and satisfying the minimum legal requirements.
4. True growth is the growth of people and their happiness and wellbeing. It goes without saying that businesses need to be financially sustainable and turn a profit, but the enterprise needs to resolve the conundrum of doing well and doing good, as both should not be at odds with each other. This will continue to be a key leadership criterion.
5. Without the natural world, there is nowhere to do business. Business leaders, practitioners, scholars, and educators need to internalize and take to heart the importance of preserving and improving the conditions of the natural world as a business imperative.

In conclusion, it is safe to say that, for better or for worse, our businesses reflect who we are. They bring our values to life and demonstrate what is important to us. After centuries of trading, exchanging, and doing business, it is clear that a purpose-driven business is not only the most sustainable and inclusive way of doing business but also the most shrewd and profitable.

Integrating market mechanisms with long-term thinking can unleash unprecedented collaborative value creation while ensuring that business institutions remain respected as a force for good in the world.

Chapter 11

Geopolitical Collaboration

> 'Throughout human history, in any great endeavour requiring the common effort of many nations and men and women everywhere, we have learned—it is only through seriousness of purpose and persistence that we ultimately carry the day.'
>
> —Ban Ki-moon

In global politics, collaboration between leaders—especially those from ideologically opposed superpowers—can sometimes stem from the most unexpected exchanges. A striking example of this occurred during a meeting between US President Ronald Reagan and Soviet Secretary General Mikhail Gorbachev. The scene was set amid the tensions of the Cold War, a period marked by deep-rooted mistrust and rivalry. However, it was during their 1985 summit in Geneva that an unusual but profound dialogue started a change in their interaction and, by extension, the relationship between their respective countries.

As the two leaders took a private walk by the lake, Reagan posed a hypothetical question to Gorbachev: What would he do if the earth were invaded by aliens from outer space? Reagan's question was not merely about extra-terrestrial threats, but was a creative way to shift perspective and break the ice on heavier topics. The underlying query tested the potential for a shared purpose that transcended earthly disputes: a theoretical yet creative way to think about mutual interests.

Gorbachev, surprised by the question, responded that the Soviet Union would undoubtedly be willing to work closely with the US to protect the planet. Reagan echoed this sentiment, emphasizing that global challenges required global solutions and collaboration. This conversation underscored a fundamental point: If two superpowers could agree on collaborating against a common 'alien' enemy, could they not also collaborate against more tangible global threats, such as nuclear proliferation, economic challenges, and environmental degradation?

The alien invasion question moved beyond being just a quirky anecdote; it became a metaphor for unexpected common ground. It facilitated a softer, more open dialogue that many believe contributed to the eventual easing of Cold War tensions.

Following this meeting, both leaders continued to engage more constructively, with subsequent agreements on nuclear arms reductions being a testament to the potential of collaboration borne from shared objectives and mutual trust.

This story shows how invoking a shared purpose can bridge vast ideological divides, illustrating that the basis of effective collaboration often lies in recognizing and embracing our common humanity and mutual interests. In the context of Reagan and Gorbachev, it was the imaginative leap into science fiction that reminded them of their responsibility towards reality—an enduring lesson on the power of collaboration across all spheres of human endeavour.

This chapter discusses how collaboration not only enables countries to satisfy their current needs but also ensures that future generations can enjoy the Earth's resources sustainably. Through analyses of both successful and failed international partnerships and policies, this chapter demonstrates that effective geopolitical collaboration is the cornerstone of global stability and prosperity. It makes the case that in a world where challenges and resources are interconnected, collaborative approaches are the most viable path forward.

International Relations

At the end of the Cold War in 1991, there was a deep sense of triumph in the West. A unipolar world seemed to be there to stay as George Bush Senior hailed what he called 'the New World Order'. Francis Fukuyama, who represented the liberal theory of international relations, developed his thesis of the End of History, which viewed the defeat of nazism, fascism, and communism as episodes in a historical progression leading towards a future world in which ideological struggles diminish and states increasingly adopt democratic reforms and that economic integration of the world will lead to an unprecedented era of peace and prosperity worldwide.[71]

This view of the world is called liberalism, and its proponents see that it is the responsibility of the great powers of the West to spread democracy, as this is the inevitable arc of history. Since then, many things happened. The American Invasions of Afghanistan and Iraq are recognized as disastrous failures, and as I write these words, there are two major wars in Ukraine and Gaza, the Asad's Syrian regime has just fallen, and the potential for more polarization in the world's geopolitics is increasing.

On the international relations theoretical spectrum, at the other extreme of Fukuyama's liberalism is the theory of realism, which assumes that continuous struggle between states is the dominant dynamic in international relations.

Professor John Mearsheimer of the University of Chicago is one of the prominent realist international relations scholars. He is best known for his theory of offensive realism, which attempts to explain and predict how states operate when dealing with each other. This theory is part of the broader realist school of thought, which emphasises the competitive and conflictual nature of international relations.

The key assumptions of this theory are[72]:

1. **Anarchy:** The theory of offensive realism assumes that the international system is anarchic. Unlike the case of individuals who can resort to the legal system, if they feel they were subjected to unfair or oppressive treatment, there is no higher authority that a state can resort to if threatened by or had a disagreement with another state. This lack of overarching authority results in a system where states must rely on their own strengths and capabilities for survival, security, and retention of sovereignty.
2. **Survival:** In such an anarchic system, states will prioritize their survival over everything else, including prosperity and economic gain. Offensive realism assumes that in international relations, states' survival is the primary goal.
3. **Offensive capability:** States aim to own and possess some offensive military capabilities, giving them the power to harm each other. Great powers possess greater offensive capabilities, enabling them to dominate the system and ensure their survivability in case of a conflict. This capability drives the fear and suspicion between states.
4. **Uncertainty of intentions:** States can never be certain about the intentions of other states. While a state might appear peaceful today, it could become aggressive in the future. This inherent uncertainty makes trust difficult to establish and maintain in international politics.
5. **Rational actors:** States are rational actors that calculate the best means to ensure their survival. This rationality

> includes understanding the distribution of authority in the international system and making strategic decisions to maximize their own security and power.

Both these two extreme views of the world, liberalism and realism, have their theoretical, ideological, and practical foundations. As is the case with any theory, these theories succeed in representing and correctly predicting the world at times and fail at others. Essentially, geopolitical collaboration, just like the collaboration between individuals and organizations, requires the presence of shared purpose and mutual trust.

Shared Purpose and Mutual Trust

'The Middle East region is quieter today than it has been in two decades.' These were the words of Jake Sullivan, the National Security Advisor for President Joe Biden, at the Atlantic Festival. What made these words remarkable was the fact that they were uttered a mere eight days before the 7 October 2023 attack by Hamas on Israel. The field of international relations is highly complex, dynamic, and at times difficult to predict.

However, with the deep mistrust between different parties in the Middle East and the lack of shared purpose or vision for a solution to the Palestinian issue, it is rather difficult to find the basis for Sullivan's prediction.

Reflecting on the core five assumptions of offensive realism theory, one can't be blamed for noticing that they seem to predict the current world of geopolitics pretty accurately. Nevertheless, political leaders need to prioritize the creation of mutual trust so that lasting peace and sustainable progress can be realized. Mutual trust will be the only real antidote to the challenge of the uncertainty of intentions, while the remaining four assumptions can be addressed to a great extent by the focus on the establishment of a deep, true, and long-term shared purpose.

Interestingly, the existence of global challenges may be the reason that will make world leaders realize that collaboration is the way to go. In a way, these challenges may prove to be a blessing in disguise. The fifth assumption of Mearsheimer's offensive realism affirms that states are rational actors that calculate the best means to ensure their survival. This will require states to widen their timescale sufficiently so that the big picture of the long-term challenges becomes clear.

A Brief History of Peace and Conflict

When we hear the term 'globalization,' many think of the period from the end of the twentieth century until now, when technological, financial, and geopolitical developments enabled many economic activities to be integrated globally. However, this state of interconnectedness is not exactly new. Economists often refer to the period from 1870–1914 as the First Age of Globalization. That era was marked by high volumes of trade between nations, substantial levels of cross-border investments, industrial collaboration, labour mobility, infrastructure development, and standardization. Sadly, all of that interdependency was not sufficient to prevent World War I. Rapid growth, accompanied by rampant inequality and rising nationalism and protectionism, may have sown the seeds for the lack of shared purpose and mutual trust and contributed towards the conditions that precipitated the eruption of that devastating war.

Viewing the situation before World War I, through the lens of Mearsheimer's offensive realism, one may observe that as nations and states become more powerful, other states start fearing for their security and exploring ways to strengthen themselves and weaken their rivals, creating an ever-present potential for conflict through arms races and increased tension.

Here, we are suggesting that creating dynamics that inspire shared purpose and fostering the conditions of mutual trust will be essential to maintaining world peace, collaboration, and prosperity.

Below is a brief description of the states of geopolitical collaboration and conflict in the modern world over the past 150 years:

First Age of Globalization (1870–1914)

The technological developments enabled by the first industrial revolution and the establishment of large-scale infrastructure projects, as well as the availability of cross-border finance and labour, resulted in the flourishing of trade and innovation, economic growth, and the creation of an interconnected world, particularly in Europe. This economic collaboration was accompanied by intense economic rivalries as countries competed for markets, resources, and dominance. Much of the economic prosperity was built on the exploitation of colonies, leading to imbalances and tensions within the global economic system. The extensive economic interdependence was not sufficient to prevent the outbreak of World War I.

World War I (1914–1918)

The war took place between two groups of nations, the Allies (France, Russia, the United Kingdom, Italy, the US, Japan, Belgium, Serbia, Greece, Romania, and Portugal) and the Central Powers (Germany, Austria-Hungary, the Ottoman Empire, and Bulgaria). Each of the warring groups managed to coordinate their war efforts, cooperate in military operations, and collaborate as they found the shared purpose of trying to defeat their enemies and build mutual trust as their survival depended on them working together. Throughout the war, each group cooperated militarily, economically, and diplomatically. They shared intelligence, coordinated their naval activities, and supported each other's propaganda efforts.

Interestingly, the level of collaboration among the Central Powers was hindered by the diverse war aims each country harboured. While Germany's dominant role within the alliance provided crucial support to its partners, it led to tensions and challenges to achieving a fully cohesive strategy. The Central Powers' inability to match the level of coordination and resource mobilization achieved by the Allies ultimately contributed to their defeat.

Interwar Period (1918–1939)

The victorious Allies formalized the peace terms by signing the Treaty of Versailles in 1919 with Germany. Historians agree that the treaty was very harsh on Germany. In its 'War Guilt Clause', the treaty placed full responsibility for the war on Germany and its allies. In this humiliating treaty, Germany was required to pay substantial reparations to the Allied powers.

Instead of being the basis of lasting peace, the Treaty of Versailles maintained a climate of mistrust and hostility towards Germany, which led to Hitler's ascendance to power on a national agenda and, ultimately, the outbreak of World War II.

Although the League of Nations was established as a forum to build mutual trust and shared purpose, it failed in achieving this objective as the League's effectiveness was limited by the absence of major powers like the US, which never joined, and the inability to enforce its resolutions.

World War II (1939–1945)

The interwar period was marked by fragile and often ineffective international cooperation as the world grappled with the legacy of the Treaty of Versailles and the challenge of maintaining peace in a deeply divided Europe, setting the scene for World War II.

Similar collaborative dynamics between the warring parties, the Allies and Axis Powers, took place, as was the case in World War I. Interestingly, the US and the Soviet Union, which was officially established in 1922, were both members of the Allied Powers. After defeating the Axis, the shared purpose between the US and USSR disappeared, and the mutual trust was replaced by a deep suspicion, starting the Cold War era.

The Cold War (1947–1991)

After the end of World War II, it was clear that in the absence of a common foe, maintaining a collaborative relationship between the US and USSR was an impossible task. The world was largely divided between countries that orbited the US and those that orbited the USSR, creating a bipolar world order. The main source of mutual trust between the two superpowers emanated from the Mutually Assured Destruction that they achieved by amassing sufficient nuclear weapons to destroy the world a few times over.

The Cold War era was a true ideological competition between capitalism and communism, affecting how shared purpose and mutual trust within each camp were established. Both sides viewed the survival of their way of life as a source of shared purpose for their respective bloc.

However, capitalism was able to deliver more freedom and abundance to the people when compared to communism, which used more oppressive means to keep the coherence in the system. On the mutual trust side, the openness, free speech, and the rule of law that are built in the market economy were able to foster better trust between the people and countries within the Western bloc compared to the Eastern bloc.

This was among the factors that led to the eventual victory of the West and the collapse of the USSR in 1991.

The Unipolar Era (1991–early 2000s)

The collapse of the Soviet Union and the dissolution of the Warsaw Pact created a special historic moment for the US, when it was the dominant superpower in the world, resulting in a unipolar world.

The Eastern Bloc states reeled under the pressures of the economic, social, and political changes, and they were in no position to compete with the US, whose relationship with China was improving. Despite tensions over human rights and trade issues, US economic ties with China were growing significantly.

China was granted the Most Favoured Nation (MFN) status, and the two countries cooperated on various international issues. The MFN status and the US support for admitting China into the World Trade Organization were direct results of the liberal US foreign policy, whose proponents believed that as China developed economically, it would simultaneously become more democratic, and this would bring it closer to the Western sphere of influence.

A Multipolar World

With China achieving unprecedented economic growth, Russia regaining its bearings and its position as a major power, and blocs such as BRICS (Brazil, Russia, India, China, and South Africa) becoming major players in the world, the unipolar moment is vanishing quickly, and the world is moving into an era of multipolarity.

This will be a new era with its own dynamics, rules, and challenges. To maintain peace and stability, address the global challenges, and realize the opportunities in this era, the role of global institutions will become increasingly important.

What Trust Means in the Geopolitical Corridors

In an article entitled 'On Trust' published in the November 2020 issue of *Foreign Service Journal*, George P. Shultz, who served as the sixtieth Secretary of State, under President Ronald Reagan from 1982 to 1989, said:[73]

> Our relations with much of the rest of the world also have become characterized by distrust bordering on hostility, even in the way Washington deals with close allies in Europe and Asia. We are nearing a Cold War II situation in our relations with China and Russia. Reliance on military threats, with little or no effort at diplomacy, is the most prominent feature of our relations with nations that we associate with anti-American sentiments and actions.

This was prophetic, accounting that almost exactly one year after his death in February 2021, the situation in Europe escalated to a full-fledged war between Russia and Ukraine.

During the darkest moments of conflict, we keep on hearing statements such as 'We do not negotiate with terrorists' or 'We do not want to have talks with an invader.' This kind of mindset, while it may portray adherence to high moral standards, ignores the eternal principle of diplomacy that states, 'You negotiate peace with your enemies, not with your friends.'

Deescalating conflicts, maintaining peace, and promoting international collaboration call for pragmatic leaders and diplomats who have the ability to empathize with their opponents and the willingness to search for shared purpose and build mutual trust even when common values seem to be nonexistent.

In the same article mentioned above, Shultz added:

> Trust among nations or between those who represent their nations in official discourse with other nations should not be equated with burgeoning friendship or a change in fundamental beliefs on either side. The idea implies a belief that what a nation or a public official commits to do will, in fact, be done. That means not only that honesty has become the accepted norm but also that what a nation or its official says will happen is, in fact, capable of being done; that is, the commitment is precise enough to measure its implementation, and the authority to carry out the commitment is assured.

Coming from a statesman like Schultz, this is highly empowering and very aligned with the four elements of trust analysis presented in Chapter 7 on nurturing mutual trust. It is also deeply diagnostic of the challenges impacting international collaboration matters, such as reducing emissions when officials and representatives of countries commit to targets that they are unable to honour.

This undermines trust and can have far-reaching damaging effects.

An Asian Collaborative Success

In a 1993 study titled 'Ripe for Rivalry: Prospects for Peace in a Multipolar Asia'[74] published by the American political scientist Aaron L. Friedberg in the *Journal of International Security*, the author argued that Asia appeared to be more likely than Europe to be the 'cockpit of great-power conflict.' Concluding that in the long run, 'Europe's past could be Asia's future.'

Clearly, the above predictions did not pan out.

Since the 1990s, Europe has experienced several conflicts in Bosnia, Croatia, Kosovo, Albania, Macedonia, Georgia, and Ukraine. In the same period, there was no major conflict in Asia, even though the countries there lacked the interconnectedness their European counterparts enjoyed.

But what explains this relative peace in Asia?

Kishore Mahbubani, the Singaporean diplomat and geopolitical expert who served as Singapore's permanent representative to the UN for more than a decade and president of the United Nations Security Council between 2001 and 2002, answers this question:

> The simple answer is that Asia benefits from a culture of pragmatism, as demonstrated by the Association of Southeast Asian Nations (ASEAN), which emerged as a successful regional organization at the end of the Cold War. While ASEAN welcomed Vietnam, an erstwhile adversary for many of its members, Europe consistently excluded its erstwhile adversary, Russia, from significant binding regional arrangements. Mikhail Gorbachev's proposal of 'a common house for Europe' was effectively rebuffed.[75]

ASEAN's success and its potential to continue to provide a platform for further progress and development stem from the ability of its leaders and member countries to articulate and communicate a clear shared purpose and maintain mutual trust, despite the history that is rife with disagreements and the present that has its fair share of disputes.

The association starts with a clear sense of purpose shared among its member countries, which is to facilitate collaboration, leading to the promotion of regional peace, acceleration of economic growth, and provision of support to member states in areas of education, agriculture, and trade. According to the association's website, the fundamental principles adopted by the member states in their relations with one another, which are contained in the Treaty of Amity and Cooperation in Southeast Asia (TAC) of 1976, are:

1. Mutual respect for the independence, sovereignty, equality, territorial integrity, and national identity of all nations;
2. The right of every state to lead its national existence free from external interference, subversion, or coercion;
3. Non-interference in the internal affairs of one another;
4. Settlement of differences or disputes in a peaceful manner;
5. Renunciation of the threat or use of force; and
6. Effective cooperation among member countries.

Mahbubani also seems to recognize an alternative style of leadership that Asian wisdom may contribute to geopolitical skillsets, where societies prioritize building trust through relationships and connections. Many predict that the twenty-first century will be an Asian century, basing this argument on the economic growth indicators.

However, there seems to be an additional element that favours Asia, which is the innate cultural capabilities of its people and leaders to favour non-confrontational approaches and emphasize the building of mutual trust and shared long-term purpose. This could prove to be essential for practising geopolitics in a multipolar world.

I am not claiming here that political leadership in Asia is perfect. The continent is still struggling with corruption, inequality, rising populism, and racial tensions in certain parts. However, the ability to largely maintain peace, in a region rife with differences and border disputes, is something to be considered and recognized.

A Missed Geopolitical Collaborative Opportunity

As pointed out by Mahbubani, Mikhail Gorbachev, at a certain stage before the collapse of the Soviet Union, proposed 'a common house for Europe'. This Russian desire, or at least pretence, to be aligned with the West was reiterated when Vladimir Putin expressed Russia's interest in joining NATO in the early 2000s, as recalled by Lord George Robertson—a British former Labour defence secretary who was the tenth secretary general of NATO between 1999 and 2003—in an interview that he gave to the One Decision podcast.

In the podcast, Lord Robertson recalled an early meeting with Putin, who became the Russian president in 2000.

'Putin said: "When are you going to invite us to join NATO?" And I said: "Well, we don't invite people to join NATO, they apply to join NATO". And he said: "Well, we're not standing in line with a lot of countries that don't matter."'[76]

This account aligns with an interview that Putin gave to BBC Breakfast with Frost on 5 March 2000.[77]

Below are excerpts from this interview:

> **David Frost:** Tell me about your views on NATO, if you would. Do you see NATO as a potential partner, or a rival or an enemy?
>
> **Putin:** Russia is part of the European culture. And I cannot imagine my own country in isolation from Europe and what we often call the civilized world. So, it is hard for me to visualize NATO as an enemy. I think even posing the question this way will not do any good to Russia or the world. The very question is capable of causing damage. Russia strives for equitable and candid relations with its partners. The main problem here lies in attempts to discard previously agreed common instruments—mainly in resolving issues of international security. We are open to equitable cooperation, to partnership. We believe we can

> talk about more profound integration with NATO but only if Russia is regarded as an equal partner. You are aware we have been constantly voicing our opposition to NATO's eastward expansion.
>
> **David Frost:** Is it possible for Russia to join NATO?
>
> **Putin:** I don't see why not. I would not rule out such a possibility. But I repeat: If and when Russia's views are taken into account as those of an equal partner.

With the Ukraine war waging since 2022, it is difficult to imagine a time when Putin indicated interest in joining NATO. Clearly, there was a deep suspicion concerning Putin's true intentions, and the trust situation was not ideal, to say the least.

Following the Orange Revolution street protests in Ukraine in 2004, Putin grew increasingly suspicious of the intentions of the West, blaming it for meddling in the country's internal affairs with the objective of undermining Russian interests. His frustration was compounded by NATO's ongoing expansion into Central and Eastern Europe, as Romania, Bulgaria, Slovakia, Slovenia, Latvia, Estonia, and Lithuania joined the alliance in 2004, followed by Croatia and Albania in 2009.

While we will never know for sure if Putin seriously saw Russia as part of the Western security structures or not, the failure to integrate Russia into the European system right after the collapse of the Soviet Union and the disintegration of the Warsaw Pact was a lost historical opportunity.

Imagine if Russia were made a member of the European Union or even NATO. This, however, would have required a level of leadership that simply did not exist. It required the mutual trust and shared purpose between the West and Russia to be developed to levels that never existed before. This would have been difficult but not impossible; politics is defined as the art of the possible, after all.

Reflecting on both the successes and missed opportunities in global geopolitics, it is apparent that collaboration is the only sustainable way forward. Political leaders will need to develop and hone their competencies and skills in building a shared purpose and inspiring a real and deep mutual trust between their governments, societies, and businesses to enable the collaborative ethos to prevail, particularly with parties that adopt different ideological, world views, or even approaches to addressing challenges.

These competencies need to become an essential part of the job descriptions of geopolitical leaders, as peace, sustainability, and progress will depend on that.

Both successful regional collaborative initiatives and projects, such as ASEAN, along with failures such as missing the historic opportunity to integrate Russia into the Western frameworks, should serve as reminders of the role and responsibility of leaders in creating a world that is equitable, sustainable, and enriching—not only for their nations, societies, and constituencies, but for all of us.

Future of Geopolitical Collaboration

Besides the active wars we are experiencing, the world continues to have multiple flashpoints that threaten to erupt if attention is not directed towards defusing them. As Schultz mentioned, world leaders will need to realize that military might is never the solution, and that diplomacy should be given ample chance. Leadership priorities should include stopping wars, deescalating tensions, and preserving peace. We need to remember that even in the case of war, the first steps in a ceasefire are the confidence-building measures that both sides need to adopt to allow mutual trust to grow.

To arrive at lasting peace or even a thriving partnership, mutual trust needs to be augmented by a shared purpose.

A report by S&P Global articulated the top geopolitical risks of 2024, identifying several high-profile risks.[78] These included US-China relations, Russia-NATO relations, climate risk, anti-globalization sentiments, and energy security. These risks can only be addressed and mitigated with authentic cross-border collaboration, which will require purpose-driven leadership and deliberate work to build shared purpose and mutual trust.

The four elements of trust, discussed in Chapter 7, would come in handy as well.

The roles of political, cultural, and educational institutions continue to be central in creating the acceptance of others, appreciation of their cultural contributions, and empathy for their points of view. We ought to, for example, continue to welcome international students and invest in study abroad and student exchange programmes, as these will prepare future leaders from various nations to be able to build mutual trust. Strengthening the institutions of the UN is another priority that the world should focus on, as this is the foundation for the rules-based international order.

Chapter 12

Collaborative Negotiation

'This division of labour, from which so many advantages are derived, is not originally the effect of any human wisdom, which foresees and intends that general opulence to which it gives occasion. It is the necessary, though very slow and gradual, consequence of a certain propensity in human nature, which has in view no such extensive utility: the propensity to truck, barter, and exchange one thing for another.'

—Adam Smith
The Wealth of Nations

Negotiation is a constant aspect of our lives—whether we realize it or not. From encouraging our children to eat their vegetables and selling a car, to acquiring a business for a multinational corporation or reaching international agreements on emission reductions, negotiation is essential. When we seek something from others or when they desire something we possess, we have three main approaches: we may coerce, concede, or negotiate.

When negotiating, outcomes can vary significantly. A poor deal occurs when one or both parties end up being worse off. A good deal is characterized by both parties gaining at least some of what they desire. The ideal scenario is a great deal, where both sides walk away markedly better off—a true win-win outcome. That is why mastering negotiation can be a key enabler of sustainable collaboration.

The work presented here is based on my experience teaching negotiation to MBA students at my university. It attempts to redefine the art of negotiation by emphasizing collaboration over confrontation, prioritizing the discovery of a shared purpose and nurturing mutual trust. It explores how adopting a collaborative mindset transforms negotiation from a combative exchange to a constructive dialogue, where all parties can achieve their goals.

The course I teach involves forty-two hours of classes, discussions, and practical sessions, so I am not pretending this chapter replaces a serious study of negotiation. Nevertheless, I hope this chapter will illustrate the importance of shared purpose and mutual trust in negotiation processes, showing how these elements facilitate more effective and satisfactory outcomes. Through practical strategies and real-world examples, readers will learn how to approach negotiations not as a zero-sum game, where one party's gain is another's loss, but as an opportunity for all involved to benefit.

This chapter provides essential insights and tools for anyone looking to enhance their negotiation skills in both professional and personal contexts, advocating for a collaborative approach to resolve differences and achieve shared goals.

Purpose-Driven Negotiation

We go to the negotiation table, driven by objectives we wish to fulfil, hopes we aspire to achieve, or fears we aim to alleviate. In the literature of negotiation, these are called 'interests' and are fundamental and non-negotiable.

In our pursuit of our interests, we are often prepared to pay money, make concessions, share resources, and accept trade-offs.

Professional negotiators refer to elements such as price, payment terms, and the distribution of resources as 'issues' as they represent the pathway to reaching mutually beneficial agreements.

Negotiating parties take 'positions' on these issues by stating, for example, the price they are willing to accept or pay for an item. Often, people haggle over their positions on issues related to the matter at hand without paying deep and conscious attention to the interests that drove the parties to the negotiation table in the first place. This can have a damaging effect on the possibility of arriving at an agreement. This failure to allocate sufficient focus to understanding and appreciating the interests and the purpose of both negotiating parties does not only happen when negotiating small deals; it can occur even when billions of dollars are at stake.

Negotiating parties may have different interests, but they should agree on the issues they are negotiating. Of course, if negotiating parties can uncover a shared purpose, this will make the negotiation much easier. Throughout the negotiation process, mutual trust should be built and sustained, as without it, the negotiation process could falter and collapse.

In an extreme instance, such as negotiating with hostage-takers, the interest of the hostage-takers is usually threefold: to stay alive, to remain free, and to achieve either a political or a financial objective—sometimes both. The hostage negotiators, on the other hand, define their interest as saving and freeing all the hostages.

From the point of each party, their interests are non-negotiable. No hostage negotiator, for example, is willing to sign off on a deal in which half of the hostages will be killed. The negotiation issues can include the ransom amount and the safe passage that will guarantee the freeing of the hostages.

Luckily, while the negotiation situations that we are involved in could be consequential, they are seldom literally a matter of life and death, like a hostage negotiation. However, complex matters that we increasingly are required to reach agreements on, such as climate negotiations, demand a whole new level of collaborative negotiation, which needs active exploration of pathways to uncover shared purpose and nurture mutual trust.

While professional negotiation practitioners follow a structured process in which they systematically identify the interests, issues, positions, and available tradeables for both their side and the other, too, often very little work is done to articulate and uncover a shared purpose between the negotiating parties.

Microsoft and Yahoo

A case in point is the 2008 negotiation when Microsoft attempted to acquire Yahoo. Microsoft needed a gateway to enter the lucrative search business, of which Google is the undisputed leader. Yahoo was then second in terms of search business market share, and acquiring it would have been a strategic move by Microsoft.

The talks about the intended acquisition alarmed Google so much that their leading legal counsel said that this buyout could hurt Web innovation. The negotiation process focused mainly on the price. In February 2008, Microsoft made an offer to buy Yahoo for $31 a share, or $44.6 billion.

However, Yahoo's leadership rejected that offer, indicating that it substantially undervalued the company's brand and worldwide assets. After a number of negotiation rounds, Microsoft raised its bid to $33 per share in May 2008. Yahoo's board held firm to its position regarding the acquisition price, insisting on nothing less than $37 per share or $53 billion.

Despite Microsoft's substantial offer, Yahoo's refusal to negotiate on the price led to a breakdown in talks and Microsoft rescinding its offer.[79]

By the 2010s, Yahoo was a shadow of its former self. The company attempted to reinvent itself through a series of acquisitions to no avail. Meanwhile, Yahoo's advertising revenue continued to decline as Google and Facebook dominated the market.

In 2017, Verizon acquired Yahoo's core internet operations for $4.48 billion—a mere fraction of its former value and approximately 10 per cent of Microsoft's offer from nine years earlier. This acquisition signified the end of Yahoo's era as an independent internet powerhouse.

While hindsight is often 20/20, one cannot but wonder if there was a better way to handle the negotiation by seriously considering the higher purpose of both companies and their leadership teams, as well as the broader interests of consolidating resources and remaining competitive in the tech industry, Yahoo focused too heavily on the position of maintaining a high valuation, which ultimately resulted in lost opportunities as both companies struggled in the evolving tech landscape.

Researching the literature describing the circumstances surrounding the negotiation, two items stood out. The first was a general concern about how challenging it would be to harmonize the two entirely different corporate cultures of Yahoo and Microsoft. The second was the perception that Yahoo's CEO, Jerry Yang, harboured personal negative preconceived views of Microsoft even before the negotiation started.

These two elements belong to the purpose and interests sphere, and addressing them could have made the position on the issue (price) less entrenched.

For example, the corporate culture challenge question could have been used to create shared purpose and common interests that may cause things to ease up in the rigid position about the price issue. The negative preconceived views of Yahoo's CEO on Microsoft represent a suitable background for investing in trust-building measures and having an open mind for the possibility of change.

Malaysia Airlines and Qantas

The nineties were the golden years for Malaysia Airlines Systems (MAS), as they enjoyed a great reputation and high customer satisfaction rates. But with increasing competition and operational costs, the airline started to struggle.

In an attempt to turn things around, the Malaysian government, which owns the flag carrier, appointed Idris Jala as CEO on 1 December 2005. A veteran of Shell for twenty-three years, Idris had a reputation for identifying and realizing operational efficiencies. During his tenure, he successfully turned around the airline from its worst financial loss to achieving record profits in its sixty-year history.

Inspired by the merger between KLM and Air France, Idris Jala proposed a merger between Malaysia Airlines and the Australian Qantas. The planned merger was based on a shares swap agreement where Qantas would own 70 per cent of Malaysia Airlines, while Malaysia Airlines would own a 30 per cent stake in Qantas, which was much larger. This would have allowed both airlines to keep their own branding and identity, while resulting in the sixth-largest airline in the world and the largest in the Asia Pacific.

The potential merger sounded like a marriage made in heaven, as both parties were poised to have sizeable wins. Because of its location in Australia, Qantas is largely considered a destination, not a network, airline. There are very few large destinations to fly to after reaching Australia. So, having access to Kuala Lumpur could have made Qantas a true network airline. Malaysia Airlines would have benefited from financial backing and the operational excellence of Qantas.

While generally, mergers and acquisitions are tricky business with a high failure rate, this partnership seemed very promising as the two parties worked out details of the synergies to result, including how to share lounges around the world, transforming Kuala Lumpur to be the centre of servicing and maintaining all the aircraft of the two airlines as well stopping Qantas flights to Changi Airport in Singapore and diverting all the traffic to Kuala Lumpur International Airport, so that the two networks are fully integrated. The two-year negotiations reached advanced stages when Australian PM John Howard met with his Malaysian counterpart Tun Abdullah Badawi, with Qantas then-CEO Geoff Dixon and Idris Jala present, and the deal seemed to be on track to be realized, until it was not.

'We had a detailed hardwired agreement that both parties signed off,' Idris Jala told me during a personal interview. 'We left nothing to chance because we knew if we did not iron out the details ahead of time, we were in for trouble when we were due to start implementing the deal. For example, both Qantas and MAS had sales offices around the world. We agreed that we would assess those based on performance and keep the best-performing offices to service the newly formed alliance, so for Jakarta, the agreement was that Qantas would close its sales office there. MAS would close its sales offices in Australia.'

When identifying their interests, the MAS team recognized a few non-negotiable showstoppers, chief among them are:

1. Malaysian Airlines needed to retain its brand and not be absorbed by the newly formed entity.
2. It will always have a Malaysian CEO, and Qantas should never impose a non-Malaysian CEO on it. 'Of course, cross-posting, where a Malaysian CEO leads Qantas while an Australian CEO leads MAS, was a possibility,' Idris added.
3. The chairperson of the new alliance should be on a rotating basis. Malaysian Airlines chair was to chair the

> new alliance for three years, followed by Qantas chair, and so on.

'Qantas agreed to all of that,' he concluded.

While the two negotiating parties worked out all the issues, including going through the operations flight by flight to make sure the details of the deal were fully agreed upon, something was missing.

The purpose and interest of the Malaysian government were thought to be to make sure that its airline was financially sustainable, which is, of course, true. But there was an even deeper, non-negotiable purpose: This was national pride. It was politically unpalatable for the government to agree that 70 per cent of the Malaysian flagship carrier be owned by a foreign entity. The highly volatile political scene of the time would have guaranteed that the Opposition would accuse the government of selling out the country's assets, particularly the airline, which many Malaysians felt emotionally and fondly about.

'The failure of this merger was the biggest corporate regret of my life,' Idris Jala continued. 'The failure was not due to the lack of a business case, but to the lack of political will. Politicians crave applause and prioritize votes, while changing the paradigm often involves pain. I believe that transformational leadership is about disappointing people at a rate they can tolerate, as Marty Linsky said. Leaders need to build trust with their constituencies so that they are permitted to do the unpopular, but necessary, acts.'

An early assessment of this deal, with a deep focus on the purpose and interests of the owner of Malaysian Airlines and Qantas, would have been a great investment as this would have resulted in either not pursuing the deal, if there was no deal to be struck in the first place, saving the two companies a great amount of time and resources, or creating a detailed and long term stakeholders engagement plan, not only to communicate the benefits of the deal but also to allay any worries and concerns that Malaysia was losing control of one of its highly prized national icons. This could have even included the Opposition in the deal to ensure bipartisan support.

If he could turn back time, what would Idris Jala have done differently?

'The challenge was Qantas insisted on complete secrecy while negotiating the transaction. We signed a nondisclosure agreement (NDA) as a condition for the talks to carry on. There was a lot of anxiety on their side, as they worried about the strict Australian Anti-Competitive Behaviour Act, and didn't want to risk being on the wrong side of the law,' he offered. 'Nonetheless, in hindsight, we could have attempted to create a platform or a safe space to engage with the Opposition in Malaysia. With some convincing, we may have been able to persuade Qantas that talking to the Opposition is an essential ingredient of reaching a deal. We could have done a version of our Lab,' he concluded.

The Lab

In 2009, Malaysia introduced the National Transformation Programme (NTP). To ensure the effective implementation of the governmental plans, the Malaysian government initiated the Performance Management Delivery Unit (PEMANDU), which literally means 'driver' in Malay, within the Prime Minister's Department to drive the successful execution of these plans. This unit was led by Idris Jala.

After all the transformational projects and initiatives are agreed upon, PEMANDU would facilitate what they called the 'Lab,' where detailed implementation plans are created. Labs are multi-key-stakeholder working sessions that can take up to six weeks and result in detailed plans of execution signed off by all key stakeholders. These labs represent ideal opportunities to identify and align the interests of different parties, leading towards the emergence of shared purpose as well as the building of mutual trust between different stakeholders.

One of these labs that took place in 2010 was to work out the plans for a modern public transport system for Greater Kuala Lumpur and the Klang Valley, the Mass Rapid Transit (MRT). The projected population growth and car numbers for the city meant that having public transport was a must.

However, there were a number of challenges:

1. **Political:** The proposed MRT line will pass through land in Kuala Lumpur (under the federal government) and Selangor (under the rule of the Opposition). The federal government and the Opposition needed to work together, which was not a straightforward thing during the highly polarized political scene back then.
2. **Technical:** The soil of Kuala Lumpur was not suitable for extensive tunnelling, some experts thought.
3. **Financial:** The cost of building the MRT was expected to be prohibitive.

Idris Jala remembered how he got the stakeholders into the MRT Lab. 'It took me three months to convince the Minister of Federal Territories (government) and the Chief Minister of Selangor (Opposition) to get into a meeting with each other,' he said. 'After completing the lab and signing the hardwired agreement, the Chief Minister gave a speech in which he said: This is a fateful day. We came from different political parties and harboured different ideologies, but now we can safely say that we have *dua bantal, satu mimpi*—a Malay proverb that means we have two pillows but one dream,' he proudly added.

One could only imagine what would have happened if a version of this lab had been conducted in the presence of the

Malaysian Opposition while the Malaysia Airlines-Qantas deal was being progressed.

The above corporate examples demonstrate the importance of prioritizing the understanding of the purpose and the interests of each party, which are non-negotiable and sometimes are not even obvious.

Of course, there are multiple examples from the worlds of politics and business, when parties were able to use the exploration of their deep interests and purpose to help them make movements related to their positions on the issues being negotiated.

India, Pakistan, and Kashmir

One of the world's oldest outstanding conflicts is the one between India and Pakistan over the Kashmir region. Positions of both parties have historically been entrenched, with both nations firmly asserting their claims. However, there have been instances where back-channel negotiations highlighted underlying interests. While both countries viewed Kashmir as an integral part of their territory, during various peace talks, they both recognized that their primary interests were national security and regional stability. Any long-term solution will need to first address these interests. This led to discussions on confidence-building measures, such as trade agreements and cultural exchanges, even if a complete resolution of territorial claims was not immediately feasible. The realization that fostering trade and stability could benefit both countries helped create an environment for further dialogue with the potential to arrive at a shared sense of purpose.

Applying collaborative negotiation requires escalating the mindset from the level of identification of interests, issues, and positions to investing in the long-term search for shared purpose and building mutual trust. In the case of Kashmir, climate change and the need for joint effective management of water resources in the region may be a way to develop this shared purpose.

'Kashmir is sitting atop the water tower of Asia, the Himalayan region, with almost 18,000 glaciers nourishing the water supply in the state.' Kashmir-based Shakil A. Romshoo, vice chancellor at the Islamic University of Science and Technology, told VOA.[80]

With both nations having rapidly growing populations, Kashmir's water is a source of conflict between India and Pakistan. Transforming the management of water from a source of conflict to a shared purpose will require truly transformative leadership and negotiation genius on both sides. This is neither easy nor quick, but potentially the only way to achieve a lasting peace.

Many of the world's intractable geopolitical flashpoints cannot be solved by military might. It is time to apply collaborative negotiation and invest in developing shared purpose and mutual trust.

Our future generations deserve that.

Once the negotiation scope is explored, and negotiating parties become aware of each other's deep purpose and interests, as well as hopes, needs, and concerns, parties will be in a better position to trade items that will help facilitate the movement of the positions taken along the issues being considered. Items that can be traded are called 'tradeables'. These are things, commitments, or concessions valued by the receiving party more than the giving one. Further details about this will be explored in the next section.

Trading Tradeables

When I first visited Paris, I made sure that I found time to get to the Louvre. I especially wanted to see two things: the obelisk of Hammurabi's Code (humanity's first written law) and the Mona Lisa. Finding the location of the latter was not challenging, as it was the most crowded room in the museum.

To tell the truth, I was a bit disappointed when I saw it: It was much smaller than I had been expecting! While the Mona Lisa is now worth $850 million, you can buy a copy from the souvenir shop in the Louvre for a couple of euros, so what, or who makes the original Mona Lisa so much more valuable than an identical copy?

The answer? Humans.

The Mona Lisa is worth that amount because someone is willing to pay that much for it—only if it's for sale. At the end of each value exchange process, there is a human being. Only humans can create and exchange value. Luckily, we also value things differently, which facilitates trading and exchange.

For example, if you buy a car for $10,000, the value and utility that the car is worth for you is more than the value you attach to the money, while for the company or person who sold you the car, they value the $10,000 more than the car. This value differential is a unique human feature and represents the very foundation for trading and exchange. It has always enabled people to work together, acting as the glue for the development of the economy at multiple levels.

Trading is a key component of successful negotiation, and being ready with items that we can trade with other parties is an essential part of the negotiation preparation process. Kennedy Rolland defines tradeables as 'items over which we have discretion, but perhaps they are not directly related to the negotiation. They are not something you are here to negotiate about, but they can be useful to consider to add movement later in the negotiation.'[81]

Remember, tradeables have little value for us, while the other negotiating party values them more. For example, a free airline ticket is valued much higher by a passenger receiving it, as part of a settlement deal, than by an airline that is offering it as it is operating the flight anyway.

BATNA

This term stands for the Best Alternative To A Negotiated Agreement. The concept, developed by negotiation experts Roger

Fisher and William Ury, was introduced in their book *Getting to Yes: Negotiating Agreement Without Giving In.*[82]

It defines the negotiator's alternative option if they do not agree to the present terms offered by the other party and the negotiations cease. BATNAs provide data on the 'walk away' or 'take it or leave it' alternative. They strengthen the negotiator to the extent that the BATNA is credible to the other party; they underscore their weakness if there is no BATNA that is at least as good as the current offer. This is why it's highly advisable that negotiators put some effort into developing and enhancing their BATNA.

For example, if a business is negotiating the rent rate of a premise they are renting, they will be better off exploring the other options available to them, so that they can readily compare their position on issues such as rental rate and other dimensions of the deal with their BATNA.

Preparation for Negotiation

Preparation for negotiation, particularly in a business context, represents an essential and very important activity. During this stage, negotiating teams establish their purpose, interests, negotiation issues, positions, available tradeables, and BATNA. Teams will also benefit from repeating the same exercise from the point of view of the opposing party, as this will enable them to understand the intentions, interests, and limitations of the other team.

Despite the importance of the preparation stage, negotiating teams often dedicate too little time to it. Collaborative negotiation requires very careful preparation and views the time dedicated to this activity as a worthwhile investment.

A key objective during the preparation stage, and throughout the negotiation process, is to make sure that your team and other internal stakeholders are fully informed and aligned at all times. This may sound intuitive, but it is often neglected. Important stakeholders such as board members and management representatives need to be regularly updated and aligned; otherwise, this could be detrimental to the whole process.

After preparing the negotiation envelopes, parameters, and strategies, it is essential to present those and sign them off internally. On many occasions, negotiators neglect to allocate sufficient time and effort to align the internal stakeholders, which could prove to be counterproductive to the whole process.

The Negotiation Preparation Template shown below can be utilized to prepare for negotiation, and also to align the internal stakeholders. It is important to recognize that completing the right-hand side of the template requires studying all the available information about the other party of the negotiation, as well as understanding the prevailing market conditions.

This Negotiation Preparation Template will need to be regularly updated as the interaction with the other party may yield further information, correct wrong perceptions, and provide new negotiation ideas. In any case, the negotiating team needs to maintain a version control system as the template is updated and keep the internal stakeholders informed about any changes made to it.

Collaborating with the Negotiating Counterparts

After preparing for the negotiation process, the time will come for the encounter with the negotiating team of the other side. This is where knowledge and skills will be tested. While the nature of the interaction will be situational and depend on the type of negotiation and the style of the team, you can adhere to a number of principles to maximize the potential of having a more collaborative encounter with the other party.

These include:

1. Enter the negotiation with a mentality that focuses on discovering a shared purpose, building mutual trust, seeking a win-win solution, and inventing options for joint gain.
2. Recall the Prisoner's Dilemma and the fact that playing nice pays off. Always start nice, but be ready to reciprocate in kind if the other party does not play nice.
3. When making an opening offer, ensure that your offer is both credible and defensible. Outrageously lowball offers that have no grounding in reality can be seen as a sign of disrespect and may derail the negotiations.
4. During the discussion with the other party, try to always separate the people from the issues. Use neutral statements, avoid attack and blame, assure the other side about your commitment to reaching a deal, use questions to understand their purpose, interests, and positions, and summarize the conversations at the end to avoid any misunderstanding.
5. Negotiating entities may not be of the same size, financial might, or market share. Regardless of the size of your organization or business compared to the other party, remember you have a seat at the table because the other

party wants something from you. This is particularly important, for example, if you are a small supplier negotiating with a big organization. This should help you hold your ground and get the best deal possible.

6. If the opponent behaves in a rude or unprofessional way, remind yourself and them, if necessary, that an agreement can only be based on the merits of the offer and the principles of trading. The way they are treating you will not impact the outcome.
7. Always trade. You can always find items that will cost you little while the negotiating counterpart would like to have. If you operate a hotel, you can always spare rooms or upgrades during your off-season period, while the party negotiate with you would love to have free rooms or upgrades to send their management team to a planning retreat. This trading exchange may help you move the position of your counterpart on some of the negotiated issues closer to yours.
8. Aggressive negotiators can use negotiation ploys to push you into agreeing to a suboptimal deal. They may claim that they have another supplier waiting to do business with them at a much lower price, or they may create arbitrary deadlines citing their internal policies or regulations. In all these cases, you will need to recognize the ploys and be ready to address them.

<table>
<tr><th colspan="2">NEGOTIATION PREPARATION TEMPLATE</th></tr>
<tr><td colspan="2">Version:

Date:</td></tr>
<tr><td colspan="2">Project Description:</td></tr>
<tr><td>Name of Our Team/ Organization</td><td>Name of Other Party's Team/ Organization</td></tr>
<tr><td>Our Purpose:</td><td>Other Party's Potential Purpose:</td></tr>
<tr><td colspan="2">Potential Shared Purpose (if it is possible to articulate):</td></tr>
</table>

<table>
<tr><td colspan="3">Our Interests:
1.

2.

3.

4.

5.</td><td colspan="2">Other Party's Possible Interests:
1.

2.

3.

4.

5.</td></tr>
<tr><td>Negotiation Issues</td><td>Our Entry Position</td><td>Our Exit Position</td><td>Other Party's Potential/ Declared Entry Position</td><td>Other Party's Potential/ Declared Exit Position</td></tr>
<tr><td>Issue 1 (e.g. price)</td><td></td><td></td><td></td><td></td></tr>
<tr><td>Issue 2</td><td></td><td></td><td></td><td></td></tr>
<tr><td>Issue 3</td><td></td><td></td><td></td><td></td></tr>
<tr><td>Issue 4</td><td></td><td></td><td></td><td></td></tr>
<tr><td>Issue 5</td><td></td><td></td><td></td><td></td></tr>
<tr><td>Issue 6</td><td></td><td></td><td></td><td></td></tr>
<tr><td>Issue 7</td><td></td><td></td><td></td><td></td></tr>
<tr><td>Issue 8</td><td></td><td></td><td></td><td></td></tr>
</table>

Our Tradeables:	Other Party's Possible Tradeables:
1. 2. 3. 4. 5.	1. 2. 3. 4. 5.
Our BATNA:	Other Party's Likely BATNA:

Negotiating Our Survival

The literature about negotiation is rich and diverse, and the practice of reaching a deal has been honed by negotiators over the millennia. Researchers and practitioners of negotiation, like Gavin Kennedy[83] from Edinburgh Business School of Heriot-Watt University and Fisher and Ury[80] from Harvard Business School, wrote a number of definitive texts in the field and taught negotiation directly and indirectly to millions of people, pioneering and framing concepts such as integrative bargaining and principled negotiation.

As mentioned earlier, this chapter is not a replacement for learning from and engaging with this rich literature and tradition. It is rather a humble attempt at extending and shifting our perspective, and to include searching for a shared purpose and working towards mutual trust in the job descriptions of our negotiators. The grand challenges we face today, like the environmental emergency, geopolitical conflicts, and lack of economic equality, require a totally new approach to negotiation.

While most of the negotiation textbooks favour the arrival at win-win agreements, they also acknowledge the human nature that has the tendency to prioritize and maximize one's own gain. There are, of course, mathematical models that describe how to truly reach agreements that will maximise the mutual gain, rather than the individual. Nash equilibrium is one of these models in an area of research called rational bargaining. The negotiation literature clearly outlines the limitations of these models as they require complete transparency and rationality of the negotiating partners and agreement on maximizing the joint, not individual, gain.

In my MBA negotiation classes, when I pit the students against each other in a Prisoner's Dilemma game, less than 5 per cent of the pairs achieve the rational win-win outcome. We have known for some time now from economic research that people are not rational agents. Hence, Rational Bargaining research can shed light on the theoretical maximum of the joint gain if players choose to be transparent and rational.

Interestingly though, addressing our grand challenges, such as the climate emergency, requires exactly the adherence to the requirements of rational bargaining, which the current negotiation literature describes as unrealistic.

This is indeed a paradox. If countries are negotiating a reduction in carbon dioxide emission to control the greenhouse effect, prioritizing individual gain by choosing to cheat and not adhere to the agreed reduction targets will be harmful to all parties, including those who are cheating. The only way forward is for all to be collaborative and transparent.

I am very optimistic that we are reaching a key moment in our history when purpose, trust, and wisdom will prevail and provide the way out as we recognize collaborative negotiation as the viable option for our species' survival.

Chapter 13

Future of Work and Careers

'Work is love made visible.'

—Khalil Gibran

This chapter explores the evolving landscape of work in an era where multiple confluences challenge the traditional value of human work. These include disruptive technologies such as AI, the disenchantment of the workforce with their employers as a force for good, and the general lack of a deep sense of purpose and meaning at multiple levels.

As we come closer to realizing AGI, the quality of the outputs created by technology is approaching and, in some cases, even surpassing human output quality. This includes writing original text, designing innovative processes, providing medical diagnosis, and even creating music and videos in a very short time and almost for free.

AI will, without a doubt, play a key role in profoundly transforming the world of work. The ability to efficiently, effectively, and safely use AI to integrate with our work will increasingly be a highly desired skill in the job market. Because an AI system is largely a black box and its inner workings are beyond the comprehension of the majority of people, it can sometimes create erroneous outputs. It is also open to manipulation and being used for less than admirable objectives.

All these factors underscore the importance of leadership and leaders who prioritize humanity and human connection and collaboration. Inspiring a collaborative mindset and developing the skills necessary to create a shared purpose and nurture mutual trust will continue to be pivotal for success, positive impact, and flourishing in a world that is both defined and disrupted by technology.

These human capacities will be even more crucial for career success in a world where uniquely human capabilities, as opposed to machine capabilities, are increasingly prized.

This chapter explores and outlines frameworks for individuals aiming to excel in their careers by capitalizing on these skills. It emphasizes that in the rapidly changing professional environment, the ability to leverage technology to connect and work effectively with others, build consensus, and lead through collaboration is not just valuable but essential.

History of our Humanity, Work, Technology, and Impact

Humans deliver work, experience life, shape their environment, and interact with each other via three essential capacities or labours: physical, cognitive, and emotional. We use these three labours to process materials, energy, and information to create systems, produce objects, and deliver services with the intention of creating and adding value.

In this section, we will tell the story of how technology shaped human work and civilization, from the invention of the wheel to the development of AI, as seen through the lens of these three human labours. This has been a journey that culminated in the age of purpose that is dawning upon us, and it is depicted in the figure below and explained thereafter. The shaded areas in the figure show how, over time, technology replaces work and tasks that humans used to perform.

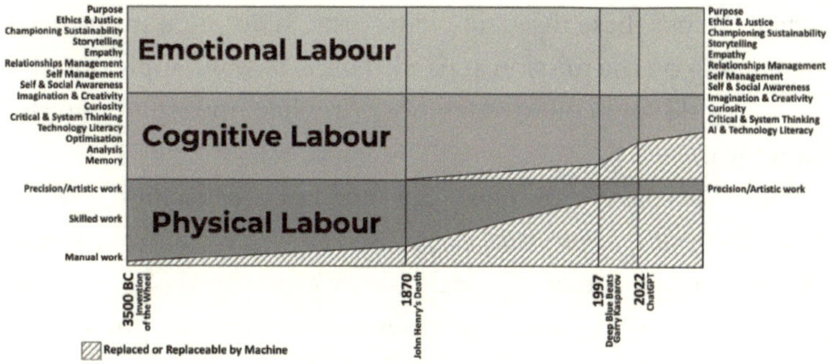

Fig. 10 – History and Future of Human Work

Whether we are cooking a meal, writing a book, making a sandcastle, building a piece of furniture, constructing a house, manufacturing a car, bathing a baby, giving someone a haircut, or telling a story, we are essentially using some form of energy to reshape and combine materials, concepts, and ideas according to desired and imaginative patterns.

The patterns in which materials and/or ideas are combined can generally be referred to as the information content of the system or product we are creating.

Generally speaking, the ultimate value of what we produce depends on the cost and worth of the materials, energy, and information needed to produce it. The rarer and the more difficult to acquire the required materials and the more original, restricted, and complex the information content of a system, the more valuable it is. Information needed to make or produce something refers here to the knowledge, experience, skills, and imagination that go into making it. If the produced item is a unique piece of art, then the value of the artist's distinct style will be scoped here, too, introducing subjectivity into the evaluation. Energy is usually more fungible, so the more energy we use to produce something, the more costly it gets.

Classifying human labours as physical, cognitive, and emotional does not imply that they occur independently of each other. We use these three simultaneously, in different proportions, depending on the mission at hand. This is how we apply ourselves in the world and collectively impact it while impacting ourselves in return.

For example, we need our cognitive capacities and our nervous system to control our muscular system to perform even the most mundane of physical tasks. We also need our emotional capacities to keep ourselves motivated to perform physical and cognitive tasks.

Each of these three labours exists on a growing scale of complexity.

The physical labour, which refers to our ability to move and manipulate objects and depends largely on our muscular strength and dexterity, can manifest itself as routine manual work, such as sweeping the floor or carrying some loads, skilled work as in bricklaying, or precision work as in tuning a piano.

The cognitive labour is founded on the bedrock of the cognitive capacity, memory, which is demonstrated by the ability to memorize and recall knowledge and information. Its complexity progresses to include analysis of information, optimization, technology literacy, decision-making, critical thinking, curiosity, and ultimately, creativity and imagination, which are the pinnacle of human cognitive achievement.

The emotional labour deploys skills and capabilities such as awareness, self-motivation, empathy, relationship-building, a sense of purpose and meaning, and behaving ethically.

Since the dawn of time, humans have worked on enhancing how these labours are delivered and deployed. This usually starts with improving personal capability to deliver labour by working towards becoming stronger, faster, and generally more effective. If the work is dangerous, dull, or difficult, or when human biological limits to process materials, energy, and information are reached, people start to look for alternatives to extend themselves, so the labour is either mechanized or transferred to domesticated animals. This trend is particularly obvious with the physical and cognitive labours.

Humans started by enhancing physical labour, they always wanted to be able to carry and move around increasingly heavier objects and do that at a higher speed; think of the work needed to lift the stones used to build the pyramids of Giza, for example.

To achieve that, humans invented the wheel, used levers, wedges, and ropes, and employed draft animals. They also harnessed nature's energy using inanimate objects such as sails, water wheels, and windmills. All of that raised the capacity to use energy to process materials to a whole new level.

From the time the wheel was invented in Mesopotamia circa 3500 BCE, the gradual inclination towards replacing human physical labour with mechanical labour intensified. Machines free humans from the limitations that biology imposes. A human body, or the body of a draft animal like a horse, elephant, or ox, for that matter, unlocks the energy contained in food through the metabolism process and uses muscles to deliver physical labour. A steam engine or an internal combustion engine, on the other hand, can process and release massive amounts of energy, stored in coal or petrol, and use that to deploy huge sums of physical labour, fuelling the building of civilization at an unprecedented scale.

The First Industrial Revolution in the nineteenth century resulted in the accelerated deployment of machines that were far stronger and much faster than any human being or domesticated animal. This was accompanied by a major loss of manual human jobs and a great deal of disruption to the social and political order. This is depicted in the increasing shaded area in the physical labour in the History and Future of Human Work figure above.

A watershed moment that represented the essence of the disruptive nature of the First Industrial Revolution is the legend of John Henry. An African American strongman who lived in the middle of the nineteenth century, he worked as a steel driving man, hammering steel chisels into rocks and making deep holes to place explosives to dig tunnels for the Chesapeake and Ohio railroad. He was the best at his job, driving one steel chisel after another as they were blunted and replaced by his partner.

During his working days, steam-powered hammers started to appear. To assess the effectiveness of these mechanical hammers, they were brought to compete against John Henry, but he always won. The power of steam seemed to be no match for the strength and dexterity of the human muscle. One day in 1870, the engineers working on the railroad brought in the latest steam-powered digger to compete against John Henry. A human-against-machine race started. At the end of it, John was able to dig 14 feet, while the machine managed only 9 feet.

However, this would be the last time any human could beat a machine at such a mainly physical task, as John Henry collapsed and fell dead at the end of the competition.[84]

Throughout the First Industrial Revolution, machines continued to improve in effectiveness, efficiency, and reliability and human jobs that were based on physical labour kept on being mechanized. Not only were many jobs lost, but the disruption also had far-reaching consequences on the very fabric of nature and society, transforming our reality politically, economically, socially, and environmentally. In the industrializing nations, many people migrated from rural areas to urban industrial centres to get jobs in the newly built factories. The notion of wealth, which was locked in the value of land for millennia since the Agricultural Revolution, transformed to increasingly include the ownership of the means of mass production, creating a new capitalist class.

The richest people were no longer the feudal owners of large swathes of land but rather the capitalists who owned factories, railroads and concessions for the coal mines and, later, oil fields that powered the Industrial Revolution. This served as the background for rapid growth in the volume of economic exchange, human population, environmental pollution, and inequality.

Educational institutions expanded their offerings to cater for the needs of the industry, and massive exercises of upskilling and reskilling of the workforce took place. The educational outcomes focused on enhancing and expanding human capability to deliver cognitive labour, as increasing amounts of physical labour were being carried out by machines.

While the trends of increasing mechanization, urbanization, economic growth, human population, inequality, and environmental degradation continued throughout the nineteenth and twentieth centuries, the scientific and technological developments of calculating and computing machines were happening simultaneously.

Starting with mechanical calculators that were able to perform simple calculations, computers kept improving in performance and speed while reducing in size and price—all the while increasingly being able to perform tasks within the cognitive labour domain. For a start, computers have superior memory compared to humans, a trend that is only increasing by the day. They are able to retain, process and analyse massive amounts of data, and with the right algorithms and computer programmes, they are even capable of learning and discerning trends much faster than us. Once again, machines are enabling humans to transcend their biological limitations. Despite all of this, many experts thought that cognitive labour would remain largely the human territory where we create and add superior value.

Just like in the case of John Henry, our superiority was to be unforgivingly tested. In May of 1997, human cognitive supremacy was put to the ultimate trial when Gary Kasparov, the world champion in chess, played a chess rematch against Deep Blue, an IBM supercomputer, in New York City. The six-game rematch came after a similar set that was played between the human master and the supercomputer in Philadelphia in 1996, when Kasparov won 4–2.

However, the programmers of Deep Blue were able to make changes and improvements to the code and the rematch was won by Deep Blue 3½–2½. A tight win, but it created another watershed moment, nonetheless.

Computers have come a long way since 1997, and the field of AI and the ability to harness and process Big Data held the potential to dominate wide aspects of the cognitive labour domain and transform the jobs market.

A 2017 study by McKinsey and Company predicted that, by as early as 2030, 800 million people could lose their jobs, while 375 million people will need to undergo a career change as a result of technological advancements.[85]

With the release of ChatGPT in November 2022, which is the first conversational AI Large Language Model (LLM) developed by OpenAI, the tale of displacing humans in the cognitive domain enters a whole new chapter. You can ask the tool to write you a speech, a computer code, a report, a song, an essay or even a whole book in a matter of seconds. Its capabilities will only grow wider, deeper, and stronger, challenging us to justify the value we can add in the area of work.

The enormous acceleration in the ability to store, process, and learn from data and information changed the nature of the economy again. Today, the largest, richest and most influential companies are not the behemoths of manufacturing with their large number of employees and huge physical assets, but rather information technology, often cloud-based, companies such as Apple, Microsoft, Meta, and Google. The consolidation of capacities in these cloud-based companies is transforming them into platform monopolies with powers similar to those of landowners in the feudal system. Yanis Varoufakis, the economist and ex-finance minister of Greece, considers this historical stage a post-capitalism era and calls it technofeudalism.[86]

What Remains Constant

It is clear from the earlier analysis that technology is increasingly and reliably able to deliver what humans used to be paid for in physical labour and cognitive labour domains. The History and Future of Human Work figure tells a clear story: most of our physical and cognitive labour tasks can, and will, be automated. It also shows that the emotional labour, with its many human capabilities, is the realm where humanity needs to focus and continue to lead. It is the domain where we can add value, make a difference, connect with one another, and ensure that we remain relevant and continue to flourish.

This can represent a profound transformation. Humans are not here to compete against machines. Humans' true role is to achieve their emotional full potential of being good, kind, wise, and compassionate. It is to build trust and purpose so that we can leverage technology for the goodness of the human family.

In the fast-changing environment we are in today, it is a fool's errand to try to predict how the world of work will look a decade or two from now. It is even more difficult to try to predict what future careers will be available for people or even how and for what people will be paid.

One thing, however, I feel confident about is that the difference we make through work will remain an essential source of identity, dignity, and purpose for many of us. So, instead of trying to predict the future of employment, I will attempt to outline what people would ideally want from their jobs, work, and careers and also the skills and mindsets needed to successfully engage in such desired work.

If given an option, most people will choose to engage in work and careers that are:

1. **Driven by purpose:** As technology is becoming increasingly more capable of delivering many of the physical and cognitive tasks, an ideal outcome would be to free humans to take on jobs that help them sharpen their sense of purpose and mobilise it into a positive impact on the world.
   Workplaces and employers that give employees the opportunity and the platform to pursue purposeful work will reap benefits in employee engagement, motivation, retention, and productivity, not to mention the ability to attract better talent.
2. **Measured by impact:** Human beings, in general, would like to do the work needed by others, the one that can have a positive impact on the world. This will increasingly become a key factor in talent attraction and retention, and corporations will need to be on the front foot when it comes to highlighting the public good that they are delivering, while they pursue their business objectives. People would want to work for entities that are not only measured by profit, but also by impact.
3. **Engaging and leveraging the strengths of the individual:** Human talent needs to be treated as a very precious resource. As human labour will increasingly be more expensive than machine labour (which continues to drop in cost with technological progress), it makes sense to use humans in a way that harnesses their unique capabilities and leverages their strengths.

4. **Stimulating and positively challenging:** Humans are easily bored when doing dull or repetitive tasks. Work that will appeal to most people is engaging and has an edge of variety and challenge. With the right support, challenging work can be a pathway towards personal growth and development.
5. **Aligned with the values and beliefs:** People would like to do work that is congruent with their values and the causes they believe in. They would want to be of service to others in a positive manner.
6. **Rewarding, both financially and otherwise:** Work can be an important part of life. People have the right to be part of work environments that are safe and respectful and do tasks that will enrich their lives, help them be connected to the communities that matter to them, and enable them to grow professionally and personally.

The above list describes the characteristics of work and careers that we aspire towards in any situation and any era. These are very aligned with the narrative depicted in the History and Future of Human Work figure. The realm in which we have a superiority over our technology is the emotional labour domain. With the latest developments in AI, we will have a real chance at making this type of work, where our desires meet our capabilities, a reality. However, this positive vision is neither predestined nor inevitable, and it requires vision, action, leadership, and collaboration to make it happen.

Essential Success Capabilities, Skills, and Mindsets

Since 2016, the World Economic Forum has periodically published its Future of Jobs Report, which surveys the world's most influential corporate CEOs, policymakers, and thought leaders as they weigh in on the future of work and the skills needed to succeed.

Since it began to be published, a trend was clear: people skills, self-management capabilities, and resilient mental attitudes are key to success. The 2023 edition of this report indicated that the importance of these skills, capabilities, and mindsets is on the rise as they are the true differentiator between work delivered by humans and that done by machines.[87]

This is largely in line with the analysis depicted in the History and Future of Work figure shown earlier, which identified the fundamental non-machine skills as AI and Technology literacy, critical and system thinking, curiosity, imagination and creativity, self and social awareness, self-management, relationship management, empathy, storytelling, championing sustainability, ethics and justice, and purpose.

These fundamental skills underpin essential capabilities such as effective leadership, collaboration and teamwork, entrepreneurial mindset, emotional intelligence, resilience and flexibility, negotiation, and consensus-building.

In the age of AI, successful individuals will be required to become even more effective in bringing to the fore human magic, discerning the quality and intention of the output of intelligent machines, and leveraging human connections. Being a catalyst for assisting people and organizations, to discover and articulate their purpose, will continue to be a highly valued skill.

Sharpening the Collaborative Talent

Our journey outlining and exploring what the future needs took us here. The destination is the development of human talent, wisdom, purpose, trust, compassion, and connections.

Below are some of the skills, mindsets, attributes, and capabilities we will need to sharpen to enhance our collaborative potential, remain relevant, and add value in a world shaped and disrupted by technology.

Articulating a Deep Sense of Purpose

The premise of this book is that shared purpose and mutual trust are the foundation for collaboration. Discovering and articulating one's deep sense of personal purpose is also essential for self-motivation, resilience, mental and physical health, and success in general. Working on the discovery of an individual's purpose is one of the key elements of establishing self-awareness and professional and personal growth. Using the techniques outlined in Chapter 6, individuals are encouraged to articulate their Impact Statements.

Articulating and communicating a personal purpose through an Impact Statement can also be a great way to attract mission partners. It can also be a powerful reminder of who we are, when we need that the most. Many of my colleagues, including myself, sign off their emails with their names and Impact Statements. Some of us even put the Impact Statement on the back of our business cards.

I still remember the story one of my colleagues told me. She was having a protracted email correspondence with another coworker who was supposed to complete some work and forward it to her. After multiple reminders and a few wasted weeks of unanswered requests and incomplete submissions, my colleague just lost her patience and decided to write him a strongly worded email. She vented all her frustration and detailed in a long email the number of times she followed up and how his less-than-professional response adversely affected the wellbeing and performance of her department.

As she was proofreading her email to make sure that it was loaded with a sufficient calibre of complaints, she noticed her impact statement that appeared automatically as part of her email signature:

'I am an optimist. My purpose is to turn uncertainties into opportunities, helping many realize their financial freedom by optimizing these opportunities.'

Needless to say, my colleague decided to rewrite the email to be more guided by her Impact Statement. According to her, that was the best decision, as later she discovered that the coworker had some challenges beyond his control that resulted in the delays.

Ethics and Justice

Imagine a runaway train heading towards five people tied up on the tracks. You are standing next to a lever that can divert the train onto another track where there is only one person. The question to you is: Is it right, obligatory, or morally permissible to pull the lever, sacrificing one person to save five?

This thought experiment, named the 'trolley dilemma', was first articulated in 1967 by British philosopher Philippa Foot in a moral philosophy paper that explores ethical decision-making.[88]

This theoretical scenario was aimed at providing a way to think about some of the moral dilemmas we face, and few thought this might become a literal practical consideration one day.

Of course, this day has arrived, and designers of self-driving cars are expected to programme them to be able to handle very similar situations. Imagine that the brakes failed on a self-driving car and a collision is inevitable, the car has two choices and a millisecond to act: stay in its current path and hit a bus with the potential of killing 10 people or veer to the right and kill one child who is playing by the roadside.

Increasingly, matters that used to be the staple of philosophy classrooms are making it to the computer science, economics, and political realms. To operate on the world's stage, it is an expectation to apply justice principles and ethical standards to frame and anchor our actions and decisions and those of the organizations and businesses that we represent and work for. The awareness and understanding of these principles and standards and the ability to implement them in a highly complex world require knowledge, skills, and mindsets that have to continually be honed, nurtured, and developed.

This can start by doing what feels right, but it does not stop there. Just as we saw with the 'Trolley Dilemma', what is right, just, and ethical may not be apparent or agreed upon. Lifelong learning and continuous upskilling will increasingly be expected from all of us.

Championing Sustainability

Driven by growing environmental concerns, corporate responsibility, and consumer demand for sustainable practices, understanding the implications of sustainability for business operations and the ability to champion and advocate for sustainable practices effectively will increasingly be highly desired skills and a requirement for success. In this context, championing sustainability is classified as part of emotional labour because it requires dealing with various emotional obstacles and hurdles.

While the science of climate change is conclusive and the behavioural, technological, and policy tools to address it are obvious, the implementation pathways, on the other hand, require collaboration, mutual trust, and shared purpose. Effective implementation requires dealing with anxiety, fear of change, and concerns about loss of profitability or market share.

As climate change and resource depletion become urgent global issues, organizations are compelled to integrate sustainability into their operations and strategies. This has led to philosophies such as sustainable development and concepts like planetary health joining the mainstream of the discourse in more domains. Consequently, the skill to account for and minimize the environmental footprint of individuals and organizations, and the ability to champion sustainability have become desirable attributes for employees across various sectors.

Besides the fact that prioritizing sustainability is the right thing to do, businesses are facing mounting pressure from stakeholders, including investors, customers, and regulatory bodies, to adopt sustainable practices. Companies that demonstrate their commitment to sustainability are often viewed more favourably and can enhance their brand reputation, attract loyal customers, and secure investment opportunities. Employees who can advocate for and implement sustainable practices are essential to meeting these expectations and driving organizational success.

So, what can we do to be effective advocates and champions for sustainability?

Below are a few actionable suggestions:

1. Familiarize yourself with the science of climate change that anchors the need for sustainable development. It is now accepted in the scientific community that the levels of emission we have, for example, are responsible for the heating up of our climate. This increase in temperature has immediate negative impacts on the climate and the lives of all living beings on the planet.
2. Get educated about the different forms of emissions resulting from organizational and business activities. The

emission of green gases is divided into three scopes: Scope 1 refers to emissions directly associated with the activities taking place on the business premises or directly by its activities. Emissions therein are the easiest to effectively account for and control. Scope 2 emission refers to those that take place away from the business and happen in the course of the generation of the energy used by the business or organization, such as the emissions that result from electricity generation plants that supply the business or the organization. Finally, Scope 3 includes all other indirect emissions that occur in the value chain of the organization, including both upstream and downstream activities. This may encompass emissions from suppliers, product transportation, waste disposal, and even the use of products sold by the business. Scope 3 emissions typically represent the largest portion of an organization's total carbon footprint and are often the most challenging to measure and manage. Understanding the holistic carbon footprint profile of the organization is a key requirement for championing sustainability.

3. Be acquainted with the latest technological advancements that can reduce the environmental burden and minimize the carbon footprint of the industry or sector that you are part of. This needs to be done with all three Scopes in mind.
4. Recognize sustainability as an opportunity rather than just as a challenge. Employees who embrace sustainable practices tend to think creatively about resource management, waste reduction, and energy efficiency. This innovative mindset can lead to cost savings, improved productivity, and the development of new products and services that align with sustainability goals, significantly benefiting the organization in the long run.

5. Promote sustainability as a way of creating the jobs of the future. The transition to a sustainable economy creates new job opportunities and roles focused on environmental stewardship, renewable energy, and sustainable supply chain management. As industries evolve, workers equipped with the knowledge and skills to support these initiatives will be in high demand. This trend highlights the importance of sustainability expertise as a competitive advantage in the job market.
6. Keep abreast of the environmental standards and legal requirements in the sector and jurisdictions in which your organization is operating. Assisting the management team to stay in compliance will make you an indispensable resource for the organization.
7. Celebrate successes and wins in the space of sustainability. This can be when the organization wins an award, achieves an accreditation, or even successfully passes an audit. Highlighting and recognizing savings and productivity improvements, as a result of using fewer resources or reducing waste, is highly desirable as well. A workforce committed to sustainability often feels more connected to their organization's values and mission. This alignment can lead to higher job satisfaction, lower turnover rates, and a more positive workplace culture, ultimately contributing to better organizational performance.

The action points above can be adopted by anyone regardless of their position. Whether you are the CEO of the organization or an intern who has been working there for a few months, you can always choose to champion sustainability. Doing so consistently can create a positive personal brand for you that will go a long way in shaping your future success.

Storytelling

Earlier, we discussed the role of stories in shaping our characters, communities, and the world we live in. In today's world, rife with complexity, uncertainty, and volatility, the importance of storytelling is not diminished but rather further enhanced as the ability to communicate clearly, effectively, and impactfully becomes an essential skill for success. Good stories are not only a source of entertainment; they can enrich our lives, inform our views, and provide a source of hope. Commanding the ability to tell our stories helps others tell their stories too. Bringing complex concepts and data to life through stories can mean mastering our destiny.

When a Native American proverb declares, 'Those who tell the stories rule the world,' I believe it refers to stories that are told masterfully. We have always known the importance of stories in shaping our lives. However, the technological advancements we experience now are making stories even more important, as they can be the sources of uniqueness and differentiation for our work at a time marked by the outputs of the machines.

Researchers recently were able to shed some scientific light on why stories are such a powerful way to communicate and shape public discourse and the general narrative. Work done by Uri Hasson and his collaborators showed that when we listen to a story that is well told, our brains have similar electrical brain patterns to those patterns detected in the brain of the person telling the story.[89]

This is confirmed by scanning the brains of the storyteller and the listeners in an fMRI machine, which can record brain activities in real-time. This is a very powerful and empowering finding. It means that a story can literally tune the minds of thousands and millions of people.

So, how can we get better at telling our stories? There are a number of techniques that we can practise to tell more empowering stories.

I will describe two of them here:

The Hero's Journey Story Structure

In his book, *The Hero with a Thousand Faces*, Joseph Campbell codified what he called the Hero's Journey by examining a large number of stories that shaped humanity's outlook, from the Epic of Gilgamesh to the stories of the Old Testament. He found a common pattern in all these stories. From Homer to Shakespeare, storytellers seem to follow a standard structure. This discovery inspired many to write highly impactful stories.

One of them was Christopher Vogler, the prominent American screenwriter. While advising Walt Disney Animation executives on developing the plot for the movie *The Lion King*, Vogler wrote an influential memo outlining a twelve-stage story structure that was inspired by Campbell's work. He later put this into a book titled *The Writer's Journey*, which detailed the twelve-stage method that has galvanized Hollywood's treatment of cinematic storytelling.

These twelve stages are:

1. **Ordinary world:** The scene is set showing the hero's ordinary life at the start of the story, before the beginning of the adventure.
2. **Call to adventure:** Something happens that disrupts the hero's normal life. This could be a crisis, conflict, or challenge that compels the hero to begin their adventure.
3. **Refusal of the call:** Initially, the hero resists going on the adventure because of their existing commitments, fear, doubt, insecurity, hesitation, or any other number of issues.

4. **Meeting with the mentor:** The hero meets a mentor who provides guidance, wisdom, knowledge, or tools to prepare them for the journey ahead.
5. **Crossing the first threshold:** The hero departs from their ordinary world for the first time, letting go of the current ways, stepping across the threshold into a realm of adventure, and accepting new ways of doing things.
6. **Tests, allies, and enemies:** The hero discovers the rules of the new world, faces challenges, forms alliances, and confronts adversaries.
7. **Approach to the inmost cave:** The hero embarks on the adventure as per the initial plan to confront the challenge, but setbacks arise, prompting them to explore new strategies or embrace different ideas and approaches.
8. **Ordeal:** Complications happen, introducing additional conflict. The hero faces increasingly challenging hurdles and obstacles, some of which may result in a life crisis.
9. **The reward:** Having survived the Ordeal, the hero claims the sword—a metaphor for a hard-earned reward that empowers them to confront the ultimate conflict. This may be a tangible object or wisdom that aids in their perseverance.
10. **The road back:** The hero perceives a glimmer of hope on the horizon, yet they are about to encounter even greater trials and challenges that will test their will to the limit.
11. **The resurrection:** The climax arrives as the hero confronts a final and ultimate challenge, applying all they have learned to tackle the conflict once and for all.
12. **Return with the elixir:** The hero returns to the ordinary world, bringing back their newfound knowledge, wisdom, power, or 'elixir'.

Overlaying the above structure on the stories that became part of the collective memory of humanity, it is fascinating to see how the structure works. Whether the hero is the customer you are trying to sell to, the beneficiary of voluntary work you are doing, or yourself as you use your story to inspire, you can use *The Hero's Journey* to craft compelling and captivating stories.

The Pixar Story Structure

Pixar has been extremely successful in producing highly acclaimed animated movies, producing twenty-eight feature films, beginning with *Toy Story* in 1995. Pixar's films have collectively grossed $15 billion worldwide. This success is not accidental, of course. It is the result of talent, investment, and technology. The stories of the movies themselves are masterfully set. Just like *The Hero's Journey* structure, Pixar has its own storytelling framework codified by Emma Coats, a former story artist at the company.

It has six components shown below:

1. **Once upon a time:** The story scene is set, describing the hero and their life views.
2. **Every day:** The hero goes about life in its typical format.
3. **One day:** The routine is broken, opening the door for a challenge that the hero has to confront.
4. **Because of that:** A crisis is introduced that changes the status quo.
5. **Because of that:** The hero is compelled to challenge themselves and take on an adventure outside their comfort zone.
6. **Until finally:** The resolution and the arrival at new heights of understanding, knowledge, wisdom, and love.

In his book, *To Sell Is Human,* Daniel Pink uses *Finding Nemo* (2003) as an example of the Pixar pitch framework as described below:

1. Once upon a time, there was a widowed fish named Marlin who was extremely protective of his only son, Nemo.
2. Every day, Marlin warned Nemo of the ocean's dangers and implored him not to swim far away.
3. One day, in an act of defiance, Nemo ignores his father's warnings and swims into the open water.
4. Because of that, he is captured by a diver and ends up as a pet in the fish tank of a dentist in Sydney.
5. Because of that, Marlin sets off on a journey to recover Nemo, enlisting the help of other sea creatures along the way.
6. Until finally, Marlin and Nemo find each other, reunite, and learn that love depends on trust.

Storytelling is an art and a craft that can be enhanced with practice. Starting with a structure for your story, delivering this structure both verbally and in writing, and seeking feedback for improvement will help you hone your craft and build your self-confidence. While telling your story, it is important to remember that every story is unique and, when told well, every story is interesting and has the potential to change the world.

Emotional Intelligence

This feature is essential for nurturing individual and relational health and enhancing harmony and productivity. It represents a set of skills and attributes that enable us to understand, recognize, predict, and appropriately respond to emotions in ourselves and others, as well as in groups and teams.

Framing the intellectual underpinning and the importance of emotional intelligence has been years in the making, particularly with the work of Peter Salovey. Daniel Goleman presented a neat and helpful framework to describe the four domains of emotional intelligence: self-awareness, social awareness, self-management and relationship management.[90]

Reassuringly, these domains are all within the human skills that have been identified as part of the emotional labour, which will continue to be a definer and differentiator for humans as we shape the workplace of the future and assert the central role of humanity as a creator and arbiter of value.

Within the four domains, there are eighteen attributes. This book does not have the space to outline all of them. However, in my other book, *Leading with Stories*, I dedicated four chapters to the four domains, suggesting multiple exercises to help hone and develop those eighteen skills and attributes. In the rest of this section, I will provide a brief description of the four domains with some practical advice on developing them.

	Self	**Social**
Regulation	**Self-Management** Emotional self-control Transparency Adaptability Achievement Orientation Initiative Optimism	**Relationship Management** Developing others Inspirational leadership Influence Change catalyst Conflict management Teamwork & collaboration
Awareness	**Self-Awareness** Emotional awareness Accurate self-sssessment self-confidence	**Social Awareness** Empathy Organizational awareness Service orientation

Fig. 11 – Emotional Intelligence Framework.

Self-Awareness

Stephen Covey, the self-improvement guru and best-selling author, once said:

> Self-awareness is our capacity to stand apart from ourselves and examine our thinking, our motives, our history, our scripts, our actions, and our habits and tendencies.

This capacity is the cornerstone of emotional intelligence. It represents awareness of the stories we tell ourselves about who we are, what is happening within us, and our strengths, weaknesses and limitations. Emotionally intelligent individuals are aware of their internal state, capabilities, and constraints. They are not only able to use language to describe how they feel in clear and precise words, but they can select the language that can positively influence how they and others feel.

Those who are self-aware can manage themselves better and can develop better relationships. Through awareness of what drives and motivates them, self-aware individuals are able to pursue aspirational and challenging goals that they manage to continue to chase, even if the obstacles are numerous, mainly because they have a clear sense of purpose.

In 2010, Green Peak Partners and Cornell's School of Industrial and Labour Relations conducted a study to examine the role of business executives' interpersonal traits in the success of achieving overall business objectives. The study examined seventy-two executives at public and private companies with annual revenues from $50 million to $5 billion.

While the research examined several executive interpersonal qualities, self-awareness seems to stand out as a predictor of success as it enables executives to inspire trust while 'still hold the bar very high and demand strong performance but with a style that incorporates strong relational skills and respect.'[91]

The study concluded that the search to fill leadership roles gives short shrift to interpersonal skills such as self-awareness, which leads to the ability to inspire trust, while these skills should actually be top criteria. Interestingly, a high self-awareness score was the strongest predictor of overall success.

In Chapters 6 and 7, we discussed how we could discover our superpowers, articulate our purpose, and cultivate self-trust and confidence. These are key components of self-awareness and appreciation.

Social Awareness

Empathy and the interest in serving others are key components of social awareness. Empathy is the ability to put ourselves in the position of others and understand their feelings and perspectives. It does not necessarily mean to agree with others, just to understand what they feel and why they feel that way.

This is extremely necessary for all social animals, and it has its roots in the biology of the brain. Italian researchers discovered specific neurons in the brain that are activated not only when we go through an experience but also when we observe someone going through something similar. That is why, for example, if we see someone accidentally hitting their finger with a hammer, we can almost feel the pain in our fingers. These neurons are now dubbed 'mirror neurons'.[92]

Empathy is not only the foundation of a more harmonious and amicable society, but also a great skill for those who build products and services for other people. Engineers, designers, builders, bankers, and other professionals who are keen on creating products and services that people would find useful and easy to operate are in for a surprise if they designed these products and services for themselves rather than for their intended users.

This is a common challenge when able-bodied designers design products for people with disabilities, for example. Empathy is also a key enabler for effective and sustained collaboration, particularly with those having different world views.

To build our social awareness and empathy muscles, we can do the following:

1. Develop the intent of being empathetic. When dealing with others and before making decisions or taking stands, ask yourself what other people would feel and think about this. Over time, this can form a habit that will strengthen your empathy and social awareness.
2. Actively put yourself in the position of others. This could be in an imaginative or actual way. If you intend to deliver a keynote for an hour, try to sit in the chair at the lecture theatre for the said duration. If the chairs are not too comfortable, you may design the lecture so that participants can stand halfway through to perform an activity.
3. Explore cultures and ways of life that are different from yours.
4. Strike up conversations with strangers, and even with people who oppose your views and try to actively listen to understand rather than listening to respond.
5. Actively use non-judgmental language when describing others, their actions, and their views. Using inclusive language can open the door to deeper empathy as it can enable people to have alternative perspectives.

Self-Management

In the 1960s, Walter Mischel and his colleagues performed a series of experiments with the pre-schoolers at Stanford University's Bing Nursery School. The test setup was straightforward: A child was asked to sit in a room and was presented with two choices: to have a tasty treat (for example, a marshmallow) right away or have two marshmallows if the child was willing and able to wait for around twenty minutes.

As expected, some children were able to delay gratification and resist the temptation to enjoy the bigger reward, while others did not hesitate to eat the single marshmallow. While Mischel, a psychologist, had been studying the dynamics of delayed gratification and self-control among children, his research resulted in some interesting insights.

In a follow-up study on the same children over a decade later, researchers found that those who were able to exert more self-control as children had better academic performance, earned more money, and were even fitter than those who were unable to exercise self-control.

In his book *The Marshmallow Test*, Mischel examined willpower and whether it can be taught and developed. His research showed that willpower is a skill that can be cultivated, and this is indeed great news.[93]

Below are some techniques and strategies that can be used to improve self-management:

1. One of the most powerful tools in the self-management toolbox is having a clear sense of purpose. A sense of purpose can serve as a guide, self-motivator, and source of inner energy.
2. Another key pathway to self-management is through reframing of situations. Remember, whenever an event happens, many times, the only thing we can control about the situation is the way we think about and respond to that event. When we are faced with a difficulty, we can see it as an obstacle or an opportunity to grow and connect.
3. Designing an environment that encourages self-management is a great enabler. For example, if we want to start eating healthily, it is advisable that we stock our

refrigerators with vegetables and fruits rather than sweets and chocolates.

4. Breathing is another powerful way to manage our body and mind. Every time we take a slow, deep breath, our blood pressure goes down, our heartbeat slows down, and we can become calmer and more aware. Cultivating the habit of breathing deeply and intentionally can help in self-management.

Relationship Management

'What keeps us happy and healthy as we go through life?' Psychiatrist Robert Waldinger started his TED talk in November 2015 with this question.[94]

In a recent survey of millennials that Wadlinger cited, over 80 per cent of respondents said that getting rich was their major life goal. Another 50 per cent of these said they also wanted to be famous.

Robert Waldinger is not an ordinary man; he is the director of a seventy-seven-year-old Harvard study on adult development, which is one of the most comprehensive longitudinal studies in history. The study was commissioned in 1938 with 724 men: both from Harvard College and Boston's poorest neighbourhoods. They are contacted annually and asked questions about their work, home life and health. When Waldinger delivered his TED talk, sixty of the initial participants were still participating in the study.

The finding of the study was simple: Good relationships keep us happier and healthier. While this sounds simple enough, and at a certain level, it feels expected; how on earth are so many people thinking of money and fame as their major life goals?

Shouldn't we all spend more time and effort cultivating great relationships with our loved ones, and with our communities at large? What resulted in this situation? And more importantly, what kind of social, educational and political leadership is necessary to enable individuals and communities to achieve their potential and live successful, balanced and happy lives?

The research done in the areas of human happiness, motivation and success in the past few decades is pointing in the direction of emotional intelligence and nurturing successful relationships as the bedrock for how individuals and communities remain motivated, resilient, happy, and connected.

Genuine relationships are built on mutual trust and shared purpose. The ability to build and nurture those relationships is also a great enabler of collaboration at all levels. In the following two sections, we will explore practical techniques to enhance professional relationships through building social capital and delivering gratitude.

Social Influence

Back in the 1960s, a PhD student at Harvard spoke to 282 men in the same town in the US and asked each of them how they had got their jobs. The surprising results were that over 80 per cent of those surveyed said they found employment through acquaintances or 'a friend of a friend'.

The findings of this enquiry were published in a paper titled 'The Strength of Weak Ties', which became one of the most cited papers in sociology. Simply put: Your social circle matters. The value of your relationships can be described as your 'social capital'.

More than sixty years later, further current research shows that developing social influence and building social capital is becoming even more important in this age shaped by technologies such as AI and social media. Not only does it help people build better careers and deliver superior job performance, but it also gives access to better information and facilitates trust. Social capital is the value of the relationships and networks that we are part of.

Acquired and used properly, social capital can leverage human capital to deliver the creation and accumulation of economic capital (money and other valuable assets).

The first step in getting ready to build better professional relationships and initiating and nurturing social capital is to realize that who we are truly connected to is not the many connections friends on social media we have.

It is who will return our phone call, email, or text if we reach out.

Scholars have shown that people do not benefit from networks passively. They need to mobilize these networks to benefit from them. To equip students with the necessary networking capabilities, universities need to transform the curriculum, the role of career services, and alumni departments to provide students with both the opportunities and the skills necessary to grow their social capital.

To build successful professional networks, the following points can prove helpful:

1. Map your existing network by identifying the people whom you already know and the networks these people belong to. These can be your family members, friends or even teachers and lecturers. Make sure that you keep good relationships with those currently in your network and be helpful to them by supporting them in achieving their professional goals.
2. Identify the networks that you would like to be part of and use your current contacts and the 'friends of friends' to introduce you. Some networks are more difficult to penetrate than others, but an introduction is always helpful. Remember that the most resourceful network that you can tap into could be the alumni network of your institution.

3. Build a professional online presence. LinkedIn is a very good platform for this. Use a professional profile picture and describe your skills, experiences and career goals in a clear manner. If you have an Impact Statement, put it there too.
4. Join suitable societies and chapters representing the professional bodies that you are interested in. Be an active member of these societies through participation in organizing events and running for leadership positions.
5. Volunteer with a charity that resonates with your purpose, core values, and the impact you wish to have on the world. Volunteering is a great tool for meeting highly motivated, supportive, like-minded individuals.
6. Help the network become stronger by introducing people you know to each other if you feel that it is beneficial to both parties to be introduced. Be generous with your support to other members of the network, support their events and send them personalized messages to celebrate their success.

Social capital can be a very valuable asset that can differentiate you from other individuals, and more importantly, it can differentiate the value you add when compared to work done by machines.

Professional Gratitude

Expressing gratitude is one of the most powerful ways of building strong personal and professional relationships. Effectively doing it is a skill that can be learned and improved. Its structure, called the 4S, is described below:

1. **Specific:** Specifically state what you are grateful for. Avoid saying things like 'Thank you for everything.' Specificity

is essential. If someone did a million things that deserve gratitude, thank them a million times.

2. **Success:** Mention how the action or behaviour you are grateful for helped you become more successful.
3. **Sacrifice:** Acknowledge the sacrifices that the person you are grateful for has made to support you.
4. **Strength:** Recognize the character strength demonstrated by the person to whom you are saying thank you.

At Heriot-Watt University Malaysia, we teach the 4S Gratitude technique to all the students as part of their Foundation Programme. We encouraged the students to write gratitude letters to their parents. As students read these letters to their parents, the impact was simply amazing. Hugs were exchanged, tears fell, and more importantly, the students learnt how to acknowledge and express their emotions. Many participants found it difficult to express their emotions at the beginning. Slowly, with training and support, they were able to be more aware of their emotions and more capable of expressing them.

This 4S Gratitude exercise can be adopted directly in professional settings. Thanking those who helped and supported you, such as bosses, mentors, and colleagues, can have a far-reaching impact on the quality and depth of your professional relationships.

Curiosity, Imagination, and Creativity

'Mama, do you like cockroaches?' my then four-year-old boy asked my wife one day.

'No!' was the emphatic reply.

Relentless as a four-year-old is, my son pursued his line of enquiry. 'Why?'

'Because,' his mother explained, 'they are ugly, brown, and have spiky legs.'

Undeterred, my son continued, 'Hmmm, what if the cockroaches were in rainbow colour, would you like them?'

It is amazing how curious, creative, and surprising children can be, even at four years old!

Creativity is the ability to bring novel and imaginative ideas into reality. It is often associated with curiosity and the capacity to see unexpected connections and discover hidden patterns. The way children think can provide a window into how creativity works and how we can nurture and develop it.

It is widely accepted that, as children, we are at our most creative and that this diminishes as we grow older. One of the most creative people who ever lived, Pablo Picasso, said, 'It took me four years to paint like Raphael, but a lifetime to paint like a child.'

So why do we become less creative as we grow older? Many blame the education systems, culture, and society as they favour answers rather than questions and sometimes stifle curiosity and imagination, which are the foundation of creativity. This argument has some basis, but there is a deeper biological reason that we need to be aware of, too.

The human brain is the most complex object in the known universe. In many aspects, the brain is still superior to the most advanced computers we have ever built. The brain's superiority stems from its ability to quickly learn and develop mental shortcuts. These enable us to perform tasks such as split-second intuitive decision-making and highly effective image processing. These are based on thinking templates that our brains create to quickly compare to future situations when needed.

In other words, the brain is a stereotyping machine. Because of this, brain superiority comes at a price: the various thinking biases it has.

The brain has more than 800 million neurons. Its power emerges from the almost endless number of ways these neurons can network and connect. For children, many fewer connections, thinking templates, and mental pathways have been cemented, and that is why they feel free to establish surprising and unusual associations. As we grow older, we learn more things and establish mental pathways that make us both very good at delivering the usual and less capable of establishing the unusual.

This is also true for experts. Often, new innovations and creative solutions come from curious outsiders to the field of expertise rather than from within. Deep expertise can be a huge asset when dealing with established frameworks, but a liability when creativity is required.

The question is whether we can maintain our creative potential while we develop mental habits that are necessary to deliver our day-to-day tasks. To put it another way, using Picasso's words, can we still paint like children while learning how to paint like Raphael? The answer is yes.

The above question and its answer are among the most important arguments we face today. The way we manifest curiosity, imagination, creativity, and innovation is part of differentiates us from our machines. Parents, education systems, employers, and policymakers ought to pay special attention to that.

Foreseeing this, back in 2010, an IBM report stated that 'chief executives believe that—more than rigour, management discipline, integrity or even vision—successfully navigating an increasingly complex world will require creativity.'[95]

In order to maintain a creative mind and foster the capability to discover hidden and unexpected patterns and associations, we need to stay curious and nurture our imagination.

The following exercises can be helpful:

1. **Always train the creative muscle.** This can be done through exercises such as thinking of an object, say a brick, and coming up with 100 different uses for it.

Edward de Bono says, 'Creativity involves breaking out of established patterns in order to look at things in a different way.' Repeat this exercise once a week for a different common object.

2. **Stay positive.** Negativity is the enemy of curiosity and creativity. An exercise that I encourage to boost positivity is to keep a journal and write daily the five things that you are grateful for; I call this Brain Rewiring.
3. **Use creative language.** Language is not only a medium for communication, but a system of thought too. When facing a challenge, replacing the P-word (problem) with the word 'opportunity' can open the doors to many possibilities, helping to reframe the challenge and unlock huge value. This is a way of positive framing that we spoke about earlier in the self-management section.
4. **Do things out of your routine.** Take a different route to work every now and then, travel, brush your teeth using your non-dominant hand or read books in a genre that you are not accustomed to.
5. **Challenge yourself.** Move out of your comfort zone by trying to learn new things, such as a new language or a new sport.
6. **Encourage diversity.** When working in teams, try to have more diversity when it comes to the members. Inviting people from outside your field or sector can potentially increase the creativity of your team.

Creativity is so important to the success and future of individuals, communities, nations and humanity at large. We cannot afford not to be able to teach it and inculcate it in our youth—and maintain it in ourselves.

Critical and Systems Thinking

A meal of fried rice and a drink costs $3. If the rice costs $2 more than the drink, how much does the drink cost? If your answer is $1, welcome to the club of the majority of people who answer this question wrongly!

The correct answer is 50 Cents. The rice costs $2.50, which is $2 more than the drink, bringing the total up to $3.

Answering such a seemingly easy question wrongly has a neurological root that is at the heart of the quest for critical thinking. The human brain represents only 1 per cent of the body mass, but uses 20 per cent of the energy in the body. It is wired to conserve its energy and avoid any computationally demanding operations. In his book *Thinking Fast and Slow*,[96] the Nobel Prize winner Daniel Kahneman identified two systems of thinking: System 1, which is fast, energy efficient, and full of shortcomings; and System 2, which is slow, deliberate, and consumes high energy.

If I ask you what 2 + 2 is, you will effortlessly answer 4. This is System 1 in action. However, if you are asked what 123 × 27 is, you will need to think carefully to do the mental math. This is when we need System 2.

As System 1 utilizes many shortcuts, it can make mistakes and has many biases. It applies the rule of thumb and thinking templates and does not go into the details of a given situation before arriving at a quick conclusion. This is adequate, indeed necessary, to deal with many of the situations we face daily until we face a question like the one I started this section with.

Critical thinking is what System 2 does. It is the disciplined exercise of systematically, objectively, and impartially considering and evaluating facts, observations, assumptions and claims before arriving at judgements, solutions, decisions, and conclusions. Critical thinking is a skill and process that can be developed and perfected, and is highly valued by employers.

As AI is poised to take on an increasing share in delivering work, critical thinking will continue to be a defining skill essential for people assessing work produced by machines. As the potential for misinformation, disinformation, and deepfakes increases, the need for critical thinking rises as well.

Critical thinking is a buzzword that everyone is talking about; policymakers promote it, employers want it, universities pledge to inculcate it, and students are supposed to acquire it. The question is, then, can we develop critical thinking? And how?

Traditionally, schools and universities assumed that critical thinking would organically emerge as students take various courses in their selected field of study. However, research conducted by New York University sociologists Richard Arum and Josipa Roska studying several thousand undergraduates throughout their years at university found that 'large numbers didn't learn the critical thinking, complex reasoning and written communication skills that are widely assumed to be at the core of a college education.'[97]

While this may not be surprising, it is not satisfactory and rather dangerous at a time when the ability to apply critical thinking skills fluently is a fundamental requirement to survive the sea of confusing and contradicting information, data, and opinions.

Clearly, the systematic development of critical and systems thinking requires carefully designed educational experiences that establish the mental habits and attitudes necessary for this skill to take root.

Critical thinking should be practised as a step-by-step systematic process that can be regularly used to make decisions and solve challenges in a variety of contexts and situations. The FRAME process proposed here can be applied to yield better conclusions, solutions and decisions. It has the following logical steps: Formulate, Review, Alternatives, Measure, and Evaluate. As the process is utilized, it is recommended that the steps are documented so that they can be reviewed and improved upon.

F	**Formulate**	Formulate the challenge being considered by writing a clear and concise Challenge Statement. The statement should be accurate and based on facts (not opinions).
R	**Review**	Gather available information and evaluate them paying special attention to examining conflicting reports of a situation or event (challenge your own assumptions).
A	**Alternatives**	Identify, propose, and create a variety of alternative options, solutions, stands, and decisions to address the challenge at hand. You can use different ideas creation techniques such as brainstorming.
M	**Measure**	Using clearly identified selection criteria, measure and assess the effectiveness and suitability of each option, solution, stand, or decision. A Decision Matrix can be used for this purpose.
E	**Evaluate**	After implementing the selected solution or the decision, evaluate its effectiveness and document the lessons learned for future improvements.

The above process can be used when assessing different offers, deals, and situations. It can, for example, be used to select your next car, house, or job. Christopher Hitchens said, 'The essence of the independent mind lies not in what it thinks, but in how it thinks.'

Critical thinking is one of the most important skills that our youth need to be future-proofed in the age of AI, and the education system should help them acquire it.

AI and Technology Literacy

To function effectively in a changing world that is defined by rapidly advancing technologies, we need to develop the capacity to understand the capabilities, potentials, and limitations of these technologies. Keeping ourselves up to date is a lifelong learning process as technology continues to evolve.

We need to understand the basic premises of technologies such as AI, the science behind pandemics, genetically modified organisms, bioengineering, blockchain, as well as the science of climate change and technologies that can provide sustainability. We are not expected to become experts in these fields, but we need to know how the evolving technological landscape is impacting our sectors and fields of interest and where to find more information if we need it.

This may sound like a lot to wrap our heads around, but it is increasingly becoming a requirement to comprehend the basics of these disciplines. For example, when using AI chatbots such as ChatGPT, Copilot, or others, knowing their limitations will enable us to compose better prompts so that we get better outcomes. Also, knowing that the output of AI systems may be confabulated will lead us to require fact-checking before accepting it as the truth. Being aware of the potential misuse of AI for misinformation is highly valuable too.

What is true for AI is true for other technological developments taking place. Regularly reading, continuously learning, and relying on reputable and reliable information sources are becoming extremely important. When we are faced with personal and professional questions, there is no replacement for spending time understanding the issues and forming our own views. We cannot farm out these matters to AI, for example.

Providing a summary of the state of the art of the technologies shaping our world is well beyond the scope of this book. It is also not feasible as by the time this book is printed, some information will become obsolete. This section is a call for the adoption of a lifelong and a life-wide learning mindset.

The Future of Credentials and University Degrees

In the previous sections, we explored a number of human skills we need to focus on developing in an age that continues to be disrupted by technology. A brief assessment of the track record of the education system in teaching and assessing the attainment of these skills shows a huge room for improvement. Universities and other institutions of higher learning have been under scrutiny over the last decades to demonstrate the value they are adding, particularly as the cost of higher education continues to escelate.

Despite that, very little transformational change was seen in universities over that period. Perhaps universities are resistant to change because their business model is still working. Students still need degrees, diplomas, and other qualifications in order for them to secure the jobs they desire. Employers, on the other hand, are using degree classifications as criteria to filter applications for the positions they need to fill.

Employers are not hiding their dissatisfaction with the outcomes of universities, and many of them is faced with the need to retrain graduates, at a considerable cost, before they can be productive members of their workforce. Though employers keep saying that their companies are after competencies over credentials, we still see degrees as requirements in job advertisements.

One may ask: Why don't employers run their own competency tests as part of the recruitment process? This will, for sure, put pressure on the education system to transform its methods and provide those who possess the competencies, but not the paper qualifications, with a golden opportunity. It turns out that there is a back story to why this is not done.

During the early 1960s, Duke Power Company in North Carolina required that job applicants possess a high school diploma and successfully complete standardized IQ tests to qualify for certain positions. While seemingly neutral, these requirements ended up disproportionately excluding African American applicants. Some questioned if these requirements were demonstrably related to some of the elementary jobs that were applied for. Willie Griggs and other African American employees of Duke Power Company filed a class action lawsuit against the company, claiming that the company's hiring and promotion practices discriminated against them. When the case reached the Supreme Court, the central question was whether such employment practices, although neutral on the surface, violated Title VII of the Civil Rights Act of 1964 by perpetuating racial discrimination.[98]

The Supreme Court, led by Chief Justice Warren Burger, ruled unanimously in favour of the plaintiffs. This established that employment practices must be evaluated based on their impact, not just their intent. It introduced the principle of 'disparate impact,' which requires employers to demonstrate that their employment practices are job-related and consistent with business necessity, even if they appear neutral.

This landmark legal case caused many companies to abandon the practice of running batteries of tests before hiring staff for fear of violating the law and being open to litigation. Gradually, this became the standard practice of most employers, and traditional qualifications became an essential part of the selection process.

I personally believe that higher education experience will remain important and can become an even more fundamental part of preparing our youth to flourish in a rapidly changing world, provided that two deep reforms are made:

1. Universities will need to make sure that their students are not only acquiring disciplinary knowledge but also helping students discover their true calling and passions and empowering them to grow skills that will be essential for the mobilization of their purpose into a positive impact on the world. This is foundational for leading a flourishing life that is characterized by both success and impact. The development of these life capabilities needs to be evidence-based, concrete, and demonstratable.
   This is very challenging to do, but it is essential to achieve. It is relatively straightforward to teach someone mathematics, testing that they have learned the required knowledge is equally straightforward, all that we need is an exam. Systematically developing people to be confident, empathetic, and motivated and demonstrating this development is a whole new ballgame altogether.
2. Universities will be required to seriously bring down the cost of educating students. Technology and innovation have made the cost of many products and services cheaper, but not education. The cost of higher education to students, their parents, and taxpayers is becoming so prohibitively high, leading to continuous questioning of the value added by higher education. This needs to be addressed.

I am confident that with the right leadership, incentives, and ingenuity, higher education will be able to rise to the occasion. In the next section, I will briefly introduce a programme aimed at equipping the students at Heriot-Watt University with what they need to succeed in a challenging future. The skills we aimed at inculcating through this programme are not new; they are what we outlined earlier in this chapter and verified with multiple stakeholders. In fact, most universities have these skills as part of the intended learning objectives for their students.

What is unique about our programme is anchoring the skills development in the purpose of the students, using the learning process to create a real impact on the world, and also the way we documented and signposted the development of these skills.

EmPOWERing the Next Generation

Recognizing the importance of nurturing human skills as a major part of our students' growth, we developed the EmPOWER programme as a structured human development and leadership initiative to inculcate, document, and signpost the individual growth journey of each student.

The programme has six domains:

1. Global Citizenship, Leadership, Ethics, and Impact
2. Emotional Intelligence, Resilience, and Happiness
3. People Skills
4. Entrepreneurship, Innovation, and Creativity
5. Critical Thinking and Decision Making
6. Employability and Industrial Relevance

The programme structure, shown in the figure below, has four stages that take every undergraduate student on an adventure of Knowing and Leading Self, Leading Teams, Leading Communities, and Leading Enterprises.

To progress through the programme, students need to accumulate Watt Points (not marks) that will enable them to move from the Watt level to the Kilowatt, Megawatt, and eventually the Gigawatt level. The students earn the Watt Points as they complete different parts of the programme requirements, some individually and most working in teams.

The name Watt Points is used to celebrate the Watt as the unit of measuring power and implying that progressing through the programme signalls a growth in being empowered.

	Global Citizenship, Leadership, Ethics & Impact	Emotional Intelligence, Resilience & Happiness	People skills	Entrepreneurship, Innovation & Creativity	Critical Thinking & Decision Making	Employability & Industrial Relevance
Watt Knowing & Leading Self	. Defining Impact (Impact Statement) . Leadership Style Awareness	. Self Awareness . Self Management . Active & Healthy Lifestyle	. Effective Communication .Time Management . Gratitude	.Divergent Thinking . Facilitating Discovery . Opportunity Finding	. Brainology . Thinking Biases . Brain Neurology . Reframing & Positive Framing	. Preparing CV . LinkedIn Profile . Career Planning . Career Fair . Prof. Dev. Plan
kilowatt Leading Teams	. Influencing through Impact . Awareness of the Global Challenges	. Social Awareness . Relationship Management . Return on Failure	. Effective Collaboration	. Lean Startup . Creating Products, Processes & Services	. Evaluating Claims . Analysing Inferences	. Business Etiquette . Applying knowledge in industrial contexts
Megawatt Leading Communities	. Widening Impact . Resolving Ethical Challenges	. Leading at the Happiness Project	. Negotiation, Mediation & Persuasion	. Financial Literacy . Appreciating Market & Customers . Raising Funds	. Weighing Decisions . Analysing Challenges	. Global Industrial Placement (Work Global)
Gigawatt Leading Enterprise	. Global Impact . System Thinking	. Supporting those under their care emotionally	. Lifelong Learning	. Running an enterprise . Blue Ocean Strategy	. Assessing Risk	. Impacting Industrial practice . Creating jobs

Fig. 12 – The Structure of the EmPOWER Programme

The foundation of the programme is the Watt level, which is about Knowing and Leading Self. It focuses on exercises aimed at getting the students to understand and appreciate themselves, learn how the human brain works, and recognize their own sense of purpose and passion.

One key exercise is the Impact Statement workshop that we discussed to in Chapter 6.

After articulating their Impact Statements and discovering their purpose, students with aligned purpose statements come together in groups of ten to run crowdfunding campaigns to raise funds for NGOs that are congruous with their purpose. This concrete mobilization of purpose into a positive impact on others not only affects the lives of the beneficiaries, but also has a transformative effect on the students themselves.

Since the start of the programme, students have raised hundreds of thousands of ringgits and directly made a difference in the lives of thousands of people.

As the students complete the tasks and activities associated with the skills covered by the EmPOWER programme, the staff team help them claim the related Watt Points and keep records of their achievements. This includes their progress from the Watt level onwards.

At the graduation ceremony, each student receives two documents: their degree testamur, which certifies their academic achievements, and their Impact Transcript, which states their Impact Statement and outlines how they mobilized their purpose into a positive impact on the world and the skills they developed doing so.

Epilogue

When invited to speak at conferences and public events, I often begin with a disclaimer that I have nothing new to teach and that everything I will share is likely familiar to the audience, or can be relatively easily discovered by them if they choose to seek it out.

However, stating this does not imply that speaking at conferences, articulating fresh perspectives, elucidating new connections, and reframing existing knowledge are done in vain. Our purpose is not merely to reiterate existing knowledge but also to encourage people to modify their behaviour, embrace new viewpoints, and act upon the best information available to us.

It is a reality of the human condition that between knowing and doing, there is often a stubborn gap. Most smokers, for instance, are aware that smoking is detrimental to their health. Sharing additional data and research findings regarding the dangers of smoking rarely motivates them to quit. This kind of change must happen at a deeper, more emotional level before the cognitive abilities are engaged. The talks we deliver, the stories we share, and the engagements we pursue should strive to bridge the knowing-doing gap by offering alternative pathways for thought, leading to reframing what we know, reimagining what can be achieved, and rewiring new possibilities.

Writing this book evoked similar thoughts.

We all seem to recognize the importance of fostering mutual trust, inspiring shared purpose, and collaborating with one another. Why, then, as the world grows increasingly interconnected, does collaboration in achieving what truly matters paradoxically become rarer while populism, individualism, and hypercompetition thrive?

The concepts presented in this book are simple, straightforward, logical, and intuitive. However, as we know, simple does not equate to easy. This book aims to encourage the adoption of collaboration as a strategic and intentional choice.

When I teach business negotiation, one of the foundational concepts we introduce is the distinction between distributive and integrative bargaining. Distributive bargaining perceives the world as a fixed pie and a zero-sum game: for one to win, another must lose. Integrative bargaining, on the other hand, regards the world as a pie that can be expanded through collaboration, striving for genuine win-win solutions.

Despite the abundant rhetoric surrounding win-win solutions in business and politics, the transactional distributive mindset appears to be the norm. Even in my classroom, when engaging in the prisoner's dilemma, the majority of students choose not to collaborate.

This book underscores the obvious and advocates for what we intuitively recognize as beneficial, yet is insufficiently exercised under life's pressures. I refer to investing time in nurturing mutual trust, shared purpose, and genuinely collaborative relationships.

In the book, we explore how collaboration serves as a profound organizing principle that operates from the level of microorganisms to multinational organizations. I hope the real-life stories, lessons from both successes and failures, and the frameworks provided here will help foster the discipline to choose collaboration and inspire others to do likewise.

Changing our behaviour is never easy, but with intentional practice, we can all strengthen our collaborative capacities. I believe this is the best way forward in building a world that is sustainable, equitable, and enjoyable.

Endnotes

Chapter 1

1 Searle, John R. (1997). 'The Construction of Social Reality.' Free Press.

2 Harari, Yuval Noah. (2018). 'Sapiens: A Brief History of Humankind.' Harper Perennial.

3 Smith, Adam. (1994). 'The Wealth of Nations.' 6th Edition. Modern Library.

4 Briggs, Charles Frederick and Maverick, Augustus. (1858). 'The Story of the Telegraph and a History of the Great Atlantic Cable.' Rudd and Carleton.

Chapter 2

5 Axelrod, Robert. (2006). 'The Evolution of Cooperation.' Revised Edition. Basic Books.

6 Meriam-Webster Online. https://www.merriam-webster.com/dictionary/trust

Chapter 3

7 Hammond, P., Heinrich, S., Hooker, S., Tyack, P. (2017). 'Whales: Their Biology and Behavior.' Comstock Publishing Associates.

8 Moffett, Mark W. (2019). 'The Human Swarm: How Our Societies Arise, Thrive, and Fall.' Basic Books.
9 Dunbar, R. I. M. (1992). 'Neocortex Size as a Constraint on Group Size in Primates.' Journal of Human Evolution. 22 (6): 469–93.
10 Wright, T. and Hope, B. (2018). 'Billion Dollar Whale: The Man Who Fooled Wall Street, Hollywood, and the World.' Hachette Books.

Chapter 4

11 Bar-On, Yinon, Phillips, Rob, and Milo, Ron. (2018). 'The Biomass Distribution on Earth.' Proceedings of the National Academy of Sciences. 115. 201711842. 10.1073/pnas.1711842115. https://www.pnas.org/doi/epdf/10.1073/pnas.1711842115
12 Tommonaro, G. (2019). 'Quorum Sensing: Molecular Mechanism and Biotechnological Application.' Academic Press.
13 Corcoran, Aaron, and Conner, William. (2014). 'Bats Jamming Bats: Food Competition through Sonar Interference.' Science 346: 745-47.
14 Moffett, Mark W. (2010). 'Adventures Among Ants: A Global Safari with a Cast of Trillions.' University of California Press.
15 Winston, M. L. (1991). 'The Biology of the Honey Bee.' Harvard University Press.

Chapter 5

16 Scarre, Chris. (2013). 'The Human Past: World Prehistory and the Development of Human Societies.' 3rd Edition. Thames and Hudson.
17 Scott, James C. (2017). 'Against the Grain: A Deep History of the Earliest States.' Yale University Press.

18 Barclay, Harold. (2003). 'The State.' Freedom Press.
19 Opello, Walter C. and Rosow, Stephen J. (2004). 'The Nation-State and Global Order: A Historical Introduction to Contemporary Politics.' 2nd Edition. Lynne Rienner Publication.
20 Hardin, Garrett. (1968). 'The Tragedy of the Commons.' Science 162: 1243–48.
21 Lee, Dave. (2013). 'Nokia: The rise and fall of a mobile giant.' https://www.bbc.com/news/technology-23947212
22 Ziegler, Chris. (2011). 'Nokia CEO Stephen Elop rallies troops in brutally honest 'burning platform' memo?' Engadget. https://www.engadget.com/2011-02-08-nokia-ceo-stephen-elop-rallies-troops-in-brutally-honest-burnin.html
23 Christensen, Clayton M., Alton, Richard, Rising, Curtis, and Waldeck, Andrew. (2011). 'The Big Idea: The New M&A Playbook.' Harvard Business Review.
24 Schleifer, Theodore. (2019). 'The Uber-Waymo Dispute Returns — This Time in Criminal Court.' Vox. https://www.vox.com/recode/2019/8/27/20835498/anthony-levandowski-uber-waymo-google-indictment-self-driving-cars
25 Waymo. (2022). 'Waymo Via and Uber Freight Partner to Accelerate the Future of Logistics.' Automotive World. https://www.automotiveworld.com/news-releases/waymo-via-and-uber-freight-partner-to-accelerate-the-future-of-logistics/

Part Three

26 Beer, Michael, Finnström, Magnus, and Schrader, Derek. (2016). 'Why Leadership Training Fails—and What to Do About It.' Harvard Business Review.
27 Shahid, Shiza. (2014). 'Why the World in 2015 Faces a Leadership Crisis.' World Economic Forum. https://www.

weforum.org/stories/2014/11/world-2015-faces-leadership-crisis/

28 Gardner, John W. (1968). 'No Easy Victories.' 3rd Edition. Harper & Row.

29 Sacks, Jonathan. The Rabbi Sacks Legacy. https://rabbisacks.org/quotes/contracts-and-covenants/

Chapter 5

30 Frankl, Viktor E. (1970). 'Man's Search for Meaning.' Touchstone.

31 Damon, W. (2008). 'The Path to Purpose: How Young People Find Their Calling in Life.' Free Press.

32 Hansen, Morten T. (2019). 'Great at Work: The Hidden Habits of Top Performers.' Simon & Schuster.

33 Quinn, R. E., and Thakor, A. V. (2019). 'The Economics of Higher Purpose.' Berrett-Koehler Publishers.

34 Dhingra, N., Emmett, J., Samo, A., and Schaninger, B. (2020). 'Igniting Individual Purpose in Times of Crisis.' McKinsey Quarterly.

35 Al-Atabi, Mushtak. (2024). 'Driven by Purpose: Your Practical Guide to Discovering Individual and Team Purpose and Mobilising it into Positive Impact.' Independently Published.

36 Kumano, M. (2018). 'On the Concept of Well-Being in Japan: Feeling Shiawase as Hedonic Well-Being and Feeling Ikigai as Eudaimonic Well-Being.' Applied Research Quality Life 13: 419–33. https://doi.org/10.1007/s11482-017-9532-9

37 PN Purpose Tracker. (2020). 'Employee Perspectives on Responsible Leadership During Crisis.'

Chapter 7

38 Arrow, K. J. (1972). 'Gifts and Exchanges.' Philosophy and Public Affairs: 343–62.

39 Maister, David H., Galford, Robert, and Green, Charles. (2021). 'The Trusted Advisor: 20th Anniversary Edition.' Free Press.

40 Blanchard, Ken, Olmstead, Cynthia, and Lawrence, Martha. (2013). 'Trust Works!: Four Keys to Building Lasting Relationships.' William Morrow.

41 Reichheld, Ashley, and Dunlop, Amelia. (2022). 'The Four Factors of Trust: How Organizations Can Earn Lifelong Loyalty.' Wiley.

42 World Values Survey. https://www.worldvaluessurvey.org/

43 Algan, Y., and Cahuc, P. (2013). 'Trust and Growth.' Annual Review of Economics 5(1): 521–49.

44 Edelman Trust Barometer. (2024). https://www.edelman.com/trust/trust-barometer

45 Sandström, Stefan. (2025). 'The Rise and Fall of Japan's Global Pharmaceutical Market Share,' Online. https://biosector.jp/the-rise-and-fall-of-japans-global-pharmaceutical-market-share/?utm_

46 World Bank Press Release. (2022). 'Lifting 800 Million People Out of Poverty – New Report Looks at Lessons from China's Experience.' https://www.worldbank.org/en/news/press-release/2022/04/01/lifting-800-million-people-out-of-poverty-new-report-looks-at-lessons-from-china-s-experience

47 Jacobs, A. (2008). 'Chinese Release Increased Numbers in Tainted Milk Scandal.' The New York Times. Online. https://www.nytimes.com/2008/12/03/world/asia/03milk.html?_r=0

48 World Bank (2023) – with minor processing by Our World in Data. 'GDP per capita – World Bank – In constant 2017 international $' [dataset]. World Bank, 'World Bank World Development Indicators' [original data] from https://ourworldindata.org/grapher/gdp-per-capita-worldbank

49 Vic Harris, V., Hart, D., Hibbard, B., Jurgensen, J. and Wells, J. 'Crisis Communication Strategies.' https://www.ou.edu/deptcomm/dodjcc/groups/02C2/Johnson%20&%20Johnson.htm

50 Khoo, Christopher. (2024) 'Singapore's integrated resorts: economic revival and social safeguards.' The Korean Times. https://www.koreatimes.co.kr/opinion/20240621/singapores-integrated-resorts-economic-revival-and-social-safeguards

Chapter 8

51 The White House. (2014). 'Remarks by the President on Research for Potential Ebola Vaccines.' https://obamawhitehouse.archives.gov/the-press-office/2014/12/02/remarks-president-research-potential-ebola-vaccines

52 Gates, Bill. (2015). 'The Next Outbreak? We're Not Ready.' TED Talk. https://www.youtube.com/watch?v=6Af6b_wyiwI

53 https://ourworldindata.org

54 Lindsey, Rebecca. (2024). 'Climate Change: Atmospheric Carbon Dioxide.' https://www.climate.gov/news-features/understanding-climate/climate-change-atmospheric-carbon-dioxide

55 Scharmer, Otto. (2016). 'Theory U: Leading from the Future as It Emerges.' 2nd Edition. Berrett-Koehler Publishers.

56 Fanning, A.L., O'Neill, D.W., Hickel, and Roux, N. (2022). 'The Social Shortfall and Ecological Overshoot of Nations.' Nature Sustainability 5: 26–36. https://doi.org/10.1038/s41893-021-00799-z

57 International Energy Agency. (2021). 'Net Zero by 2050 A Roadmap for the Global Energy Sector.' https://iea.blob.core.windows.net/assets/7ebafc81-74ed-412b-9c60

-5cc32c8396e4/NetZeroby2050-ARoadmapfortheGlobalEnergySector- SummaryforPolicyMakers_CORR.pdf
58 Ritchie, Hannah, Rosado, Pablo, and Roser, Max. (2023). 'CO_2 and Greenhouse Gas Emissions' Our World in Data. 'https://ourworldindata.org/co2-and-greenhouse-gas-emissions'
59 Kagels, R. T. (2024). 'ISS: International Space Station: The Marvel of Human Ingenuity.' Independently Published.
60 Fuller, R. Buckminster. (1969). 'Operating Manual for Spaceship Earth.' Southern Illinois UP.
61 M. Senge, P.M., Smith, B. Schley, S., Laur, J., and Kruschwitz, N. (2008). 'The Necessary Revolution: How Individuals and Organizations are Working Together to Create a Sustainable World.' Doubleday Publishing.

Chapter 9

62 The Epic of Gilgamesh. Online. https://www.ancienttexts.org/library/mesopotamian/gilgamesh/tab1.htm
63 Franck, James. (1948). 'The Franck Report.' https://fissilematerials.org/library/fra45.pdf
64 Clark, Stuart. (2014). 'Artificial intelligence could spell end of human race – Stephen Hawking.' The Guardian. https://www.theguardian.com/science/2014/dec/02/stephen-hawking-intel-communication-system-astrophysicist-software-predictive-text-type
65 Future of Life Institute. (2023). 'Pause Giant AI Experiments: An Open Letter.' https://futureoflife.org/open-letter/pause-giant-ai-experiments/
66 Anderson, Janna and Rainie, Lee. (2017). 'The Future of Truth and Misinformation Online.' Pew Research Centre. www.pewresearch.org/ internet/ 2017/ 10/ 19/ the-future-of-truthand-misinformation-online/

Chapter 10

67 Friedman, Milton. (1970). 'A Friedman Doctrine—The Social Responsibility of Business Is to Increase Its Profits.' The New York Times. Online. https://www.nytimes.com/1970/09/13/archives/a-friedman-doctrine-the-social-responsibility-of-business-is-to.html

68 Cameron, William Bruce. (1963). 'Informal Sociology: A Casual Introduction to Sociological Thinking.' Random House.

69 Mayer, Colin. (2024). 'Capitalism and Crises: How to Fix Them.' Oxford University Press.

70 Griffith, S., Uratani, J.M., Ríos-Galván, A., Andresen, J.M., and Maroto-Valer, M. (2024). 'Green Flight Paths: A Catalyst for Net-Zero Aviation by 2050.' Energy & Environmental Science 17: 9425-9434

Chapter 11

71 Fukuyama, Francis. (1992). 'The End of History and the Last Man.' Free Press.

72 Mearsheimer, John J. and Rosato, Sebastian. (2023). 'How States Think: The Rationality of Foreign Policy.' Yale University Press.

73 Shultz, George P. (2000). 'On Trust'. Foreign Service Journal. November.

74 Friedberg, Aaron L. (1993). 'Ripe for Rivalry: Prospects for Peace in a Multipolar Asia.' Journal of International Security.

75 Mahbubani, Kishore. https://mahbubani.net/how-asia-keeps-the-peace/

76 Dearlove, Richard and Kosinski, Michelle. (2021). '9/11, the Big Gamble and Putin.' One Decision Podcast with Lord George Robertson. Apple Podcast.

77 BBC Breakfast with Frost. (2000). http://news.bbc.co.uk/hi/english/static/audio_video/programmes/breakfast_with_frost/transcripts/putin5.mar.txt

78 S&P Global. (2024). 'Top Geopolitical Risks of 2024.' Online https://www.spglobal.com/en/research-insights/market-insights/geopolitical-risk

Chapter 12

79 Mitarai, Shoji, Ogasawara, Haruno, and Rambelli, Fabio. (2008). 'Lessons from Microsoft vs. Yahoo Negotiation.' Online. https://core.ac.uk/download/pdf/230304631.pdf

80 Voice of America (2023) Manmade water crisis in Kashmir tourist spot. Available at: https://www.voanews.com/a/manmade-water-crisis-in-kashmir-tourist-spot-/7539573.html

81 Kennedy Rolland, Florence. (2020). 'The Persuasive Negotiator.' Routledge.

82 Roger Fisher, R., Ury, W.L. (1992). 'Getting to Yes: Negotiating Agreement Without Giving In.' 2nd Edition. Houghton Mifflin Harcourt.

83 Kennedy, G. (1984). 'Everything Is Negotiable.' Barrie & Jenkins.

Chapter 13

84 Nelson, S.R. (2006). 'Steel Drivin' Man: John Henry: the Untold Story of an American Legend.' Oxford University Press.

85 McKinsey Global Institute. (2017). 'Jobs Lost, Jobs Gained: Workforce Transformations in A Time of Automation.'

86 Varoufakis, Y. (2023). 'Technofeudalism: What Killed Capitalism.' Jonathan Cape and BH.

87 World Economic Forum. (2023). 'Future of Jobs Survey 2023.' Online. https://www3.weforum.org/docs/WEF_Future_of_Jobs_2023.pdf

88 Foot, Philippa. (1967). 'The Problem of Abortion and the Doctrine of the Double Effect.' Oxford Review Journal. https://philpapers.org/archive/footpo-2.pdf

89 Hasson, U. (2010). 'I Can Make Your Brain Look Like Mine.' Harvard Business Review, 88(12), 32–33.

90 Goleman, D. (2006). 'Emotional Intelligence: Why It Can Matter More Than IQ.' Revised Edition. Bantam.

91 Flaum, J.P. (2010). When it Comes to Leadership, Nice Guys Finish First – What Predicts Executive Success. Green Peak Partners. http://greenpeakpartners.com/what-we-think/what-predicts-executive-success-green-peak-and-cornell-university-study

92 Iacoboni, M. (2009). 'Imitation, Empathy, and Mirror Neurons.' Annual Review of Psychology 60(1): 653–70.

93 Mischel, W. (2015). 'The Marshmallow Test: Why Self-Control is the Engine of Success'. Paperback Ed. New York: Little, Brown and Company.

94 Waldinger, Robert. (2015). 'What Makes a Good Life? Lessons from the Longest Study on Happiness.' TED Talk. Online: https://www.ted.com/talks/robert_waldinger_what_makes_a_good_life_lessons_from_the_longest_study_on_happiness?subtitle=en

95 IBM Newsroom. (2010). 'Creativity Selected as Most Crucial Factor for Future Success.' Online. https://fr.newsroom.ibm.com/2010-05-18-Etude-IBM-Global-CEO-Study-2010?utm_source=chatgpt.com

96 Kahneman, Daniel. (2013). 'Thinking, Fast and Slow.' Farrar, Straus and Giroux.

97 Arum, Richard and Roksa, Josipa. (2011). 'Academically Adrift: Limited Learning on College Campuses.' University of Chicago Press.

98 Martin, Jonathan. 'Griggs v. Duke Power.' NorthCarolinahistory.org:AnOnlineEncyclopaedia,NorthCarolinaHistory Project. https://northcarolinahistory.org/encyclopedia/griggs-v-duke-power/